The Literary Lorgnette

The Literary Lorgnette

ATTENDING OPERA IN IMPERIAL RUSSIA

Julie A. Buckler

STANFORD UNIVERSITY PRESS
STANFORD, CALIFORNIA

Stanford University Press
Stanford, California

Printed in the United States of America
on acid-free, archival-quality paper.

Library of Congress Cataloging-in-Publication Data

Buckler, Julie A.
The literary lorgnette: attending opera in imperial
Russia / Julie A. Buckler
p. cm.
Includes bibliographical references and index.
ISBN 0-8047-3247-7 (cloth : alk paper)
1. Opera–Russia. I. Title.
ML1737.B83 2000
782.1'0947–dc21 99-086375

Typeset by BookMatters in 10/15 Caslon

Original Printing 2000

Last figure below indicates year of this printing:
09 08 07 06 05 04 03 02 01 00

To my parents
Marilyn L. Buckler
Sheldon A. Buckler
And to the memory of my grandmother
Gertrude Lebow

Acknowledgments

I would like to acknowledge the people who played a part in making this book possible. First and foremost, I thank William Mills Todd III, who has been there from beginning to end. It is no exaggeration to say that every page owes something to his intellectual influence and unparalleled brilliance as a guiding star. My thanks and appreciation go also to John Malmstad, whose careful readings and performing-arts expertise shaped this project. I am deeply grateful to Caryl Emerson, Helena Goscilo, and Louise McReynolds for their readings of the manuscript. Their comments inspired re-visionings and rearticulations at the very heart of the book. I would also like to thank Stephanie Sandler for sharing her ideas about gender and identity in literary texts. Finally, I'd like to note that it was in Irina Paperno's spring 1992 seminar on *Anna Karenina* that the first piece of this project came to life as a presentation.

Friends and colleagues in Russia also offered me a great deal of support and guidance. I would particularly like to thank the staff at the St. Petersburg State Museum of Theater and Musical Art (SPbGMTMI), especially Marina Godlevskaia and Elena Grushvitskaia. Staff at the Russian National Library in St. Petersburg (RNB), the Russian Institute of the History of Art (RIII), the Russian State Archive of Literature and Art (RGALI), and the Russian State Historical Archive (RGIA) were extremely hospitable and helpful. I also appreciate the interest that Russian scholars Abram Gozenpud, Boris Kats, and Albin Konechnyi took in my project, and thank them for directing me to relevant texts and materials.

Helen Tartar at Stanford University Press deserves a special thank you for all her support and guidance.

I offer my thanks to the people in my life who made the process of researching and writing this book a very happy one: Eve Buckler and Michael Geissler, Melissa Feuerstein, Ksenia Dmitrievna Friedberg, Karina Gukasyan, Jane Harrison, Deborah and Sandy Isenstadt, the Ivanovs (Ira, Volodya, Olya, and Sasha), Isabelle Kaplan, Tatiana Pavlovna Korzh, Marie Macomber, Firouzeh Mostashari and Saeid Farivar, the Rutimanns (Marjorie, Hans, Sophie, and Daniel), and the Welcomes (Sarah, Jim, Leah, and Phoebe).

Most of all, I would like to thank my husband Dmitri Nerubenko. His high standards have been a constant source of inspiration.

J.A.B.

Contents

Illustrations

The Literary Lorgnette

Chapter One

Introduction

Opera represents the culture that stages it. The operatic form brings together expertise in musical composition, poetry, drama, singing, declamation, gesture, dance, scenery and costume design, as well as in logistical, technical, financial, and administrative matters.[1] In encompassing myriad artistic genres, opera transcends and confuses the relationships between forms that neoclassical aesthetic theory sought to establish. But opera's "travels" along the spatial, social, and aesthetic continua of the urban landscape reveal the features of its host culture in other ways. Operatic forms and practices permeated Russian cultural life during the nineteenth century, as reflected in literary texts from the imperial period. As a marker of taste, opera provided a subject for social satire and parody, particularly in hybrid literary forms such as vaudeville, sketch, and feuilleton. As an object of desire and nostalgia, opera figured in poems, stories, novels, and memoirs.

Many literary-operatic encounters treat the relationship between Russian and Western traditions, since the Imperial Theater directorate generously funded the latter during most of the nineteenth century, to the detriment of the former. But viewing Western opera merely as a usurper of Russian operatic loyalties, as some Russian critics did, obscures the essential role Western opera played in the evolving patterns of Russian social life, particularly in creating pervasive "trickle-down" effects. These operatic influences stretch across the vast and inclusive middle space of cultural life, long an underexplored area for Russia, whose historical particularities inhibit discussion of categories like "middle estate" and "middlebrow culture." As Louise McReynolds and James von Geldern have recently suggested, pre-revolutionary Russian popular culture seems intrinsically more "middlebrow" than "lowbrow," representing an eclectic sphere of popularized elite art and entertainment forms for a rapidly growing number of city dwellers. The "middle" in Russian culture "suggests not so much a stable site where culture can be generated as a point of transition and transfer," often negotiated via commercial, as well as social channels.[2] The cultural middle ground in Russia provides the real theater for opera in the nineteenth century, the place where opera could truly circulate socially.[3]

Opera, of course, has represented the consummate symbol of high art for middlebrow consumers ever since the advent of what Anselm Gerhard calls the "bourgeoisification" of post-revolutionary France.[4] Opera's troubled mediation between high and middle cultural strata appears as a frequent preoccupation in aesthetic treatises from the eighteenth century onward, notably in Friedrich Schelling's *Philosophy of Art* (1805), which describes opera as a "caricature" of antiquity's ideal.[5] Although opera's late-sixteenth-century inventors conceived this new form as a return to the perfect synthesis of arts in Greek drama, the realities of producing and staging opera proved all too pragmatically based in market factors. In another, less derogatory sense, nineteenth-century Romantic opera represents a kind of *aesthetic* middle ground, providing a meeting place for the exalted subjects of *opera seria* and the comic effects of *opera buffa* on a lyrical, often melodramatic terrain that suited urban audiences.[6] Opera offered a flexible middle space in which artistic genres and social beings could interact.

Opera-going was a decidedly creative endeavor for its Russian practitioners. But before the urban Russian population could insinuate itself into the field of operatic consumption, Western opera culture first had to be appropriated from abroad. In this sense, Russian opera-going represents a horizontal, cross-cultural import, as well as a socially vertical, internal one. As Michel de Certeau asserts, the cultural consumer is actually a producer, involved in a dispersed form of "making" that "insinuates itself everywhere, silently and almost invisibly, because it does not manifest itself through its own products, but rather through its *ways of using* the products imposed by a dominant economic order."[7] In Russia's case, this dominant order was imposed primarily by Italy and France, nineteenth-century centers of the operatic cosmos.

Western theater and theatergoing practices came late to Russia, a culture with no previous history of such forms. Theater as a secular institution began in Russia with Tsar Aleksei Mikhailovich, who supported the training of actors and commissioned works for the stage during the 1670s. Russia largely lacked a tradition of medieval liturgical plays such as the mystery plays of thirteenth- and fourteenth-century Italy, which were performed in outdoor public spaces. Furthermore, the ban on Russian itinerant minstrels (*skomorokhi*) in the mid-seventeenth century suppressed one of Russia's few native traditions of virtuosic individual performance. Theater in Russia instead evolved out of the imported tradition of the Latin Jesuit school drama with its staged versions of religious stories. The abstraction and allegory of this dramatic form enabled the Russian theater to treat military, imperial, and mythological themes without provoking the church.[8]

Peter the Great constructed the first public theater in Russia in 1701 with the idea of making theatergoing a regular pursuit for "civilized" Russians. During the reign of Peter's daughter Elizabeth (1741–62), theater attendance became a regular part of court life, and theatrical offerings broadened to include Italian opera and French neoclassical drama. It has been noted that the Russian monarchy itself resembled a theatrical institution during the eighteenth century, staging elaborate coronations and pageants that extended across the entire city of St. Petersburg.[9] During the second half of the eighteenth century, theater in all its aspects spread still further in Russia. Nobles built private theaters on their estates, mounting lavish productions with trained serf performers. The public aspect of theatergoing was the least developed, although basic structures and resources, most particularly St. Petersburg's two main public theaters, the Bolshoi and the Malyi, did exist.

Russia was initially inhospitable to opera, a synthetic, dramatic, and essentially secular art form that dates roughly from Monteverdi's early-seventeenth-century opera *Orfeo*. The Russian Orthodox Church opposed musical instrumentation as part of religious ritual and as public entertainment, and it was hostile to the notion of secular performance. And yet, the fact that the Orthodox Church favored the sung word over the played phrase prepared the ground for opera's becoming far more important to Russian imperial culture than instrumental music was.

In 1803, Tsar Alexander I reorganized the public theaters of Russia under an imperial monopoly and sanctioned public performances of operas by foreign troupes. Urban cultural life soon comprised a logical and conceptual grid of aesthetic possibilities. In 1826, for example, the Russian Imperial Theater directorate allocated the use of the Petersburg Bolshoi and Malyi Theaters among the German, French, and Russian troupes according to the days of the week and the various dramatic genres. This schedule provided a temporally and spatially segmented forum for comedy, tragedy, opera, ballet, and vaudeville.[10] The division of troupes, days, and genres implied a corresponding separation of the theater audience, since each configuration attracted a particular public. Within the theaters themselves, independent of the genre being performed, a hierarchy of seating practices defined social space. This hierarchy evolved further over the decades, affording a degree of mobility to spectators while refining the social semiotics connected with specific seating areas.

By the 1840s, Italian Romantic opera, and most especially the works of Bellini, Donizetti, and Verdi, dominated the opera stage in Russia. The 1850s prolonged the hegemony of Italian opera, to the disadvantage of the slowly developing Russian operatic tradition, and this imbalance continued until the 1880s. Western operatic plots, motifs, and vocabulary infiltrated Russian cultural life, providing suggestive structuring devices for Russian realia, often ironically rendered. Bellini's opera *Norma* (1831), the story of a druid priestess and her forbidden love for a Roman official, permeated local society in the Black Sea port of Odessa during the 1830s, for example:

> I arrive at a salon; what is the subject of conversation? . . . It is Norma. A virtuoso arrives, he plays variations on motifs from *Norma*. In the summer, when music calls me to the boulevard, the echo of the military band playing a duet from *Norma* carries all the way to the sea. For my own part, during quadrilles I must perform var-

> ious maneuvers to the most bathetic airs from *Norma*. Poor Bellini. . . . If I am invited to an amateur concert (God save me!), I will endure four hours of this lovely music, executed in such a manner! All the worthy mamas who have marriageable daughters compel their offspring to sing "Casta Diva." This is because there is a particular air of success associated with all that is Norma.[11]

As part of Russian social fabric, *Norma* lost its high-culture aura of inaccessibility and merged with elements of the ordinary and everyday. The motifs and structures of Bellini's opera even infused the conventional rhythms of the courting ritual. An 1848 article about the Italian opera similarly attributes to Donizetti's opera *Lucia di Lammermoor* at once a universal and a contemporary relevance: "The contents of *Lucia*, if you discard the local color and certain private details, are for the most part close to our everyday life. This is a page torn from the youth of almost every one of us . . . if not every one of us can find in our lives a story with madness and a dagger, many have loved as Edgar and Lucia loved."[12] The opera world itself even seemed to exist self-referentially in terms of operatic tropes. The theater chronicler A. I. Vol'f combined motifs from the operas *The Barber of Seville*, *Norma*, and *Les Huguenots* to relate a possibly apocryphal story about soprano Giulia Grisi, who surprised her husband, the tenor Mario, with a pretty music student:

> Teacher and pupil took a seat at the fortepiano, exactly like Almaviva and Rosina. The lesson took its normal course, when suddenly, just as in *The Barber of Seville*, Norma, who had returned from a rehearsal, stole up to them, and "slap, slap" resounded. Not "bang, bang" from *Les Huguenots*, but only its corresponding sound from the contact of the powerful right hand of the jealous Norma against the girlfriend's cheeks.[13]

The relationship between two Western opera celebrities transforms itself into Rossinian comic farce, shot through with the darker threads of Romantic tragic opera. The mixing of operatic genres in the Russian context often involved this sort of playful blending of the everyday and the extraordinary, enacting the "domestication" of opera. This process of cultural assimilation lies at the root of Russian opera-going practices, but also of the multi-genre Western operatic works themselves. In articulating a "poetics of culture," Stephen Greenblatt has observed that art comes to life in "a subtle, elusive set of exchanges, a network of trades and trade-offs, a jostling of competing representations." The textual remains of culture are furthermore the result of "moving certain things—principally ordinary language, but also metaphors, ceremonies, dances, emblems, items of clothing, well-worn stories, and so forth—from one culturally demarcated zone to another."[14] Greenblatt's sense of culture as a comprehensive system in which, by definition, everything circulates offers a means to reconciling the ostensible gap between literature and opera that this project seeks to bridge.

The "Golden Age" of opera-going in Russia—the period extending from the 1840s to the 1880s—does not coincide with the Golden Age as conceived for Russian cultural history as a whole. As Monika Greenleaf and Stephen Moeller-Sally note, the "Golden Age" in Russia refers to the period 1762–1855, from the reign of Catherine the Great to the death of Tsar Nicholas I, or the term may simply denote the "Age of Pushkin" (1799–1837).[15] In fact, the Golden Age of opera-going more or less parallels the era of Russian prose realism, the period during which the "thick journals" flourished, publishing serialized segments from the novels of Tolstoi, Dostoevskii, and many other writers. Opera and prose fiction coexisted during these decades, two voracious meta-genres that swallowed and appropriated many diverse artistic forms.

The attempt to translate opera into the prosy matter of contemporary lives and loves is characteristic of nineteenth-century Russia, since the country's literature provided an alternative cultural theater, a public forum to which the opera theater was analogous. The drawing room (*gostinaia*) represents the central site of the confrontation staged between the novel and opera in Russian literature. In the drawing room, famous prima donnas interacted directly with their public, and amateur female singers could perform without sacrificing social approbation.

The opera prima donna, a figure for aesthetically organized self-presentation and self-expression, helped negotiate the transition from a poetry-oriented arts culture to a prose-oriented one in nineteenth-century Russia, enabling opera to infiltrate the lower strata of the generic hierarchy. Just as studies of the "poetics" of behavior reveal a spectrum of social personae for men in Russian culture, the Western opera diva offered a model for women, embodied in roles such as Donna Elvira, Mozart's Countess, Juliet, Lucia, Norma, and Violetta.[16] These assimilated roles point to the process of social negotiation and exchange that Greenblatt asserts as a defining feature of mimesis.[17]

Significantly, there had been no secular female cultural icons in pre-Petrine Russia, no female forms inspired by the Western Renaissance, as embodied by Dante's Beatrice and Petrarch's Laura. But Russian women faced few obstacles to mounting the stage, once theater arrived in Russia. The first male *and* female stage performers in Russia date from the early eighteenth century, since Russian religious authorities never prohibited women from participating in the dramatic arts. Of course, the predominance of female rulers in eighteenth-century Russia, represented in odes and visual genres as quasi-divinities, complicated the Russian cultural response to the female form on display. But with the importation of neoclassical conventions in allegorized female statuary and paintings, as well as the appearance of pre-Romantic portraits by artists like F. Rokotov and V. Borovikovskii, Western attitudes and gestures infused Russian aesthetic sensibility.

According to scholars Yuri Lotman and William Mills Todd III, fictional literature in early-nineteenth-century Russia emphasized its characters' aesthetic recombination of elements from their environment to conscious theatrical effect.[18] Russian society tales of the 1820s to the 1840s exemplify this phenomenon, depicting aristocratic Russians attending opera, ballet, and theater as part of the drama of their personal lives. As Elizabeth Shepard's analysis of this fictional subgenre makes clear, the society tale details the "intimate, small-scaled . . . world of feelings which must be kept secret, of thoughts which are concealed, in short, of 'things which no one would ever reveal to anyone.'"[19] Literary characters' inner life contrasts with public life, where "with such accessories as mirrors, opera glasses, and telescopes commonly at hand, the means and opportunities for observation are further augmented. The society tale thus tends to record close observations of people who themselves are closely observing each other (or, to their misfortune, failing to do so), while they are observing, or appearing to observe, the proprieties (*nabliudat' prilichiia*)."[20] Clearly, theatrical accessories such as the lorgnette help their bearer decode both operatic and social spectacles, perhaps even providing access to telltale signs of secret inner lives, much as literature itself does. The opera in particular, which during Tsar Nicholas I's reign became the most fashionable and most scrutinized form of theatrical entertainment, offered Russians a mirrored environment for enacting "cultural performances."[21]

Following in Theodor Adorno's footsteps, Susan McClary declares that "Opera was one of the principal media through which the nineteenth-century bourgeoisie developed and disseminated its new moral codes, values, and normative behaviors."[22] Although opera-going in the West did not correspond exactly to opera-going in Russia, where an aristocratic rather than a bourgeois public frequented the opera theater until the mid-nineteenth century, opera did represent the dominant musical and theatrical institution in imperial Russia.[23] As in the West, opera-going in Russia came to represent what David J. Levin calls "a cultural hand-me-down of the elite, . . . effecting the orderly transfer of the cultural trappings of power from one generation of the 'entitled' to the next."[24]

The culture of opera-going and the development of an integrated operatic repertoire in Russia also provide a productive site for observing what Herbert Lindenberger calls "the interactions between the aesthetic order and the social order."[25] After the failed Decembrist uprising of 1825 and well through the nineteenth century, Tsar Alexander II's legal and social reforms notwithstanding, imperial Russia offered few truly public spaces; those that did exist were provisional and theatrical.[26] In fact, the more explicitly theatrical the setting, the greater the opportunities to use this space for cloak-and-dagger manifestations of the forbidden. Richard Taruskin points to the fact that the radical students of the 1850s and 1860s could meet and congregate at the Bolshoi Theater: "Nowhere but at the Tsar's own Italian Opera, in other words, did Russian radicals have the right of assembly."[27] Taruskin's observation underscores the multiple, not always compatible uses to which the opera theater could simultaneously be dedicated.

Operatic sites invoke social and generic hierarchies not only to enforce but also to challenge these structures. Opera-going culture could be dynamic, at times even anarchic. In this, the reception of opera as an art form in Russia resembles the impact of the early cinema on Russian audiences at the beginning of the twentieth century, since opera and film both brought about an aesthetic reconfiguring of social space.[28] The opera theater represents a space in de Certeau's sense of "a practiced place," produced by "the ensemble of movements deployed within it."[29] In other words, opera-going culture transforms the opera theater as reading revisions a written text.

Opera-going exemplifies the New Historicist notion that individuals collectively, not single-handedly, create cultural artifacts, and are themselves constituted by networks of cultural relations. Opera-going inspired debates over the nature of Russian national identity, tellingly structured by tropes of cultural production and biological life. In 1897, Russian opera advocate N. Dmitriev asserted the importance of the Moscow Imperial Opera Theater, since, he claimed, its position "at the center of Russian life in the most natural fashion gives [the opera theater] the significance of a model national institution, which ought to serve both as an artistic museum and as a guiding light to Russian art, for which an epoch of luxurious flowering is coming or has already come."[30] Dmitriev urges that the management of this "museum" be entrusted to "specialists, among whose duties will be the preservation of the collections and their replenishment." Dmitriev evokes a corps of devoted curators who service the operatic repertoire and act as a guiding force for Russian culture. For historian S. Sviridenko in 1912, the St. Petersburg Mariinskii Theater similarly exemplified the organic nature of the national opera theater, an institution that, he believed, required support and intervention from its host culture:

> A long-lived opera theater is just like a gigantic tree, on which innumerable leaves come and go, flowers appear and wither, and where there are many ovaries, but many are barren. And on that tree, birds flying in from foreign lands build their nests, and branches break and die off; and sometimes a hollow forms, and the trunk is cracked, so it is necessary to protect it with a iron band.[31]

Sviridenko's "iron band" refers to increased state subsidies for the Russian opera troupe, and to the dissolution of the Italian opera troupe in the 1880s.

Like the "specialists" who preside over Dmitriev's art museum, Sviridenko's gardeners ensure that the Russian operatic tradition remains viable. Both Dmitriev and Sviridenko anticipate (albeit in a much more positive spirit) Theodor Adorno's influential essay "Bourgeois Opera," which links operatic form with museum as well as with natural world. Adorno finds opera to have been silenced by the decline of the high bourgeoisie, "founded on so many conventions that it resounds into a vast emptiness as soon as these conventions are no longer vouchsafed to the audience through tradition." For Adorno, opera in the twentieth century resembles a museum, created "to help something threatened by muteness to survive," a repository of "bygone images and gestures, to which a retrospective need clings."[32] At the same time, opera expresses a "hope for reconciliation with nature: singing, the utopia of prosaic existence [*Dasein*], is at the same time also the memory of the prelinguistic, undivided state of Creation," because "in song, people experience themselves as nature, which their prejudice against nature resists."[33] It might thus be said that opera represents the consummate form of artful artlessness.

The extended metaphors of Dmitriev and Sviridenko—art museum and tree of life—call for a unified sense of opera-going culture in Russia. In fact, by the early-twentieth-century period, Moscow and St. Petersburg had both established Russian opera troupes offering the public a mixed repertoire of native and Western works. An eclectic blend of operatic works by Mozart, Rossini, Glinka, Dargomyzhskii, Meyerbeer, Verdi, Tchaikovskii, Wagner, Bizet, Musorgskii, and Rimskii-Korsakov, the opera repertoire in Russia resembled no other in world opera culture. Russian opera troupes ultimately identified themselves as part of the Western operatic tradition, while asserting their unique status within this context.

Russian opera-going culture includes the reception histories, mythologies, and apocrypha that adhered to specific operatic works and performers, Russian *and* Western. In this vein, memoirist A. A. Stakhovich meditated upon the number of different Rosinas he saw at the same stage window during performances of Rossini's *The Barber of Seville*: "How many Rosinas I remember, all at that same little window. Angri, Grisi, Persiani, Viardot, Lagrange, Bosio, Patti. That famous stage wing existed for more than twenty years."[34] Spectator accounts like Stakhovich's are often the only extant artifacts of an operatic event. As the semiotician Marco de Marinis points out, the object of study in theatrical performance is doubly absent: "In the first instance, it is missing as a scientific or epistemological object . . . in the second instance, it is absent as a material, prescientific object."[35] All that remains after an opera performance is what de Marinis calls "traces": written accounts, director's notes, photographs, critical reviews, fictional and nonfictional responses. Opera-going survives in fragments as memoir and lithograph, repertoire and biography, architecture, anecdote, and souvenir. The history of opera-going *is* literature, not in the sense that this culture exists solely as written literature, but because opera-going must be written in order to be constituted as an object of study.

Opera is one of the youngest arts, and this is particularly true in Russia. It is striking, therefore, that opera culture in Russia should have been so paradoxically gripped by nostalgia for itself almost from its inception. Perhaps this operatic nostalgia seems less misplaced in light of early opera's guiding mission to resurrect Greek tragedy, a lost artistic unity. In this sense, Russian opera-going reproduces the quintessential expressive gesture of opera itself. Like Monteverdi's Orpheus, that first iconic figure for operatic form, Russian opera-going culture is defined by the impulse to look back.

Chapter Two

Attending Opera
A Literary Ethnography of the St. Petersburg Bolshoi Theater

As a contested and self-regarding social space, the opera theater in imperial Russia offered its visitors a rare public forum, if a provisional one. The textual artifacts of Russian opera-going culture reflect the multiple angles of vision within the theater, whereby spatial and social perspectives derive from literary genre. Vaudevilles penned by aristocratic *litterati* use elegantly rhymed couplets and verbal play to satirize opera devotees from the lower classes. Sketches and feuilletons establish their insecure scribbler narrators as "reporters" from the cultural front. These liminal literary forms—part fiction, part journalism—translate the lofty pretensions of opera into the prosaic particularities of the operatic event. Memoir literature elaborates the social codes that constituted each seating region and made attending the opera a performance in its own right. Private raptures shape themselves into middling verse tributes. Lithographs and drawings comment on the presence of a large neoclassical opera theater in a landscape of Russian church spires, the spectacle of a large theater in flames, and the meaningful structures of the theater interior.

OPERATIC NOSTALGIA

Although it shared a continent with the European centers, St. Petersburg was a remote point on the map of nineteenth-century Western operatic life; it was analogous to far-flung operatic communities in Cairo, Buenos Aires, and the American West.[1] This geographical distance from European opera capitals seems to have inspired Russians to become inventive producers, as well as consumers, of opera culture. St. Petersburg audiences "russified" operatic terms, creating linguistic hybrids with diminutives such as *primadonnochka* and *koloraturka*. Newly coined verbs such as *lornirovat'* captured the spirit of that consummate operatic practice, "surveying the social scene through one's opera glasses." Russian audiences linked operatic motifs and themes with aspects of national life, as in the modishly fervid response that early Rossini operas with freedom-loving subtexts evoked in young Russian reformists.[2] Going to the opera could represent a definitive feature in social identity, as it did for the *Bertramisty* in Apollon Grigor'ev's story "Robert le Diable" (1846). These young men attend every performance of Meyerbeer's opera to pay homage to its demonic hero, Bertram.

Quite simply, Russians were passionate about opera. At the end of the nineteenth century, memoirist Konstantin Skal'kovskii speculated on why opera-going took hold with such intensity in St. Petersburg: "Petersburg is one of the most boring and bored cities in the world. The climate precludes outdoor entertainments during the greater part of the year, which is why indoor diversions are essential, and among these, of course, one must grant a leading place to the pleasure of listening to the European operatic repertoire, rendered by first-class performing artists."[3] A. I. Vol'f, a nineteenth-century theater chronicler, claimed that Russian citizens lived for art because the Russian autocracy discouraged them from pursuing other civic interests, a commonplace regarding Russia's magnificent nineteenth-century literary tradition as well.[4] Poet and memoirist A. N. Iakhontov echoes this sentiment, declaring the Italian opera of the 1840s to have been the passion and solace of the "thinking part" (*mysliashchaia chast'*) of the St. Petersburg public. The Italian opera was of such all-consuming interest that salon hostesses regularly insisted that their guests speak of other things.[5] But the alternative social and intellectual space that opera culture afforded its Russian audience became increasingly fragmented as the nineteenth century wore on. Opera yielded to public entertainment's ever-proliferating forms. More important, the cultural consensus on opera's power to affirm national and individual identity disintegrated in the face of powerful competing social forces in Russia.

In place of consensus, a powerful nostalgic impulse invoking the "Golden Age" of Russian opera-going became evident toward the end of the nineteenth century. Journals such as *Historical Herald*, *Russian Archive*, and *Russian Antiquity* featured retrospective histories of operatic events and performers. Book-length memoirs described youthful opera-goers' formative aesthetic experiences, and recounted operatic anecdotes. Collective memory extended to visiting international operatic celebrities such as Pauline Viardot, Giovanni Rubini, Giovanni Mario, Angiolina Bosio, and Adelina Patti, as well as to the defunct site of their triumphs: the old Bolshoi Theater in St. Petersburg.

A preoccupation with memorabilia and artifacts characterizes the literature of opera-going, as a 1916 piece in *Russian Antiquity* that performs a fetishistic "reading" of operatic objects illustrates:

> Here is a handkerchief of Bosio's, yellowed with time, sheet music received at a concert from her hands, here is a scrap of Tamberlik's handkerchief—a trophy from a post-concert attack on the great performer—a fragment of his comb, posters, tickets, a countless number of portraits of famous Italians with their sometimes touching autographs, dried flowers from their bouquets, flowers . . . from their graves. These are, to wit, relics, objects of a cult, lifeless monuments to that living force, that with such strong threads joined the theater seats with the stage during the "Golden Age."[6]

The reader of this text wanders through a museum of the imagination, where the relics of Golden Age opera lie moldering.[7] This written exhibit emphasizes the spectator's role as a creative force in the culture of opera-going and a linking agent for its material remnants.[8] This "living force" that allows the scraps and fragments to speak their history is re-animated by the reader's attention.[9]

The past pleasures of opera-going are preserved in individual accounts, most particularly in memoirs, reviews, and letters. Some of these texts have themselves become artifacts, and are kept in Russia's literary archives. K. I. Zvantsev's unpublished "Letters Concerning Madame Viardot-Garcia" comprise nine packets of tissue-thin colored ticket stubs and programs, accompanied by the author's handwritten responses to Pauline Viardot's 1853 performances in St. Petersburg.[10] Viardot's return to St. Petersburg after an absence of nearly ten years offered a collective occasion for reminiscing about the legendary Italian opera seasons of 1843–45. Zvantsev's ruminations suggest that, for him, individual experience rendered in writing makes opera culture tangible, and this textual artifact literally represents the operatic event:

> During Madame Viardot-Garcia's second stay in Petersburg from 29 December 1852 through 1 May 1853, I conveyed the impressions that the great performing artist produced on me to several of my acquaintances and relatives, not paying the slightest attention to the gossip of strangers and even less to the local censor; moreover, in the following nine letters the most timid musical sensations might be too crudely and boldly disclosed. An unbuttoned soul appeals to few people. What is one to do: such is the singing of Madame Viardot, and such are its consequences![11]

Accounts of opera-going like Zvantsev's reveal a preoccupation with asserting a point of view that captured an essential aesthetic truth. These operatic "souvenirs" used literary means, both innovative and hackneyed, that claimed to transcribe an unmediated reality.

The opera spectator, like the reader, is *not* a passive consumer whose predetermined experience of the performance resides within the operatic text, but rather the primary site of the theatrical event and a co-producer of the experience.[12] In this way, the spectator creates a unique and unrepeatable "text" for each opera performance. The protagonist-narrator of Grigor'ev's "Robert le Diable" illustrates this principle with a characteristic rewriting of Meyerbeer's eponymous opera: Grigor'ev's narrator wanders in and out of the hall, absenting himself during scenes he doesn't like, artfully mixing social and musical elements.[13]

Some spectator accounts evoke a complicated layering of memories that insert themselves into the description, just as the performance leaves its mark on the listener. An 1836 review of *Norma*, as sung by the soprano Tassistro, encodes the spectator's response: "you hear: *Oh! rimembranza!* which will forever echo in your ears . . . you rest only with the falling of the curtain, because the rapid cohesion of feelings and their reflection in your soul do not give you the opportunity to take a breath . . . she answers, and the expressiveness of the answer pronounced by Tassistro lies forever in your memory."[14] Here, the memory of past performances of Norma intersects with the operatic character's own invocation of memory. And an 1849 review of Giulia Grisi in *Norma* encompasses an entire tradition of Normas in asserting the power of memories shared by the audience: "*Oh! rimembranza!* was said with such deep feeling that the entire theater burst out in a cry of amazement."[15]

The nineteenth-century opera theater represents a physical and imaginative space in which multiple performances occur simultaneously. The theater interior lends itself to cultural monumentalization as well as to individual recollection. A Soviet-era study of St. Petersburg's Theater Square accordingly peoples the nineteenth-century Bolshoi parterre with Russian luminaries: "Among the true connoisseurs and admirers of the theater, those who generally gathered in the parterre behind the expensive seats, one could often encounter Pushkin, Griboyedov, Glinka, Zhukovskii, and later, Gogol' and Lermontov."[16]

The interior of the opera theater resembles the scene of culture itself, where ordinary citizens mingle with gods from the Russian cultural pantheon. The St. Petersburg Bolshoi Theater also provided a site for Russian literary monuments: Eugene Onegin made his celebrated late entrance to the ballet at the Bolshoi, and Anna Karenina endured social disgrace at the opera there. Outside of literary fictions, "going to the Bolshoi" similarly referred to a social performance composed of particular rituals and literacies.

THE BIG STONE THEATER

The St. Petersburg Bolshoi Theater was the first public theater in the city not constructed of wood, and therefore it was often referred to as the Stone (*Kamennyi*) Theater. A severe-looking neoclassical structure completed in 1783, the St. Petersburg Bolshoi could boast of being forty years older than the Moscow Bolshoi and only five years younger than La Scala. The construction of the Bolshoi signaled the spread of theatergoing beyond the court and the private domestic theaters at estates like Kuskovo and Ostankino, and into St. Petersburg public life.[17]

The Bolshoi was the site of a terrible fire in 1811, after which the theater was closed for six years. Subsequent reconstruction of the Bolshoi made the theater more imposing and more decorative: it acquired a grand portico with eight Ionic columns, as well as a statue of Minerva in Carrara marble, which was later replaced by a bas-relief of Apollo in his chariot, that graced the main

Figure 1. Moscow Bolshoi Theater in flames. The spectacle of a major theater burning was as vivid as any stage performance.

entrance. Carriages could drive right up to the columns and allow passengers to make a grand entrance into the foyer.

The Bolshoi showcased the Russian, German, and Italian troupes on different nights of the week and featured performances of opera, ballet, and drama. In 1832, with the completion of the Aleksandrinskii and Mikhailovskii Theaters, where Russian drama and the French theater, respectively, took hold, the Bolshoi was free to concentrate on ballet and opera.[18] The Bolshoi's raspberry-velvet and gold interior underwent major renovations, and the theater reopened in December 1836 for the premiere of Glinka's opera *A Life for the Tsar*, a major St. Petersburg cultural event.[19]

The history of St. Petersburg theaters during the eighteenth and nineteenth centuries comprises a choppy narrative of structures built, reconstructed, renamed, and consumed by fire. The construction of the Aleksandrinskii Theater necessitated the destruction of the old wooden Malyi, or little, theater (1803–32), so called in its relation to the Bolshoi (big).

The demise of the Malyi thus brought about a rift in the coherence of the names and relationships that made up the cityscape.[20] The Malyi also represented the last site of theatrical eclecticism in St. Petersburg, offering theatergoers a varied menu of tragedy, drama, comedy, comic opera, and vaudeville, and showcasing both touring and hired troupes.

After the Malyi ceased to exist, the Bolshoi lacked a theatrical complement until 1859, when the stone circus building opposite it on Theater Square burned down. This structure was quickly reconstructed and reincarnated as the Mariinskii Theater, which was intended to be a suitable home for the Russian opera. While the well-funded Italian opera troupe had occupied the Bolshoi since the 1840s, the Russian troupe had contented itself with sharing the circus's performance space next door. But once the Russian opera acquired an appropriate venue in the form of a dedicated theater, this long-overshadowed troupe sought to challenge the Italians' cultural dominance in St. Petersburg. The Mariinskii opened in October 1860, pointedly echoing the Bolshoi's 1836 reopening with its own performance of Glinka's *A Life for the Tsar*. The nineteenth-century rivalry between St. Petersburg's two opera theaters played itself out as the struggle between Italian and Russian opera troupes to establish cultural primacy. The Mariinskii eventually won the war.

The St. Petersburg Italian opera troupe, long the darling of the Imperial Theater directorate, ceased to exist shortly after the directorate's monopoly dissolved in 1882. And during the mid-1880s, city authorities sanctioned the destruction of St. Petersburg's Bolshoi Theater, the city's main opera theater, in preparation for its conversion to the present-day Conservatory of Music. With the Bolshoi's demise, the Mariinskii became the city's only dedicated opera theater, and the Russian opera troupe reigned supreme in St. Petersburg. The Mariinskii still stands on Theater Square opposite the former site of its vanquished rival.

The Bolshoi Theater, an exemplar of late-eighteenth-century architecture, served for a time as a pseudo-classical St. Petersburg ruin, standing partially demolished until the early 1890s. Its remains symbolized the fierce nineteenth-century theater politics, which were fueled by the increasing critical and public support for Russian national opera.[21] Skal'kovskii noted that

"Every large city has its own ruins. . . . In Rome—those of the Collosseum, in Tunis, those of ancient Carthage. Someone had the idea of creating in the midst of St. Petersburg our own ruins of ancient Carthage, for which very purpose the building of the Bolshoi Theater served."[22] Skal'kovskii evokes Carthage ironically, to suggest arriviste St. Petersburg's aspirations to rival the ancient cities' architectural glories. But Skal'kovskii's metaphor also brings to mind the imperialist cultural chauvinism that incites one tradition to destroy another. The Italian opera troupe nearly squeezed the life out of the Russian troupe, which retaliated by sacking the Bolshoi, appropriating the Italian operatic repertoire, and taking its devoted audience prisoner. In consigning the 100-year-old Bolshoi Theater to the remote past of antiquity, city officials laid waste the Western-dominated vision of St. Petersburg city culture.

The memoirist A. A. Stakhovich similarly invoked antiquity to describe the remains of the Bolshoi, but to a different purpose. Stakhovich characterized the ruins of the Bolshoi not as a deliberately staged feature of the cityscape, but as a monument to personal history: "How sad I was, already an old man, to drive past the wrecked Bolshoi Theater . . . how many marvelous memories were experienced in it, how much happiness perished with it. For a long while I tried not to drive through Theater Square or I turned away from its ruins. If only they had left it in ruins, like the Collosseum."[23] Not unlike the collection of yellowed opera-culture relics, Stakhovich's imaginary ruins offer a tribute to individual memory. Stakhovich re-performs his acts of remembering by writing his memoirs. The connections between nineteenth-century opera in Russia and nostalgia, literally, a painful longing for home (*nostos*), serve as a reminder that a performance itself represents "a reiteration of a norm or set of norms" that only pretends to be a singular act.[24] Performances are by nature nostalgic acts. This is why Stakhovich declares the sight of the ruined Bolshoi an unbearably painful one, and then asserts perversely that the ruins should have been left as a permanent feature of Theater Square. For those whose true aesthetic home was the Italian opera, the performance of nostalgia provided a form of consolation.

In grieving for their beloved Bolshoi Theater, St. Petersburg music lovers (*melomany*) sourly recalled that the Mariinskii stood on the former site of a

Грав. П. Куренковъ.

ОПЕРА ВЪ МОСКВѢ.

Онъ. Вы не были такъ нарядны въ прошлый разъ, когда ѣхали въ оперу.

Она. Это другое дѣло. Nous allons aux italiens.—Посмотрите афишу.

Онъ. *(Читаетъ)*: Владиславлевъ, Бобовскій, Легошина.... Воля ваша—это не Итальянцы!

Она — Они русскіе, но поютъ по итальянски — теперь понимаете?

Figure 2. Russian opera cartoon from "The Spark." This cartoon, entitled "Opera in Moscow," represents a conversation between "He" and "She." Through its humor, it illustrates one of the only ways a Russian opera troupe could get the better of a rival Italian troupe: by hijacking the Italians' popular repertoire.

Figure 3. St. Petersburg Pony Circus. For supporters of Russian opera, it rankled that the Russian troupe had to perform on the site of the former pony circus, while the Italian troupe performed in the city's best theater across the square.

pony circus. But the Bolshoi's ardent supporters had conveniently forgotten that their theater, too, had replaced a form of popular entertainment: a large carousel amphitheater from the 1760s, the early part of Catherine the Great's reign. Before the construction of the Bolshoi, Theater Square had been known as Carousel Square, evidence of the proximate, yet often hostile relationship between elite Western forms of entertainment and their popular native counterparts. In fact, the tension between elite and popular art forms plagued opera in its expansion throughout the Western world and its colonies. Swedish soprano Jenny Lind's 1850–51 American tour, brilliantly organized and publicized by Phineas Taylor Barnum, offers a vivid example. The circus entrepreneur publicly auctioned tickets to create excitement, forced cities to compete with one another before deciding on concert sites, and orchestrated a major media frenzy around Lind's movements.[25]

The general unwillingness to accord cultural legitimacy to the neglected Russian opera troupe persisted in the Mariinskii's continuing association with the old circus hall. The remains of the Bolshoi, in contrast, evoked a stage set, serving as an arresting visual manifesto that decried the old Western-influenced aesthetic standards for music. The war between the two theaters dramatized the clash of values between high art (severe, neoclassical architecture) and low art (the circus), between a conception of the theater as temple to the arts or as lively place of entertainment. Paradoxically, however, it was the Italian opera that Russian critics reviled as a succession of mindless trills and merely virtuosic display, and the Russian opera they characterized as artistically serious. But the denigration of Italian opera and the destruction of the Bolshoi did not alter that theater's status as primary site for nineteenth-century opera-going memoirs. The Bolshoi's demise and remembered triumphs underscore the essential nature of performance as a "completed event framed in time and space" that is always "remembered, misremembered, interpreted, and passionately revisited across a pre-existing discursive field."[26] The Bolshoi/Mariinskii war thus speaks to the "essential contestedness of performance" in relation to social space.[27]

The histories of both the Bolshoi and the Mariinskii Theaters belong to that of the Kolomna District, which comprises the area between the Moika, Fontanka, and Kriukov Canals, and includes Theater Square within its boundaries. Kolomna dates back to the first half of the eighteenth century, when workers at the Admiralty built their small wooden dwellings in the area. During the nineteenth century, the Kolomna District endured a protracted identity crisis. Although the Kolomna section was home to the Bolshoi Theater, one of the city's foremost cultural institutions, its residents included workers from several factories nearby, as well as urban indigents. In contrast, the Kolomna streets closest to the adjacent Kazanskaia District were filled with elegant private homes. Even without the social skirmishes that occurred in Theater Square between ragged inhabitants and well-heeled visitors, Kolomna represented a negotiated urban space.

Visual representations of the Bolshoi Theater tell a story about the theater's evolving relationship with its physical setting. A late-eighteenth-century painting shows the Bolshoi at a distance, from across the Neva River. The Bolshoi stands in the center of the painting, in Theater Square, which is noticeably free of other architectural structures. In the foreground, St.

Figure 4. St. Petersburg Bolshoi Theater, eighteenth century. The Bolshoi was not a particularly imposing structure during the first decades of its existence, although the fact that it was chosen as represented subject indicates its growing importance for St. Petersburg's citizenry.

Petersburg citizens in bright clothing stroll along the embankment, while other small figures traverse the frozen surface of the Neva. The Bolshoi of this period had not yet acquired its impressive portico, and the distant perspective emphasizes its dense, compact silhouette. The unmediated head-on view of the theater, moreover, does not provide a sense of its architectural contours, without which its form appears further deflated. While a centrally situated feature of St. Petersburg, the Bolshoi does not dominate this landscape in any sense. Thatched hutlike structures with smoke emerging from chimneys surround it, representing the sole evidence of human activity in Theater Square. These huts remained a feature throughout the nineteenth century, used by coachmen to stay warm while their patrons were inside the theater.

In contrast, an early-nineteenth-century drawing depicts the Bolshoi from a ground perspective, surrounded by human traffic. This drawing shows the Bolshoi from an angle that includes the front view, including the new portico, the balustrade, and one of the projecting side wings. The perspective is also

Figure 5. St. Petersburg Bolshoi Theater, nineteenth century, #1. The Bolshoi was an integral part of the urban landscape, visible from a stroller's ground-level perspective.

Figure 6. St. Petersburg Bolshoi Theater, nineteenth century, #2. The Bolshoi appears in a winter landscape, surrounded by respectable St. Petersburg residents who appear dwarfed by the theater's pillars and walls. The bas-relief of Apollo in his chariot is visible over the entrance.

close enough for the viewer to make out the Minerva statue at the theater's front peak, as well as the smaller statues at the sides. The drawing integrates the Bolshoi into its setting in architectural terms, showing a driver's hut on one side of the theater and a three-story structure on the other. Theater Square teems with commercial and social activity. The Bolshoi stands harmoniously in this physical setting, in an intimate relationship with its surroundings. The tradition of representing "scenes" around the Bolshoi's exterior continued throughout the nineteenth century, with lithographs that represent the theater within a living urban landscape and literary *physiologies* that similarly teem with words and living images. Over time, the lithographs alter the scale of the Bolshoi's relationship to the human figures and buildings around it, transforming the theater into a looming edifice that dominates its environment. Visual representations of the Bolshoi thus assert an ever-increasing physical and cultural prestige for the theater. Literary representations stage a similarly nuanced set of confrontations between opera theater and opera-goers.

THE SOCIAL GEOGRAPHY OF OPERA-GOING

Opera-house architecture, with its meaningful distribution of interior space, manifests the connection between art and society that opera-going practices elaborate further.[28] The dizzying rate at which the interiors of the main St. Petersburg theaters were redone during the nineteenth century speaks to the reigning uncertainty about the best way to arrange space to suit theatergoers' needs and desires. The principal changes effected in the 1830s renovation of the Bolshoi included the shift from three rings (*iarusy*) to five, and the increase in seating capacity to about two thousand socially diverse spectators, "from the Court and the Senate, from Collegia and Guards barracks, from editorial offices and lycées, from German bakeries and merchants' stalls."[29] Scholar Leonid Grossman describes the theater as a "many-ringed temple" (*mnogoiarusnaia khramina*), a phrase that conveys the opera-goer's characteristic reverence of high culture, combined with an ironic sense of the "temple's" unwieldy dimensions.

The invention of the ringed theater in seventeenth-century Italy coincided with the rise of opera and the need to fit more people into the theaters, albeit in spatially and socially differentiated areas.[30] After an initial period of open balconies in Italy, the boxes (*lozha* in Russian, after the Italian *loggia* and the French *loge*) within the rings were closed. This system prevented other theatergoers from looking in, and created an intimate, private atmosphere in each box. French theaters of the eighteenth century favored a more public, inclusive atmosphere than did the earlier Italian opera houses, opening up the boxes so that audiences could survey the social landscape. In this way, individual opera boxes took on the character of salons. This conjunction of private and public as a defining feature of the theater interior determined the behaviors of the nineteenth-century opera-going public in both Russia and the West. Subscriptions (*abonementy*) to specific boxes were treated as private property, passed on as part of family inheritance. Boxes could even be decorated with wallpaper and curtains according to their owners' taste.[31] During the eighteenth century, official stipulations governed who was eligible, according to rank, to purchase seats in particular parts of the theater. During the nineteenth century, however, the cost of tickets, in combination with a set of unwritten theatergoing commandments, determined that spectators would sit where they belonged in the social hierarchy.

The interior of the nineteenth-century opera theater consisted of the following areas, specified by French terms that were variously appropriated by Russian opera-goers.

1. The *parterre*, or orchestra seats, located behind rows of more expensive, numbered chairs (in Russian, *kresla*).
2. The *baignoire*, which referred to the ring of boxes on the same level as the parterre.
3. The *bel-étage*, which represented the best, most expensive seats in the theater, usually in the second ring of boxes. The bel-étage commanded an excellent view of the entire theater interior.
4. The various rings, referred to by number (in Russian, *pervyi iarus, vtoroi iarus* and so forth).
5. The galleries, areas with benches or individual seats in the uppermost rings of the theater. The gallery areas might include an *amphitheatre*

Figure 7. St. Petersburg Bolshoi Theater interior. This interior view shows many of the Bolshoi's features, including the tsar's box at the back, the side boxes near the stage, the various tiers of the theater, and the immense chandelier.

or *paradis* (in Russian, *raëk*), which offered the cheapest seats in the theater.

6. The Tsar's box, located in the center of the theater opposite the stage, surrounded by caryatids. During the middle part of the nineteenth century, the Tsar paid out an annual sum of thirty thousand rubles to the directorate for this opera box, "as an allowance for the maintenance of the Italian opera."[32] The Tsar's box represented a modification of the ducal loggia in Renaissance Italy, when the city ruler surveyed both his subjects and the performed spectacle from a uniquely privileged, elevated seating area at the rear center of the theater.[33]
7. The side boxes, located on either side of the stage. These boxes offered the closest view of the stage, and were themselves visible to all audience members. Members of the imperial family or highest nobility might occupy these boxes for casual attendance, but would sit in the Tsar's box on state occasions.

The renovations to nineteenth-century theater interiors replaced middle-ring boxes with individual seats in order to use space more efficiently. On the one hand, these spatial reforms corresponded to a general "democratization" of both audiences and dramatic genres throughout the city's theaters; there were more seats available, and the directorate staged fewer classical tragedies, grandiose operas, and ballets, and more melodramatic plays and comedies.[34] But while the higher parts of the theater became more accessible, the lower regions grew increasingly exclusive.

According to Raphael Zotov, an important figure in St. Petersburg theater administration, the disappearance of the old-style parterre had far-reaching implications for the culture of theatergoing.[35] At the end of the eighteenth century, the parterre consisted of six rows of expensive seats and additional, inexpensive standing room for a thousand more spectators. During the first decades of the nineteenth century, however, the expensive seating area extended back into the parterre, until there was room for only four hundred spectators. The inexpensive seating area close to the stage vanished, inhibiting participation in theater life by those of modest means, such as teachers and journalists. These parterre viewers had vigorously expressed their admiration or disapprobation during performances, and kept the actors in good form. The only surviving artifact of the parterre culture were the old vaudeville couplets that addressed the extinct standing parterre directly, an example of the way that theater structure exerted a shaping influence on imaginative dramaturgical space, just as it had in Shakespeare's time.[36]

The restructuring of social space in the theater heightened the marked high/low division among spectators, with its exchange of glances, judgments, epithets, and even small flying objects. Vladimir Losskii's opera-going memoirs from Kiev during the latter part of the nineteenth century capture this social dynamic. The expressive but modulated gestures of the fashionable lower regions in the theater translated themselves into tangible form in the upper regions:

> Between the democratic gallery and the bourgeois parterre there existed an irreconcilable class antagonism. Whenever the gallery expressed its delight too loudly

> and ardently, the parterre became irritated, indignantly shrugged its shoulders, threw furious glances upwards, and finally pointedly stood up and left the theater hall. The gallery did not lag behind: onto the parterre fell accidentally-dropped apple cores, orange peels, pieces of sausage, and even weiners from the gallery buffet.[37]

The highest galleries "were peopled by shabby scribes, assistants from fashionable shops, lackeys, servant girls, valets, clerks from accounting artels, and customs watchmen."[38] These spectators were joined by those forced out of the old-style parterre, who brought with them the attributes of the now-extinct parterre by actively asserting their aesthetic preferences.

A review of *Don Giovanni* from 1838 relates an incident by which the occupants of the upper gallery (*raëk*) create what the author called a "new ending" for Mozart's opera:

> You know that at the end of the opera, the hero of the piece is seized by Furies and demons, who carry him off to the gaping mouth of hell. Unfortunately, a visiting actor made his debut in the leading role, and played the part with great ardor, waving his arms violently and singing rather off-key. However, the *lower order* of the public, which always occupies the *highest seats* in the theaters, liked him extraordinarily well. Before the closing of the curtain, from the *paradis* resounded numerous, loud cries; the judges on high were summoning the performer. Don Juan tried to tear himself from the Furies' arms, but in vain: they would not release him. "Let me go! Let me go!" he cried in a despairing voice. "No! To Hell! To Hell!" they answered. "What do you mean, to Hell! Can't you hear that *heaven* [*rai*] is calling me!" His answer struck home; the parterre too called the actor out for a bow.[39]

The narrator in the preceding excerpt implicates himself in the high/low dynamics of the theater interior: he adopts a tone of amused disdain toward the provincial Don Juan and his admirers in the upper gallery, allying himself with the Furies in their attempt to humble the operatic hero. The more discerning parterre grants its approval to the visiting actor only when he wittily juxtaposes operatic plot with cultural context.

Like the occupants of the plebian upper gallery, young officers found themselves segregated from socially prominent audience members. As a young cadet, Skal'kovskii sat in the gallery of the first ring or the balcony of the French theater at the Mikhailovskii, since "Cadets in those days did not have the right to frequent the floor seats."[40] He continues, "During the performance, we were not shy about unbuttoning our clothes, we took off our ties, and applauded in such a way that our uniforms were constantly patched under the arms. During the intermissions, we drank water with a dipper right out of a bucket, and violently argued as to the merits of one or another performer."[41] As Skal'kovskii makes clear, young officers evolved their own set of theater behaviors, replacing formal conduct with an ease of manner in a self-conscious, even theatrical way. N. A. Geineke similarly recalls that among young guard officers it was considered the height of form to walk into the hall after the performance had started, "emphatically jingling one's spurs."[42]

Women were represented in nearly all theatergoing subgroups, subject to rules for specific social stations. Skal'kovskii recalls that at the Mikhailovskii Theater, "Women of the *demimonde* could not sit any lower than the bel-étage."[43] The floor of the theater represented forbidden territory for *all* female opera-goers. Avdot'ia Golovacheva-Panaeva's memoirs describe a woman who dared to venture onto the all-male parterre alone, literally making a spectacle of herself: "In those days, women did not frequent the parterre; but one female pioneer created a great stir in the theater with her appearance; from the boxes and in the parterre everyone watched her through their opera-glasses and a buzz even ran through the hall, as each person remarked upon this bold personage."[44] As Panaeva's language makes clear, this "female pioneer" issued a challenge to the aristocratic portion of the audience, provoking their disapproving response as if to draw attention to the strictly demarcated zones this very response created. This incident illustrates the collective self-policing intrinsic to opera-going culture, as exemplified by the public censure of Anna Karenina.

As Tolstoi's novels amply indicate, aristocratic women felt themselves the primary spectacle of the operatic occasion, appearing in daringly cut evening gowns and holding court in their boxes. Still, the standards for women's behavior were known to all, and were even codified in conduct books:

> It is permissible to look freely through one's lorgnette at the stage. However, it is better for young women to look primarily at the actresses, they should avoid watch-

> ing the love scenes or looking at low cut gowns. Moreover, they should refrain from looking around the hall as much as possible through their lorgnettes; their role is to stimulate delight and admiration. In fact, the majority of women envy them this role, and that is why they are watching others through their lorgnettes! Men and women alike should equally refrain from looking around at the audience during the performance; this is considered showing off because it attracts attention to the self. . . . Men and women who occupy a high place in society must applaud very quietly; a slight gesture connotes approval from them. . . . In general it is quite risky for men to pay attention to women escorted by another man; such attentions might arouse jealousy, and can have unexpected and unhappy results.[45]

Young women should display themselves to best effect, but should observe neither stage nor audience too closely. Looking in the wrong direction draws improper attention to the self, whose goal is to appear blissfully unaware of others' much-desired notice. The opera theater resembles a hall of mirrors, with glances aimed through lorgnettes rebounding off impenetrable social surfaces.

Nikolai Nekrasov's poem "The Ballet" (1866) inverts the lorgnette by offering a biting tribute to the *arriviste* members of one female subculture that transforms the much-vaunted glamour of the bel-étage into a vulgar display of family assets. *Not* looking around the theater might have signaled high breeding in a woman, but no woman could prevent other theatergoers from looking at her and passing judgment:

> For example, how magically beautiful
> Is the bel-étage—a real flower-garden!
> There are still millionaires in Russia,
> You just have to look at the boxes,
> Where the bankers' wives have taken their seats,—
> A hundred thousand rubles on each breast!
> Swanlike necks in pearls,
> Diamonds the size of nuts in their ears![46]

In Nekrasov's poem, a woman begs a pawnbroker for the temporary return of a necklace so that she can wear it to the theater. Nekrasov satirizes the woman's need to dress up a dire financial situation by invoking theatrical illusion. His theatrical tropes implicitly question the bourgeois woman's right to sit in the aristocratic bel-étage, since she must strain to create the effects of aristocracy. But these tropes also point to women's respectably untheatrical behavior at the Bolshoi, behavior that denied the reality of the occasion by pretending women were not on display. How could women attending the theater be unaware that everyone was watching them? At the opera, women strove for social performances that produced the effect of the natural.

The spatial disposition of the St. Petersburg theater interior could accommodate changing social circumstances. Writer Faddei Bulgarin's feuilleton "Journey from the *Paradis* to a Box in the First Ring" (1825) uses the structure of the theater to describe the progression of life and career in a dramatic monologue. The literary narrator of the "Journey" transcribes the oral autobiography of an old acquaintance, called K., who as a young man sat in the upper gallery and looked with envy at the privileged figures sitting below. When K. becomes secretary to a pawnbroker, he moves to the parterre to mingle with minor civil servants, which creates the need to "play without fail the role of a *respectable* man, that is, to dress tidily, to show oneself in public in a circle of respectable people, to play Boston and whist, to loan out money, and to treat one's friends. Of course, under these circumstances, I moved over from the parterre to the floor seats, where I peacefully remained until my very wedding day."[47] Each of the elements in K.'s list of social obligations is public and performative, with the exception of lending money, the social skill on which his theater-interior mobility depends.

Once K. is married, he must insert himself into a different subculture: "You know that a respectable man of middling means with a wife must find room at least in a box in the third ring. That is no misfortune, but one must have dress clothes for a box; for the maintenance of dress clothes and coiffure, one must have a carriage, and for a carriage, one needs an apartment with stables and sheds."[48] The life journey of the unfortunate K. continues as he moves from the third ring to the second to keep up appearances, and then from the second ring to the first to display his marriageable daughters. He longs for the happy old days when he sat in the upper gallery and enjoyed the performances, unencumbered by expenses and cares. The downward trajectory of K.'s career as a theater spectator offers a spatial analog for upward social mobility.

A nostalgia for the lost realm of pure aesthetic satisfaction structures K.'s "progress."

Beginning in the 1830s, as the number of theaters proliferated and the attending public grew more socially diverse, periodical pieces and literary works reflected a prevalent anxiety over who should be sitting where. These writings exhibit an almost ethnographic focus, a strategy that resembles the use of a lorgnette in emphasizing the social distance between the narrator and the new classes of opera-goers. An 1848 article called "The Theater Public" provides a social geography of the three main St. Petersburg theaters, describing a single week in which the narrator and a friend visit the Aleksandrinskii, Mikhailovskii, and Bolshoi Theaters. This text does not describe the performances at all, but instead surveys the audience as the primary spectacle of interest.

At the Aleksandrinskii, the narrator and his friend observe a noisy, inattentive crowd of minor civil officials, merchants with their families, and simple folk, noting that "ballets, comedies, and melodramas of their own making are performed among the spectators."[49] At the fashionable Mikhailovskii Theater, which offers French drama in the original, there are no raucous encores (*bisy*), and the audience is quietly well behaved. The narrator makes a sharp distinction between those who create a spectacle and those who observe decorum. The audience at the Aleksandrinskii, a milieu unfamiliar to the narrator, resembles a jumble of living stories and entertainment genres, whereas the Mikhailovskii audience represents (for him) the unmarked norm.

In contrast, consider this sketch alongside Vissarion Belinskii's "Aleksandrinskii teatr," a written description included in Part II of Nikolai Nekrasov's well-known compendium, *Physiology of Petersburg* (1845). Belinskii defended the St. Petersburg dramatic troupe against that of Moscow, claiming that the Aleksandrinskii actors exhibited the lifelike truthfulness typical of the new Russian literature. Belinskii also declared that Moscow had no real theater public, but only a motley assortment of theatergoers from diverse social backgrounds. The St. Petersburg public at the Aleksandrinskii, he claimed, was homogeneously composed of middling service ranks, with moderate, bourgeois tastes, who warmly supported certain actors and authors. Belinskii insisted that anyone wishing to know "the inner Petersburg" must visit the Aleksandrinskii.[50] Belinskii's desire to champion the emerging social and cultural "middle" results in a view of the Aleksandrinskii public that differs radically from that in "The Theater Public."

The longest section of "The Theater Public" describes the audience in the upper regions of the Bolshoi Theater during an Italian opera performance. From the side gallery of the fifth ring, notes the narrator with distaste, "resounds the horrid applause of gloveless hands."[51] The inexpensive seats in the fifth ring made this theater region attractive to a variety of spectators, who nevertheless found their position awkward: "practically every one of the visitors tries to assure the other that he is sitting there by chance, that his real place is in the parterre, but that he ended up here completely unexpectedly."[52]

The social imposture that surrounds the narrator is so threatening that he transforms his neighbors into abstractions and linguistic flourishes: "Here there are so many stories, fictions, fairy tales, and fables in the faces, jokes, witticisms, obtusenesses, vulgarities, cries for encores, bravòs, bràves, bravàs, bràvis, da capo and fuora, that one can't stand it any longer; at times, despite onself, one laughs nearly to the point of tears."[53] Such ascription of familiar literary genres to human behavior frequently shapes the literary *physiologie*. If the narrator of "The Theater Public" perceived the public at the Aleksandrinskii theater in terms of the main entertainment genres of his day, he sees the public in the Bolshoi gallery as a series of increasingly abbreviated gestures, motifs, and generic fragments whose literary referents translate into operatic exclamations. His recitation resembles a literary aria, a virtuosic play with the conventions of nineteenth-century opera-going.

"The Theater Public" concludes with the narrator's description of Theater Square after the performance, when all audience members stand briefly on the same level. As well-born ladies await their carriages, "there begins here a sort of outdoor fête, consisting of a crush of nameless fellows and other admirers (*liubitelei*) who love to look more closely at those whom fate has placed at that height in society, to which it is painful for those fellows even to look."[54] The experience of theatergoing emphasizes the social distance from which fifth-ring viewers observe the female audience of the bel-étage and baignoire.

Inside the theater, viewers who sit in the uppermost regions may look down on their betters. Once outside on common ground, however, the real hierarchy expressed by the inverse structure of the theater interior asserts itself. Fifth-ring viewers represent nameless amateurs (*liubitelei*), who are not real "players" in the drama of social life. Nevertheless, the operatic occasion offered an opportunity for Russian society to view itself as a scene resembling the diverse parade at the opening of Gogol's short story "Nevsky Prospect" (1835). The feuilletons and sketches originally designed to maintain an aristocracy of opera-goers also served to disseminate operatic etiquette throughout the literate Russian urban population.[55]

One way of coping with theater-seating anxieties was to imagine a balanced social cosmos, as Raphael Zotov did. He urged Russian citizens to attend the theater in order to educate themselves and find their rightful place within this divine order:

> The spectator of the *paradis*, who cracks nuts during the performance, looks upon the theater, the play, and the acting completely differently from the modest visitor to the places behind the floor seats, who pays his last ruble for the pleasure of being at the theater; and this amateur is never of one mind with the wealthy youth, who has not yet completed his studies, and who, sprawling in two-ruble armchairs, looks with scorn upon the other public, boldly gazing through his lorgnette at actresses and female audience members of the *baignoire* and the first ring, loudly yelling, furiously clapping, calling to the actors during the performance itself, yawning through the touching moments, delighting in double entendres and telegraphic gestures. All of these orders of spectators, with thousands of subdivisions, each have their own opinion, which they consider indisputably right; and each is right, because each judges on the strength of his own understanding.[56]

Zotov suggests that multiple theater-interior perspectives could coexist, each offering a legitimate, uniquely coherent view of the spectacle. What is more, his description posits a provisional, collective social body, the product of intersecting views and glances. But such integrated visions of the opera-theater audience were rare. The obsessive interest in classifying the ethnographic regions of nineteenth-century St. Petersburg theaters extended to the audiences who attended performances of the French, German, Italian, and

Russian troupes, and to the conceptually separate audiences for genres such as drama, opera, and ballet. Nineteenth-century St. Petersburg theatergoing can be characterized as a cultural cacophony, cross-sectioned by genre, theater, troupe, and theater-seating area. Within individual groupings, however, there could exist a remarkably unified spirit among spectators, as was the case at the Italian opera.

ITAL'IANSHCHINA: THE ITALIAN OPERA CRAZE

Russia's passion for the operas of Rossini, Bellini, Donizetti, and Verdi reached its zenith during the period 1843–86. The Russian public made Italian opera synonymous with a finely developed aesthetic sensibility and thronged to the Bolshoi to partake of Western musical delicacies. As the appetite for Italian opera spread downward from the upper reaches of Russian society, literary works satirized the new public's malapropisms and comic misperceptions of Italian operatic convention. The Russian public's taste for operatic pleasures sometimes gave rise to antisocial behaviors: citizens sought to obtain box subscriptions through personal connections, and they trampled one another in ticket lines. Nineteenth-century Russian opera-going culture manifested itself in the most developed form at the Italian opera, as a rich cultural admixture captured in diverse literary forms.[57]

Italian opera first came to Russia in 1731, when the Russian state invited a troupe from abroad to perform at the coronation of Empress Anna Ioannovna. The influence of groups like the popular Locatelli touring troupe brought a number of Italian operatic works into the repertoire of Russian performers at court. During the first part of the nineteenth century, French *opéras comiques* by Monsigny, Grétry, and Dalayrac enjoyed greater popularity on the Russian opera stage than did Italian opera seria. But French opera fell from favor after the War of 1812, and with the evolution of Italian comic and early Romantic opera, musical fashion turned again to favor Italy.

In the 1820s and 30s, Italian opera in Russia was a sometime thing. Moscow maintained an Italian opera troupe privately funded by the Society of Music Lovers during the period 1821–27, when aristocratic Russians thrilled to the operas of Gioacchino Rossini, including *Tancredi*, *The Barber of*

Seville, and *Semiramide*. The St. Petersburg directorate made a brief, unsuccessful attempt to maintain a resident Italian opera troupe in the late 1820s, but the venture was unprofitable. Individual Italian opera stars played before the Russian public during visits by Angelica Catalani in 1820, 1825, and 1830, and by Giuditta Pasta in 1841.[58] The famed soprano Henrietta Sontag performed in St. Petersburg in the late 1830s during an extended stay with her diplomat husband, Count Rossi. As befitted the wife of such an eminent personage, however, Sontag appeared only for select audiences in private concerts.

Italian opera took hold in the Black Sea port city of Odessa as early as 1809, well before it did in St. Petersburg and Moscow. Skal'kovskii claims that Italian opera simply "raged" in early-nineteenth-century Odessa, and that he was rocked in his cradle to the strains of Rossini, Bellini, and Donizetti.[59] Poet Alexander Pushkin frequented the Italian opera in Odessa during his Southern exile in the 1820s, as evidenced by two oft-quoted stanzas from "Eugene Onegin's Journey," in which the movement of the poet-spectator's roving lorgnette connects a series of fleeting impressions:

> And what of other fascinations?
> And what of keen lorgnettes, I say . . . ?
> And in the wings . . . the assignations?
> The prima donna? The ballet?
> The *loge*, where, beautiful and gleaming,
> A merchant's youthful wife sits dreaming,
> All vain and languorous with pride,
> A crowd of slaves on every side?
> She heeds, and doesn't heed the roses,
> The cavatina, heated sighs,
> The jesting praise, the pleading eyes . . .
> While in the back her husband dozes,
> Cries out from sleep *Encore*!—and then
> Emits a yawn and snores again.[60]

The narrator's lorgnette, a figure for his imagination, carries him backstage to a meeting with a female performer, returns him to the audience, and subjects a local beauty to his amused, critical scrutiny. These interludes are a product of the narrator's creative fancy, however, since the unusual social mixture in the Odessa Theater stirs the narrator's curiosity, but keeps him in his seat.

As Pushkin's verse makes clear, visitors from St. Petersburg and Moscow considered Odessa's public to be inelegant. According to the memoirist F. F. Vigel', local merchants bought up opera boxes at low season-subscription rates, then resold them at a huge profit to summer pleasure seekers.[61] But Odessans themselves never forgot that Italian opera flourished early in their city, and they enjoyed reminding Russians from St. Petersburg and Moscow of this historical fact: "Don't we have the right to say with a certain pride that Italian opera took root here, while it still was unable to take root in our capitals?"[62] Odessa provided a hospitable environment for Italian opera by virtue of its warmer, more Southern climate and holiday atmosphere. But the provinces could not hope to maintain operatic supremacy for long.

Ironically, the Russian opera troupe seems to have done a great deal to introduce the St. Petersburg public to the pleasures of Italian opera in the 1830s, beginning with a successful 1836 production of *Semiramide*. In the 1830s, Russian and German troupes also staged operas by Bellini and Donizetti, which Russian audiences found intellectually accessible and emotionally appealing, particularly as performed in Russian translation, as was the norm for foreign opera during this period. By the 1840s, St. Petersburg's opera lovers were eager to experience first-class European operatic voices.

The "Golden Age" of Italian opera in Russia began with the tenor Giovanni Rubini's visit in 1843. After an initial season performing with local Russian singers, Rubini concluded an agreement with the Imperial Theater directorate, enabling him to form his own troupe in Italy and return to St. Petersburg for full opera seasons. The troupe initially featured the famous trio of Rubini, baritone Antonio Tamburini, and mezzo-soprano Pauline Viardot-Garcia, famous in Russia for her long, romantic friendship with writer Ivan Turgenev. Tsar Nicholas I proved himself willing to provide abundant financial support for Rubini's Italian opera project, a decision that scholar Richard Taruskin characterizes as "a diplomatic move" intended to assert St. Petersburg's status as a major cultural capital.[63] The well-subsidized Italian opera in St. Petersburg soon had little trouble attracting major Western opera stars, who easily won over the Russian public.

Still, not everyone was pleased by the Russian public's appetite for Italian opera, or, as it was called, "the Italian craze" (*ital'ianshchina*). As early as the late 1820s, writer and music critic Vladimir Odoevskii spoke out in favor of Mozart's more "serious" and intellectually challenging music over what he considered the merely entertaining music of the Italian composers. And Odoevskii never changed his views on the matter. In an 1867 article about the troupe's limited repertoire, he mocked the entire Italian operatic enterprise in Russia: "One cannot constantly feed upon Verdi-fare (*verdiatina*). We might just as well break into this melancholy little ditty, which the Petersburg ladies composed to the tune of 'La donna è mobile'":

> If we don't hear Trovatore,
> Then we'll hear Rigoletto;
> If we don't hear Rigoletto,
> Then we'll hear Trovatore.[64]

In critic Vladimir Stasov's view, Italian opera was among the "brakes (*tormozy*) on Russian art." Stasov considered Italian opera a limited, popular art form that stifled the Russian public's taste for serious art with its "insincerity, banality . . . given to everything trivial and conventional."[65] Stasov considered that supporting the Italian opera was unpatriotic, since *ital'ianshchina* clearly hampered the development of Russian national opera.

During the 1840s, the Italian opera in St. Petersburg was frequented by the aristocracy, who considered themselves the city's aesthetic standard bearers. As Skal'kovskii recalls, "Not missing a single opera performance was considered a sign of good taste."[66] These opera devotees took both opera and themselves very seriously. One memoirist characterized the Italian opera public of this period as "high priests, coming to the temple of art, as if to a real place of worship."[67] But the culture of the Italian opera eventually gave rise to a kind of transcendence in spatial, experiential, and social terms. From an acoustic standpoint, the best seats in the St. Petersburg Bolshoi were in the fifth ring, and this circumstance inspired people "who had never been higher than the bel-étage" to climb to the upper rings and the paradise.[68] Since the chandelier completely blocked the view of the stage at these dizzying heights, Italian opera fans reclined on the wooden benches in the fifth ring, unable to see, but blissfully content. This sort of operatic "slumming" represented the ultimate sign of good taste, theatrically signaling a devotion to music uncontaminated by social motives.

Although the great chandelier of the Bolshoi proved a visual obstacle for some opera-goers, its existence allowed the most intrepid opera lovers to overmaster the social map delineated by seating arrangements. The spectators in this transcendental realm were invisible to the rest of the audience, but they enjoyed the finest acoustics in the theater:

> the chandelier, as it still is today, was lowered from a wide, circular opening in the decorated ceiling, so that a free space of fourteen inches, if not more, remained around it, and this very opening was used by many people to hear the opera. They climbed up into the attic of the Bolshoi Theater by means of a two-*grivennik* coin given to a theater watchman, and settled themselves there on the upper side of the ceiling around the opening, a half-hour before the beginning of the performance, when the chandelier was lit (in those days they still used oil lamps). You can imagine their position: there were, of course, no chairs there, and moreover, the ceiling and the edge of the opening were somewhat sloped. At first, all of the lights of the enormous chandelier shone right into their eyes at the closest possible proximity. Later, when the chandelier was lowered, the heat from those lights was concentrated up into the ceiling opening. The stage, of course, was not visible, but everything was audible, down to the tiniest little note.[69]

The legendary *melomany* who experienced Italian opera performances from the upper reaches of the theater ceiling proved their devotion to art with their willingness to endure discomfort. Sitting in the uppermost regions of the theater could be equally a matter of pride, or at least of sophisticated self-mockery. The memoirist Ivanskaia records that the spectators from the fourth and fifth rings expressed their appreciation to the diva Christine Nilsson by sending her the following token: "A silver-gilt laurel wreath from pooled contributions of the fourth and fifth theater rings, with an inscription on the cover of the case: 'The enthusiasts from the tropics.' The card was signed with a thousand names, and to it was fastened a gold ring with a diamond teardrop."[70] Stakhovich declared the upper gallery the domain of genuine opera lovers: "How glad I am that when I attended the Italian opera for the first time, I was in the paradise, where the true *connoisseurs* and *judges* always sat."[71] If sitting in the uppermost regions constituted a form of social transcendence, this behavior also represented its own kind of snobbery.

Periodical pieces about opera-going from the first half of the nineteenth century adopted the perspective of a well-born narrator to describe the upper reaches of the theater. The narrator of Dmitri Mamin-Sibiriak's novel *Features From the Life of Pepko* (1894), in contrast, makes his distant perspective from the top of the theater stand for a sense of social dislocation. Mamin-Sibiriak signals this orientation in the novel's opening section, when his narrator, an undistinguished St. Petersburg student and would-be novelist, sees from the window of his grim rented room ("from my bel-étage") that a neighborhood workman has hanged himself, and hears unsavory "scenes" from the landlord's private life through the thin walls.[72] The narrator and a friend visit the Bolshoi Theater to hear the prima donna Adelina Patti. Tickets are unavailable, so they bribe an usher who leads them along passages in the ceiling to the opening through which the chandelier is raised and lowered. "Our adventure took on a fantastic character, recalling an escape from some prison of the Middle Ages," notes the narrator, as they are compelled to crawl part of the way.[73] The two friends peer through the chandelier opening directly above the stage: "Finally, we caught sight of the stage, that is, a weak, light spot, which glimmered slightly at the bottom of the abyss." From this perspective, the legendary Patti is transformed into a tiny, vaguely female figure.[74] The narrator and his companion move along the ceiling passages to the backstage area, where they gaze with alienated eyes at the pampered St. Petersburg public. The narrator barely mentions his response to Patti's singing. His focus in this passage is on the bizarre, estranged angles of vision from which these disenfranchised young men view St. Petersburg opera-going society.

Mamin-Sibiriak's fictional account of an opera performance rewrites the rampant, all-encompassing nostalgia of Italian opera lovers by means of an outsider's perspective on the cultural life of St. Petersburg. Visual representations of grand theater interiors from the earlier nineteenth century, in contrast, survey audience and stage from a box in the baignoire or bel-étage. The tradition of visually representing the theater from the best seats in the house, by no means unique to Russia, unconsciously reflects the view that spectators in the upper galleries were merely part of the scenery.

The arrangement and distribution of acoustical space in the nineteenth-century opera theater modeled the cultural drift of motifs and behaviors, but in reverse. Music in the opera theater rose from the parterre to the upper gallery, whereas operatic motifs descended from the best theaters to public taverns, where organ-grinders and harpists played excerpts from Italian operas.[75] Italian opera so thoroughly diffused itself throughout mid-nineteenth-century Odessa society that even the cab drivers could sing the Verdi aria "La donna è mobile."[76] Apollon Grigor'ev's story "Lucia" (1846) juxtaposes the rendering of melodies from *Lucia di Lammermoor* by itinerant musicians in a St. Petersburg tavern and a performance of Donizetti's opera at the Bolshoi Theater. The unexpectedly moving performance of Donizetti's music by a consumptive tavern harpist prepares the narrator to respond "sincerely" to Italian opera in the theater. The narrator's response actually reverses the expected direction of influence.

The St. Petersburg opera-going audience developed practices that further promoted cultural drift by institutionalizing the spontaneous excesses that opera inspired, and by choreographing individual responses. These operatic practices led to the coining of new terms, the most notable of which were "flower frenzy" (*tsvetobesie*), the unquenchable urge to toss bouquets to one's favorite performers, and "gift mania" (*podarkomaniia*), the passionate desire to present performers with expensive presents. Reviewers and memoirists described these gifts in great detail: enormous wreaths with compliments spelled out in tiny white roses, sets of diamond bracelets, and engraved souvenirs made of precious metals. As Russian literature testifies, these behaviors were subject to the same kind of downward cultural drift as was the language used to discuss and describe opera.

"Flower frenzy" became a full-fledged fad during the 1844–45 opera season,

Грав. П. Куренковъ.
Въ Оперѣ.
Ложа въ сосѣдствѣ съ райкомъ.
Жена. Не смотря на высоту, я нахожу, что здѣсь очень удобно — всякая высокая нотка доходитъ.
Мужъ. Это неудивительно, что высокая доходитъ, а вотъ низкая какъ сюда дойдетъ?

Figure 8. Upper Theater cartoon from "The Spark." This cartoon, entitled "At the Opera: In a Box Adjoining the Paradis," highlights the vertical axis of cultural drift. As a married couple peer down through the chandelier fixtures in the direction of the stage, the wife declares, "In spite of the height, I consider that it is most convenient here—every high note reaches us." Her husband replies, "It isn't surprising that high notes reach us, but how will the low notes get up here?"

as Vol'f describes in his chronicle of nineteenth-century St. Petersburg theatergoing: "The most abundant rain of flowers poured forth from the reserved and endmost boxes of the first ring. . . . The boxes were all filled with flowers from private hothouses, and, by the end of the evening, they had all been thrown at the feet of popular divas."[77] "Flower frenzy" expressed the fullness of spirit inspired by the Italian opera. Iakhontov's memoirs describe how he flung a bouquet ecstatically at the stage, and saw it land unexpectedly elsewhere: "not having flown as far as the stage, the bouquet fell right onto one of the orchestra lamps and burned up, like a sacrifice (hecatomb), brought to the altar of art."[78] Having expended their energies and financial resources on these perishable tributes, opera lovers symbolically hurled themselves onto the stage at the feet of their idols.

According to Zotov, love of the theater moved down into the Russian middle classes beginning in the 1830s and 1840s, ending the exclusive access of the educated elite to professionally staged dramatic arts.[79] This development provoked the obvious derision directed at lower-middle-class opera devotees in stage vaudevilles such as P. I. Grigor'ev's "Chipping in for a Box at the Italian Opera" (1843) and Count Vladimir Sollogub's "Bouquets, or Petersburg Flower-Frenzy" (1845).[80] This flourishing dramatic trend depended on the juxtaposition of high opera and the prosaic Emperor's-new-clothes observations of the newer audience members, with a particular focus on jarring stylistic elements in the spoken text.[81]

Sollogub's "Bouquets" emphasizes the abandon and general silliness that attended the paying of flowery tributes to opera divas. The luckless clerk Triapka ("Rag") has been entrusted by his superior with attending the Italian opera regularly and tossing flowers to the requisite prima donna. But Triapka finds it nearly impossible to purchase bouquets, since he must vie with the St. Petersburg elite, who buy up every flower in town.

Sollogub's vaudeville depicts the audience recreating opera culture in its own image, despite the declaration of Triapka's superior that, "with the Italian opera I've become a completely new man." The flower shop is the scene of the following conversation about the relative merits of two prima donnas:

1: Trash! Trash! What kind of a singer is that! Simply trash [*drian'*]!
2: No, she's not trash! No, she's not trash! But yours, now *she's* trash! She's really trash![82]

The comic device in this excerpted dialogue is the insistent repetition of the word "trash," which is clearly inappropriate to the lofty discourse of opera culture. Italian opera's tunes, phrases, and postures permeate the local vocabulary in odd ways, creating malapropisms such as one character's misrendering of the famous Bellini aria "Casta diva" as "How are you, Diva" (*Kak ty, diva*). Sollogub's vaudeville concludes with musical numbers in Russian sung to tunes from well-known Donizetti and Rossini operas. These songs offer yet another example of downward cultural drift, integrating musical motifs from Italian opera with the cadences of Russian verse. Sollogub's songs recall the convention in eighteenth-century Russian comic opera of composing new words to the tunes of already-familiar ditties, a widely used Russian cultural shortcut.

Grigor'ev's vaudeville "Chipping in for a Box at the Italian Opera" similarly emphasizes the social dynamics of St. Petersburg's new opera culture. Physical settings underscore the vaudeville's social perspective: the first act takes place in the living room of an official named Chernushkin, and the second act is set, as precisely noted, in the corridor of the fourth ring of the St. Petersburg Bolshoi Theater. These two settings provide the vaudeville audience with an eavesdropper's perspective on the opera-going public of the fourth ring: the merchantry, lower grades of the civil service, servants, and assorted young swells (*franty*). "Chipping in" winks at the vaudeville audience over the heads of the characters, who are heard to exclaim over Tamburini's beautiful teeth and declare that Viardot has an "instrumental voice!" In its structure and physical staging, Grigor'ev's vaudeville presents the byplay among audience members as the primary spectacle in the opera house.

The first act opens with Chernushkin's wife and daughters Vavachka and Shanichka begging him to buy a season subscription to the Italian opera. Chernushkin's wife assures him that attending the opera will improve their daughters' marriage prospects, and suggests that the family invite a few knowledgeable cavaliers to their box, "who will whisper to us which passages should send us into raptures, and which to let pass by our ears."[83] Competition between Vavachka's three suitors becomes suspenseful when Chernushkin's wife declares that whoever can get them an opera box will marry Vavachka. The tension increases when the company learns that an elderly opera lover has passed away. Chernushkin's assembled guests agree to buy his box as a group, thus the title "Chipping in." The act closes with the guests crying out "Off to the Italians! . . . How happy I am! I shall perish from joy! To the opera! To the opera!"[84]

The stage directions for the second act specify a view through an open door of the fourth-ring corridor into the opera hall; a part of the great chandelier is visible, and through the door sound bits of music, applause, and cries of "Bravo!" Grigor'ev's second act makes a collage of fourth-ring Italian-opera ethnography: audience members arrive in time for the second act, splitting a box with friends who attend only the first act. A group of lackeys lounge in the corridor, listening to one of their number complain that he never gets paid on time: "just start asking, and the master takes a look at you, and instead of your salary, he sings you some 'talian song!" Another lackey confesses that his master made the household move from Muddy Street to Italian Street, and "Now they call the cook Tereshka *Terentini*! And I, sinner that I am, I'm no longer Makar these days, but *Macarini*!"[85]

This second act features many vignettes of vulgarity, and culminates with the settling of Vavachka's fate. Her father, Chernushkin, initially unenlightened about opera, is completely won over: "I am a different person! . . . Harmony . . . melody . . . have penetrated me through and through!"[86] European culture has worked its magic, and the vaudeville audience can only concur with the closing verse:

> He who is at the opera experiences all blessings!
> He's on view, and moreover held in great honor,
> And if not, he's ridiculous and a miser,
> And a decidedly bad person!

Vaudevilles such as "Bouquets" and "Chipping in" were very likely performed at the selfsame Bolshoi Theater they depicted, and their audiences probably included the works' actual objects of derision. The staging of meta-theatrical dramatic works such as the vaudevilles of Sollogub and Grigor'ev made explicit the self-regarding nature of opera culture, as well as the spectacular aspects of opera-going. These works emphasize the commodification of operatic experience, despite or perhaps *because of* its transcendent properties, and the participation of diverse social groups in St. Petersburg's growing operatic economy.

The fundamental change in the Italian opera's fortunes also measurably affected the operatic economy. When the Italian troupe moved to the Mariinskii in 1882, ticket prices increased by 25–50 percent in response to the directorate's waning support, which in turn forced a number of changes in the disposition of longtime opera-goers:

> According to the new prices, those who sat, for example, in the second row, were compelled to sit in the sixth row, and so forth, which was already in itself unpleasant, but was made extremely distressing when the composition of the troupe turned out to be worse than before. But if those who sat in the first rows moved back several rows, then where could those who had previously sat in the last rows go? Obviously, there was no place left for them in the theater.[87]

With the move to the Mariinskii, the Italian opera audience felt itself both more and less elite. Although fewer members of the St. Petersburg public could afford to buy tickets at the new prices, the Bolshoi's code of self-policing did not survive the move across the Theater Square. As Skal'kovskii does, the memoirist Ivanskaia remarks on how uncomfortable the old Bolshoi public felt after the move to the Mariinskii:

> For us, the old-timers, it was not what we were used to, somehow awkward. Torn away from our former, long-occupied seats, we lost something dear, something that dwelled within those walls that had seen so many delights for so many years! We roamed about the new corridors during the intermissions like shadows . . . meeting the unfamiliar public . . . which introduced . . . here the "partisan" ways and clumsy applause that always distinguished the public of the Russian opera.[88]

The Russian opera audience with its unrefined theater demeanor seemed to transform the entire history of Italian opera in St. Petersburg into a ghost story. The lost paradise of the Bolshoi represented a lost unity of operatic response. Although Skal'kovskii and Ivanskaia emphasize distinctions among that opera-going public, however, the distinct subcultures of the opera audience could fuse to form a crowd whose responses were by turns exhilarating and overwhelming.

THE AUDIENCE'S RESPONSE: CONVENTIONAL AND DISGRACEFUL SPECTACLES

It might seem that the popularity of Italian Romantic opera in the 1840s contradicted the move toward realist, socially conscious modes of representation in literary works such as Dostoevskii's novel *Poor Folk* (1846) and Nekrasov's anthology *Physiology of Petersburg* (1845). But, in fact, the Italian opera afforded its patrons an opportunity to revel in uninhibited emotional response to the performances, which opera-goers insisted was "genuine" and "true," the same code words invoked by the new artistic realism. Italian opera and its effects could not simply be dismissed with recourse to obsolete Romantic fashion and its middlebrow proponents.

The Italian opera provided an opportunity to represent the social order in visual terms, and, at the same time, it offered a cathartic experience in which all could share. Perhaps this is why the intensity of the operatic experience sometimes reflected the darker aspects of crowd psychology, giving rise to spectacles of public unruliness and political unrest. Depictions of the assembled opera audience as an unpredictable entity grew out of early, rapturous accounts of the thrilling effects opera produced on its listeners.[89] Reviews from the 1840s and 1850s describe transports of ecstasy experienced by the audience, as in the following account of Viardot singing in Bellini's *La Sonnambula*: "During those minutes, a feeling of unconscious rapture overcomes you (pl.), for which you cannot account; it is almost painful, because it overstrains your nerves, and by the end of the performance, you recover and enjoy the memory of the sensations, which do not leave you for a long, long time."[90] In the passage cited, the spectators are made equal by a democratic physical response that overcomes all of them in distinctly sexual terms. Iakhontov's memoirs contain similar descriptions of the unifying power of a performance, also by Viardot:

> such a powerful wave gushed forth, such a storm broke out, the likes of which I had never seen or heard before. . . . And I myself and everyone around me screamed, clapped, stamped with their feet and chairs, went wild . . . it was a kind of intoxication, a kind of contagion of enthusiasm, which instantly seized hold of everyone, from the bottom to the top. . . . Those who were not present in the opera hall that evening cannot imagine to what degree a mass of listeners can be electrified.[91]

Iakhontov locates himself within a roaring crowd, offering a single viewpoint that represents a unified whole. The participle "electrified" (*naelektrizovana*) occurs frequently in 1840s descriptions of the Italian opera, in spite of the fact that electric lighting would not be available until the final years of the Bolshoi's existence in the 1880s. For Iakhontov, opera represents an elemental force that lights up the world.

Battling against the furious bursts of applause that regularly interrupted performances, the Imperial Theater directorate instructed audiences not to clap until the end of each act. Skal'kovskii, among others, objected to this dictate, declaring applause to be a natural, reflexive action: "Forbidding applause is just as naïve as forbidding sneezing, yawning, or blinking."[92] Opera performances evoked in listeners responses that were far from behavioral norms, however. Stakhovich describes how he rushed out of the theater when Giulia Grisi played Norma: "it would not have been fitting for me to sob while wearing my Hussar jacket."[93] Aleksei Pleshcheev's poem to Viardot, entitled "To Desdemona" (1843–44), sets the poet-listener apart; he does not clap, cry out, or throw flowers, but lets a different sort of flower bloom within:

> While the noise of applause
> And cries filled the hall.
> Only I sat in silence,
> And did not express delight in any way.
>
> I did not throw you bouquets.
> I did not throw you a wreath;
> But a poem ripened in the poet's soul—
> Accept it: here is my flower![94]

The poet's response to Viardot, like so many literary tributes to opera culture, insists on the individual nature of the operatic experience. But, ironically, composing a poem in honor of the opera diva, not to mention tossing the scroll onto the stage along with the rain of bouquets, itself represented a highly conventional gesture in the repertoire of opera-going practices. The communal catharsis often swept up the performing artist as well, resulting in tearful expressions of gratitude and further delays in the performance: "How many times has one had occasion to see that the public's delight knew no bounds and the performer, touched by the sincerity of its display, unfeignedly wept."[95] Especially interesting here is the adverb "unfeignedly" (*nepritvorno*), meant to separate the performer's rendering of an operatic character from her genuine, unperformed response to the audience's delight. Other behaviors expressing a unified response included groups running alongside a diva's carriage as she returned to her hotel after the opera. Young men would even harness themselves to a beloved performer's carriage and pull it through the St. Petersburg streets. Groups of admirers waited by the Bolshoi exits for hours in hopes of glimpsing a diva and receiving from her a single flower or a glove.

The behavior exhibited by an opera audience had a darker side, too. During the second part of the nineteenth century, claques of supporters distributed themselves throughout the opera theater, organizing demonstrations of their support, whistling, calling out insults, and generally interfering with performances. The intensity of such displays, which were particularly common in the provinces, suggested an uncontrolled mob. Mass disarray in an operatic context by no means confined itself to the provinces, however. Ivanskaia describes the unseemly scene that transpired in St. Petersburg during the 1869 season, when citizens tried to purchase tickets for a performance by Adelina Patti:

> A real battle took place when the crowd, having gathered during the night in front of the Bolshoi Theater, began to besiege it when the box office opened. There was such a stampede that thirty people were carried out of the crowd unconscious, and two, they say, were completely crushed. Foot policemen took to their heels, and it became necessary to send for mounted gendarmes, who dispersed the crowd with their horses.[96]

The Theater directorate had created a new, fourth subscription for the 1869 season in anticipation of tremendous demand, since both Pauline Lucca and

Adelina Patti would perform with the Italian opera troupe that year. This Theater Square riot coincided with a famine in several Russian provinces, a juxtaposition that inspired "Ode on the Occasion of a Fourth Subscription to the Italian Opera," published in the newspaper *The Voice.* The poem begins by describing what appears to be a public demonstration in response to news of the famine:

> Where are the noisy waves of people flowing
> During these days of repentance, prayer, and fasting?
> Everyone is so alarmed, everyone is full of impatience;
> Their eyes burn with fire, their lips keep silent . . .
> Are they not all indignant at the people's calamity,
> About which news has traveled across all Russia?
> Are they not hurrying to help their hungry brethren
> And to bring a sacrifice to the altar of the Fatherland?

The poem describes the spectacle of public unrest from the perspective of a baffled onlooker standing apart from the riot, a surrogate for the reader. The crowd itself resembles a natural phenomenon ("noisy waves") that has arisen as an appropriate response to the famine. But the poem goes on reproachfully:

> But what is the reason for this so gigantic struggle!
> No, the people here are not hurrying to save the hungry?
> This is a sacrifice carried to the Italian opera—
> To open its fourth subscription.
> You see how deeply we respect Art!
> In a calamitous time, we are ready to forget all . . .
> We bring our last *grosh,* fracture ourselves,
> Just so we manage to get a ticket to the opera.

In a striking reevaluation of the opera-goer's passion, the poem views the crowd's desire to hear two popular prima donnas not as evidence of an unquenchable love for art, but as a display of barbarism. The all-consuming search for a ticket to the Italian opera, a matter for satire in the vaudevilles of Grigor'ev and Sollogub, here becomes the stuff of social outrage. And the Italian opera, which once consoled Russians for the lack of full participation in public life, now prevents educated citizens from fulfilling their civic responsibilities. The author's ironic choice of the odic genre for this social critique underscores the poem's rejection of an exalted status for opera.

In the West, opera audience unruliness represented a response to the events transpiring on stage. French *grand opéra* from the first half of the nineteenth century frequently included large-scale choral scenes depicting an unruly mob or a chaotic battle scene, as in Auber's *The Mute Girl of Portici* (1828), Halévy's *The Jewess* (1835), Meyerbeer's *The Huguenots* (1836) and *The Prophet* (1849), and Berlioz's *The Trojans* (1856–58).[97] Social and political conflicts appeared on the Russian opera stage much later, in Musorgskii's *Boris Godunov*, which was staged for a few years during the 1870s and then not again until Rimskii-Korsakov's second revision of the opera in 1908, and in Musorgskii's unfinished *Khovanshchina*, which had its first major production in 1911. Throughout the nineteenth century, Russian censors subjected Western operas with overtly political themes, *Les Huguenots* and Rossini's *William Tell* (1829) among them, to drastic cuts and elisions before these works were declared appropriate for Russian audiences. But as the "Ode on the Occasion of a Fourth Subscription to the Italian Opera" proves, opera could inspire the very sort of demonstrations the censors sought to avoid. In this, Russian opera audiences gradually came to resemble the restless proletarian and petty bourgeois spectators at the Paris theaters after 1830.

At the beginning of the twentieth century, opera performances in Russia began to coincide with actual spectacles of explicit political protest and marked social unrest.[98] In a fusion of political and operatic spectacle, a group of students staged a demonstration in the gallery during a 1905 Mariinskii theater performance of Wagner's *Lohengrin*, crying out "Down with autocracy!" A fight broke out between the students and a group of officers, transforming the theater into a battle arena and interrupting the performance. The Russian diva Maria Kuznetsova-Benois, who was singing the role of Elsa that evening, convinced the crowd to settle down by singing the national anthem, compelling all to participate in a staged display of unity.[99] The opera theater offered an ideal setting for a dramatic event such as an assassination attempt, since an audience of witnesses was already assembled. In September 1911, Prime Minister Peter Stolypin was assassinated during a performance of

Rimskii-Korsakov's opera *Tale of the Tsar Saltan* (1900) at the Kiev Opera House. Tsar Nicholas II himself was witness to this most famous opera-house spectacle of social disarray.

At the end of Alexander Amfiteatrov's novel *Twilight of the Little Gods* (1908), an angry mob takes over the opera theater that serves as the central setting for the literary work. The mob overruns all boundaries between the spectator zones: "The wild, drunken commotion flowed into the theater in waves of street filth. . . . In the boxes, prostitutes made faces, playing at society ladies."[100] Amfiteatrov's mob desecrates the temple of art, chasing performers and management from the theater. But the protesters are reactionaries who object to the troupe's new, "revolutionary" opera *The Peasant War*, not radicals who seek to topple the rule of Western art and aesthetics. Amfiteatrov's final spectacle represents a logical extension rather than a complete overturning of the traditional performer/spectator dynamic, since the boundaries between audience and performers were always highly permeable.

BOUNDARY CROSSINGS

Russian literature consistently emphasizes the similarities between performers and spectators with theatrical metaphors characterizing nineteenth-century society. Bulgarin's feuilleton "A Philosophical Glance Behind the Scenes" (1825) develops such a metaphor in detail, declaring that the function of theatrical scenery in society is fulfilled by "wealth, family connections, a well-known name, the favor of important personages." Theatrical lighting corresponds to "ringing phrases, puns, the art of bowing and scraping, and beauty," and the role of the orchestra to "flattery and hypocrisy."[101] Witty phrases and fluid bows direct the viewer's attention as the performer chooses. Bulgarin's lighting metaphor makes free with the boundary between spectator and performer, and in doing so reveals the affinity between the two positions.

The operatic experience often transcends the traditional boundary between spectator and performer. Vladimir Benediktov's poem "Madwoman" (1853) enacts the merging of subjective response and objective perception within the poet-listener as he hears Viardot sing Dargomyzhskii's eponymous romance:

"I still love him, madwoman that I am."
"I still" . . . Just those [three] words, and you
Took them and poured them into my soul—
I foresaw it all: Already ahead of time, my soul is ready
for the last: "I love."
"I love" is not yet sung, and already a hundred times
The question has died out in my breast: "Whom?"
And you respond: "Him." Now everything is clear;
No name is needed—O yes, him, him![102]

The poet-listener anticipates the coming notes of the romance, hearing the previous phrase reverberate and incorporating these echoes into his lyric. With the poet's fevered cry "O yes, him, him!," which stages a performance of spontaneous response, the personae of spectator and performer merge completely. Benediktov's poem continues for an additional three stanzas beyond what is cited here, intensifying the creative interplay of the poet-spectator with the unfolding performance.

The self-awareness of the operatic spectator could also take comic form. Skal'kovskii's description of a fire that broke out during a performance of Auber's *Fra Diavolo* (1830) equates the theatricality of the opera audience's behavior with the theatricality of opera itself. According to Skal'kovskii, spectators were carried away by the drama of the threatened conflagration, and enacted their hurried exit from the theater as a sort of performance: "There were ladies who stood as if rooted to the spot and screamed, 'We are burning!' and a gentleman lowered his wife by her arms from the bel-étage to the floor seats, although it would have been simpler to exit through the corridor."[103] But the popular public masquerades held during the Christmas holidays and Shrovetide (*Maslenitsa*) represented the most explicit manifestations of the ambiguous relationship between spectators and performers, and the officially unofficial nature of theatergoing culture. The Imperial Theater directorate organized these masquerades in the St. Petersburg public theaters, often at the Bolshoi, which could accommodate twelve thousand guests.[104] During masquerades, a false floor placed over the seating areas on the main floor of the theater transformed the entire theater into a stage, upon which masked and gowned guests could disport themselves. But only those guests properly attired in masks and robes were permitted onto the main floor for dancing and socializing. Uncostumed guests observed the proceedings from their boxes and maintained a more "conventional" relationship between spectators and performers. But the presence of these observers itself represented a convention of the masquerade event. And the fact that the Theater directorate organized these masquerades naturally added to the sense that every aspect of the event was part of a staged performance.[105]

Any person who could afford the cost of a masquerade costume and the modest admission fee might attend, conceal her true identity, and perhaps try on an unaccustomed social role. In the words of Arbenin, the hero of Lermontov's play "Masquerade" (1835): "Under a mask, all ranks are equal. A mask has neither a soul nor a title—only a body. And people conceal their features with a mask, they boldly remove the mask from their feelings."[106] Masks offered a means to disguise and reveal oneself simultaneously, and an opportunity to transcend a limiting social self. Count Sollogub's story "High Society" (1839) depicts a masquerade in the St. Petersburg Bolshoi Theater, an event that the narrator describes as a procession of various costumes: "Over the staircases thronged dress suits wearing round hats, uniforms with multicolored plumed hats, and around them spun and squeaked masks of every color and appearance."[107] The narrator's description does not distinguish at all between the theatricality of social life and the conventions of masquerade dress. Sollogub's use of the masquerade setting enables him to stage an exaggerated, almost parodic, confrontation between public image and private yearnings, the confrontation often staged by society tales.[108]

The constraint of the society tale provides an effective contrast to the conventionalized abandon characteristic of opera-going: sobbing, tossing extravagant bouquets, clapping frantically, and pulling carriages through muddy streets. Nineteenth-century opera-going confronted questions of social hierarchy and public life, creating opportunities to transcend these bounds, if only for the duration of an opera performance. The alternative perspectives provided by parody and social satire also challenged the distinctions between theater regions. In this negotiation of generic and social hierarchies, Russian audience members became both the producers and the products of opera-going culture.

Many operatic anecdotes suggest the existence of a communal "opera-space" in imperial Russia, the stage for a temporary, ephemeral sort of society that managed and expressed itself in the absence of state interference.[109] Opera-goers who violated the codes of this space could be swiftly and cruelly punished. Public self-governance within "opera-space" was possible because the opera audience was an entirely artificial, largely performative social body, which enjoyed a concomitant measure of time-limited freedom to express its rapture and outrage. The resulting behaviors represented a controlled frenzy that nevertheless offered a much-needed release, particularly from the repressive environment created by Tsar Nicholas I during the first half of the nineteenth century. The presence of the tsar himself, or even the reminder afforded by his empty box in the opera theater, prevented audience members from forgetting that the relative freedom of "opera-space" *was* officially sanctioned.

Chapter Three

Embodying Opera
The Prima Donna in Russia

The nineteenth-century opera prima donna was a living art object, a composite of operatic heroines that she imbued with her own personal qualities.[1] The roles developed and played by the prima donna were known as "images" (*obrazy* in the Russian tradition) and "impersonations." Lithographs and drawings show the prima donna in varied poses and costumes, suggesting that she could recreate herself artistically ad infinitum. The advent of photographic images re-conceived the prima donna's roles as tangible aesthetic creations whose symbolic likenesses could be purchased and contemplated in private. Angiolina Bosio's Traviata, Maria Slavina's Carmen, and Medea Figner's Tatiana represent finished "works" that occupy a permanent place in the Russian cultural pantheon.

Although stage deities such as the ballerina and the opera tenor shared the nineteenth-century limelight, the opera prima donna reigned supreme. The diva's primacy began in the late eighteenth century, when she supplanted the castrato, a surgically created adult male soprano or contralto. Opera seria's heroic male roles had called for high voices, parts that could also be sung by cross-dressed women. Roles gradually improved for female characters, as Mozart and Rossini structured operatic works around female star performers, and major opera composers such as Meyerbeer, Bellini, Donizetti, and Verdi followed suit. Opera historian Ethan Mordden notes "the Romantic era's escalating hunger for dramatic urgency in heroines. . . . One might expect such an era to raise up a squad of male avatars—signing pacts, breaching gulfs, shaking the world. But it was the diva who became opera's Romantic icon."[2] Since the prima donna who gave the premiere performance of a given role was said to have "created" the character, she could play Romantic genius-creator along with the opera composer and literary author. Moreover, the titles of operatic works often reflect the diva-heroine's centrality in Romantic opera: *Lucia di Lammermoor*, *Anna Bolena*, *Norma*, *Lucrezia Borgia*, *La Traviata*, *Luisa Miller*, *Aida*. The female figure had become central to nationalist discourse, with the appearance of gendered national symbols such as Marianne, Britannia, and Germania.[3] This development counterbalanced opera's transnationalist aspirations, casting the opera prima donna as precious national resource and ideal national representative.

The nineteenth-century opera diva, a figure emphatically, even exaggeratedly female, resembles the Romantic male hero, who was defiant, isolated, and larger than life. In contrast, Russian memoirist K. A. Skal'kovskii attributed the prima donna's predominance to her amplification of ordinary female traits:

> When appearing on the stage, women seem to lose less in their human dignity than men do. This can be explained by the fact that women are very often actresses in life. From them one does not expect the straightforwardness demanded of men. Therefore women must lie less in order to play their roles well. On the other hand, in displaying themselves before the public on the stage boards, women violate one's feeling of propriety less than men do, since one of the obligations of a woman in society consists of exhibiting herself to delight the eye.[4]

In Skal'kovskii's view, the opera prima donna was a woman doing what comes naturally; thus, theater provided a logical extension to gender. Visual representations of the opera diva in both stage costume and everyday dress reflected her dual role as actress and real-life woman. But this conflation of femininity and performance did not seem natural to everyone. Originally viewed by Romantic convention as an otherworldly figure with transcendent artistic powers, the prima donna also came, most ambiguously, to exemplify female self-determination, and even financial independence.[5] The "discourse" of the opera prima donna marries aristocratic and democratic pretensions, rendering her at once poetically untouchable and prosaically accessible. The prima donna, an earthly, feminine embodiment of the divine in its relation to art, manifested the longstanding association between artistic muse and female beloved, but in increasingly self-contradictory terms.

Figure 9. Giuditta Pasta. This lithograph of the opera prima donna, with its accompanying verse tribute in Italian, represents her as muse and quasi-deity. Dressed in flowing white and coiffed in the classical manner, she plays a celestial harp.

Skal'kovskii's characterization also evokes the dramatic actress, who emerged as a public figure and respectable professional during the last quarter of the nineteenth century.[6] The famed Sarah Bernhardt performed in Russia during several tours beginning in 1881, exciting critical controversy over the acclaim and profit she expertly generated. Actresses Maria Savina and Maria Ermolova made themselves widely known to the theatergoing public during the final years of the Imperial Theater monopoly and into the early years of the twentieth century. The most famous Silver Age Russian actress was Vera Kommissarzhevskaia, the "Russian Duse," who captivated the public in the 1890s and 1910s. Kommissarzhevskaia achieved greater fame in her own country than did any female Russian opera singer.[7] Although Russian actresses enjoyed more opportunities to engage with contemporary women's themes, however, they were bound by reasons of language to the stage of their own country. The Russian actress's artistic identity represented an uneasy blend of translated Western roles and native dramatic "types."[8] The opera prima donna, in theory, was a cultural emissary who possessed the power to traverse national, linguistic, and social boundaries. But she rarely played a woman of her own time on stage.

ROLES AND RECEPTION

Some divas transformed themselves with each role. Pauline Viardot, who dazzled St. Petersburg audiences with her whole-souled renderings of Rosina, Desdemona, and Lucia in the 1840s, was compared by one reviewer to "the legendary Proteus."[9] But Adelina Patti was always herself, no matter which role she played; her coloratura flourishes and fashionable toilettes commanded far more attention than did her dramatic interpretations.[10]

The legal contracts Western prima donnas like Viardot and Patti made with the Russian Imperial Theater directorate provide a historical context for the prima donna's formal relationship to her roles. According to Viardot's 1843–45 contract, the prima donna reserved for herself alone the right to play "les rôles de prima-donna," which included all major soprano and mezzo-soprano parts in the Italian troupe's repertoire.[11] Viardot had the right to renounce specific prima donna roles if she wished, and could perform freely in

Figure 10. Pauline Viardot as Rosina. Viardot's Spanish ancestry was particularly apparent when she was costumed in this way. But the legendary songstress and accomplished dramatic actress could play nearly any role for a mezzo, including "breeches" parts.

public concerts and at soirees that fell outside the directorate's purview. She could not refuse to play prima donna roles in additional operas the directorate decided to stage, nor could she prevent the directorate from hiring a replacement, should she become indisposed. The contractual structure that allowed a prima donna to *be* a prima donna balanced her primary status within the troupe against protections for the directorate. The "boilerplate" included in all contracts regarding the performing artist's legal rights to costumes and accoutrements attempted to distinguish the prima donna's "person" from roles that constituted the directorate's own property: "The Directorate . . . will furnish . . . those dresses, head apparel, gloves and shoes termed 'characteristic' [in connection with stage roles] . . . the performer [*artistka*] is herself obligated to provide those dresses, head apparel, gloves and shoes termed 'everyday.'" The language and tone of this boilerplate differs strikingly from that in a contract the directorate made with Russian singer Daria Leonova in the late 1850s. Leonova's contract stated that she would receive costumes, and must be satisfied with them "in the state that they are given to me." The more severe language deemed appropriate for a native Russian artist indicates the directorate's wish to manage Leonova's stage persona, unchallenged by the singer's own rights and judgments.[12]

The boundary between the prima donna's artistic and personal identities was an arbitrary one as far as the opera-going public and the prima donna herself were concerned. An 1836 Odessa newspaper asserted a perfect identity between the diva Tassistro and Bellini's Norma, for example: "She *is* Norma, she is the realization of the poem that achieved immortality through Bellini's touch."[13] A verse tribute to Viardot by Aleksei Pleshcheev, entitled "To a Singer" (1846), typically merges the prima donna's image with her best-known roles. The poem does not name the vocalist, except in parentheses after the title, and renders Viardot as a pastiche of effects and characters.

Artistic reflections on the prima donna's relationship to her roles became increasingly self-conscious during the course of the nineteenth century. Several Western operas call for the prima donna to play the part of a singer: Ponchielli's *La Gioconda* (1876), Offenbach's *The Tales of Hoffmann* (1881), and, most famously, Puccini's *Tosca* (1900), in which the performing artist sings the aria "Vissi d'arte," declaring "I lived for Art," as she simultaneously tells her own story and that of Puccini's eponymous heroine. Anastasia Verbitskaia's novella *The Abandoned Man* (1925/26) similarly reflects upon the possibilities of assuming roles in social, literary, and artistic terms. Verbitskaia's heroine Vera grows bored with the roles available to her: popular Muscovite conservatory student, first lady of a provincial community, teacher, wife, and mother. She abandons this life to become an opera prima donna. When she returns to Moscow after years spent performing in Europe, she has learned to play the performing artist (*artistka*) with consummate skill, and has reinvented herself as "Lola." She impersonates a great lady of the stage at a musical evening: "Lola arrived . . . dressed very simply, all in black, without a single diamond. The women with the manner of connoisseurs looked over this severe, but exquisite toilette down to its tiniest details. . . . Respect for the performing artist rose by several degrees."[14] Vera projects a public self appropriate for "Lola," the persona that represents her greatest creative achievement. The assembled women interpret her impeccable taste in dress as confirmation that she is an artist.

Reviewers' preoccupation with physical appearance could entirely eclipse their view of a female singer's talent, as illustrated in the following dismissive assessment of the soprano Venturi playing Adalgisa in Bellini's *Norma*: "she has a pretty voice, but this does not justify her appearance costumed as a Druidess in the bloom of youth, whom a Roman, accorded the highest dignities of the empire, seeks to seduce."[15] Venturi's creditable soprano does not compensate for her failure to look fetching in a Druid costume. The reviewer assumes the quintessential "attitude" of the male opera-goer, with his merciless gaze fixed upon the prima donna's feminine and artistic attributes. Even an ostensibly flattering account of a singer's appearance might obscure her other gifts, as demonstrated by the following blizzard of enthusiastic diminutives: "As concerns . . . Mademoiselle Colti . . . she is an extremely pretty petite blonde [*prekhoroshen'kaia blondinka]*, with a sweet little voice [*s milen'kim golosochkom*], rounded and small [*kruglen'kim no malen'kim*] like this interesting songstress herself."[16] Colti's voice serves as an analogue for her physical self, emphasizing that Colti-the-performing-artist *is* Colti-the-woman. As one reviewer put it, "beauty in a woman is in itself already half of her gift for the stage."[17] Even Viardot's artistry could not exempt her from severe assessments of her feminine charms: "Perhaps, [she] is the only female performing artist, who, with the expressiveness and plasticity of her acting, could make one forget about her physical ugliness."[18]

Although the prima donna sometimes seemed lacking in requisite womanly attributes, opera chroniclers excuse her with reference to a burning goddesslike or queenlike temperament. The passionate natures of performers such as Giuditta Pasta, Maria Malibran, and Pauline Viardot were legendary. When Viardot played Norma in 1844, one Russian reviewer declared, "She displays so much heat and passion that during some moments, one becomes terrified for her."[19] Another reviewer characterized the diva Pauline Lucca as a small, perfectly formed woman, "who was all passion and fire."[20] The majestic mezzo Maria Slavina almost exclusively played women with strong, willful natures such as Carmen, Dalila, Amneris, and Ortrude. Images of the prima donna as a goddess are brought to earth in a number of Russian literary works from the later nineteenth century, however. According to these works, the diva's outsize nature, which can express itself fully only in a room the size of a theater hall, makes her unfit for personal happiness.

The prima donna's historic connection with the nine Muses, daughters of Zeus and the Titaness Mnemosyne, who visit and inspire mortals on earth, offers one explanation for the opera diva's quasi-deification. "Who are the Muses?" asks Robert S. Dupree in his essay on Euterpe:

> Originally goddesses of song and, according to some sources, only three in number, their inspiratory character encompassed a single art that the Greeks called "music" and that included the combined elements of what we would call music, oral poetry, and dance. Their first mythopoeic names—Preparation (or practice), Memory, and Song—stand clearly for the three necessary components of the art. We might call them "technique," "tradition," and "performance." Their later mythological elaboration into nine rendered the salient differences between various kinds of song more prominent. In the early Greek world the transmission of knowledge was carried out through the "technology" or craft of song; it was, for all practical purposes, the equivalent of what today we would call "culture."[21]

In the Western tradition, the opera prima donna represents a return to a classical conception of culture itself, embodied by female incarnations of song.

Russian periodicals and memoirs play with the common linguistic origin of the Russian words "*diva*" (female opera singer) and "*divo*" (marvel), both of which are related to the Latin *divus* (god).[22] The theater chronicler Vol'f declares that Pauline Viardot was "marvelously good" (*divno khorosha*) in both comic and tragic roles, Stark characterizes Evgenia Mravina's coloratura as "marvelously developed" (*vydelana na-divo*), and Ivanskaia claims that Pauline Lucca was "marvelously well-formed" (*slozhennaia na divo*).[23] Vladimir Nemirovich-Danchenko's novel *Stage Wings* (1899) employs words formed from the root *div-* to describe a sunrise scene in the mountains near Ravenna, and to refer to the diva-heroine herself, appropriately named Raevskaia (from *raiskii*, or heavenly). During a span of nine pages, the reader learns that "The night was marvelous" (*divnaia*), "Marvelous vistas [*divnye dali*] stretched out all around," "With marvelous speed [*s divnoi bystrotoi*] the colors and shadows changed," and finally, that Raevskaia "was marvelously pretty [*divno khorosha*]."[24] With these linguistic figurations, the author links his heroine's artistic identity with the stylistic register required to describe her. Nemirovich-Danchenko represents the prima donna as both a natural wonder and a phenomenon in excess of nature. The prima donna simultaneously embodies, etymologically speaking, the divine being come to earth and the earthly being striving for divinity.[25] She re-incarnates herself with each role.[26]

The fact that individual prima donnas "ruled over" particular nineteenth-century social sectors reflected the prima donna's status as queen of the arts. In the late 1840s, the St. Petersburg Bolshoi Theater divided itself into factions supporting the rival sopranos Erminia Frezzolini and Giuli Borsi, called Frezzolinists and Borsists. Frezzolini was the favorite of the aristocracy, who sat in the bel-étage and the baignoire, whereas Borsi was beloved by the more democratic upper rings of the theater. Frezzolini joined the Italian troupe after Borsi, eventually stealing away the latter's roles: Lucrezia, Giselda, and Elvira: "The struggle manifested itself most particularly during performances in which both prima donnas took part—for example, in *Robert* or *Don*

Figure 11. Maria Malibran. Malibran, who died in her twenties after a riding accident, was famous for her vivid diva's temperament and unusually charismatic stage presence. She became the subject of several biographies after her untimely death.

Giovanni. Each faction tried to summon its goddess for an extra bow and to throw her as many bouquets as possible."[27] Frezzolini eventually prevailed, and Borsi left the St. Petersburg Italian troupe. The arrival of the soprano Giulia Grisi for the 1849–50 season, however, proved too strong a challenge to Frezzolini, who soon left St. Petersburg herself. The existence of two prima donnas within a single troupe represented both a linguistic and a cultural impossibility.[28]

Every prima donna had to contend with the public's changing response to her as she aged. Reviewers could be merciless toward a female vocalist past her prime. In the early 1840s, St. Petersburg served as a regular stopping-off point for prima donnas trying to hold back the ravages of time, most notably Giuditta Pasta at the end of her career. Russian critics emphasized the flaws in Pasta's voice and technique, as though refusing to bow down before the West's operatic leftovers (see chapter 4). The aging prima donna eventually served as a figure for the waning nineteenth century itself. Ivan Leont'ev-Shcheglov's story "Min'ona" (1881) depicts the discomfort of a provincial audience receiving the fictional Italian soprano Fiorentini, now dumpy and middle-aged. "Min'ona" illustrates the diminishing power of nineteenth-century art, particularly Romantic opera, within a changing social context. Romantic opera remained fashionable long after the decline of literary Romanticism, but finally came to seem socially and aesthetically anachronistic during the last part of the century.

A series of operatic roles for older women, foremost among them the old Countess in Tchaikovskii's *Queen of Spades*, offered a respectable end to a stage career. It was critical that the prima donna sense the appropriate moment for this transition, however. One opera historian praised Maria Slavina for recognizing that she had reached this point: "Slavina offered a splendid example of self-awareness and at the right time calmly shifted to 'nanny' roles [*roli 'nian"*], as she expressed it."[29] In the novel *Twilight of the Little Gods* (1908), Alexander Amfiteatrov's portly mezzo Svetlitskaia shows less discernment, stubbornly continuing to play cross-dressed parts in unbecoming short tunics and tights.

An aging prima donna's gradual loss of both her feminine allure and her status as operatic deity shapes A. N. Davydov's unpublished recollections of Adelina Patti. Davydov first heard Patti perform in 1890, and was struck by an unnatural quality in the famous soprano's voice: "when she sings, some kind of special instrument has been placed in her mouth, and she simply controls it. Much as I regret to say it, I thought that it was some kind of 'trick' [*fokus*]."[30] Davydov's characterization of Patti's voice as a kind of accessory to her public self offers an apt metaphor for youth, beauty, talent, and celebrity.

Years later, Davydov attended a cycle of opera performances at the Bayreuth festival, and noticed "a heavily made-up old woman, all covered with diamonds and other precious stones." This old woman, Davydov learned, is the celebrated Patti, now relegated to the audience on operatic occasions. Elegant young men approached the ancient Patti during the intermissions, kissed her hand, and offered to escort her about the theater.

Davydov's account of Patti recalls Pushkin's famous story, "Queen of Spades" (1833), the literary inspiration for a Tchaikovskii opera that was well known by the time of this encounter during the early years of the twentieth century. Patti reigned in her time as the most famous of divas, just as late-eighteenth-century society celebrated Pushkin's old Countess as the "Muscovite Venus." And, like Pushkin's old Countess, Patti reluctantly surrendered the privileges she enjoyed as reigning queen of a bygone era, making a negative, inverted spectacle of herself. Pushkin's ancient countess attends balls, rouged and dressed in the fashions of the 1770s, sitting all evening in a corner, "like an ugly but necessary decoration of the ballroom."[31] The young hero of Pushkin's story finds himself a reluctant, unseen witness to the "repulsive secrets" of the countess's toilette as he hides in her rooms. As her final role, Patti transforms herself into a hideous parody of a prima donna and satisfies her insatiable vanity by requiring that her admirers observe the external forms of obeisance.

Davydov became acquainted with the aged Patti during the six days of the operatic cycle, and reports her affectionate, if self-absorbed words about the Russian public: "I have traveled over nearly the entire world, but I never encountered such applause and such enthusiasm in any other country." The opera historian H. Sutherland Edwards amplifies Patti's fondness for Russia, including the following alleged instance of diva overstatement:

> Ah, how I dote on Russia! So many of my happiest hours have been spent there. One never sees such audiences as those in St. Petersburg . . . Do you remember how the dear old Empress used to make tea for me between the acts? God bless her! and that grand old gentleman, the Czar, who used to let me call him "papa!" Ah, me! How I shall miss them both. They were so dignified, and yet so gentle with little me. I shall always love Russia and the Russians for their sakes.[32]

Figure 12. Portrait photograph of Adelina Patti. Patti might well be the most often represented nineteenth-century diva. She is the subject of countless photographs, lithographs, and drawings. As this portrait does, most images of Patti feature elaborate ornaments and fashion accessories.

Patti's reputed evocation of Tsar Alexander II and his wife literally turns the prima donna's socially problematic career into a tea party, and makes her the godchild of the Russian nation. She casts herself as the grandly condescending, pampered darling of the world. The tsar's 1881 assassination and the social unrest in early-twentieth-century Russia do not register in the prima donna's history of self.

As the Wagner cycle neared its conclusion, Davydov requested an autographed photograph of the living operatic relic. He ceremoniously presented himself at Patti's hotel, noting drily that he "conversed, as befits a gallant cavalier, for fifteen minutes," then "received the promised photograph, and withdrew." In return for a souvenir of Patti's vanished greatness, the image in which she continues to trade, Davydov offers her the observance of forms she treasures. His description of Patti suggests the overdevelopment and decay of nineteenth-century opera culture, a notion further supported by the Wagner opera cycle of several days' duration that Davydov attended at Bayreuth, home of the Richard Wagner Festivals.

WESTERN AND RUSSIAN PRIMA DONNAS

The prima donna as a native cultural phenomenon in Russia began to develop in the eighteenth century, largely in response to touring and resident Western troupes. The first Russian female opera singers were quite literally slaves to their cultural setting. Eighteenth-century Russian private estate theaters featured serf women performers such as the celebrated Praskovia Ivanovna Koval'ova (Zhemchugova) in elaborate productions of Western and Russian opera, ballet, drama, comedy, vaudeville, and tableaux. The tradition of estate theaters, whose performers, theater buildings, costumes, and scenery belonged to their titled landowners, continued up to the 1861 emancipation of the Russian serfs.[33]

The notion of a distinct operatic "school" for Russian female vocalists was long in appearing, as it was hindered by the general lack of professional training and by the challenges of shaping Russian voices to Western models. Neither the St. Petersburg nor the Moscow Conservatory was established until the 1860s. As Raphael Zotov declared, Russia's northern climate did not produce "the flexible and tender voices of Italy . . . these were all northern, Petersburg voices, developed solely through zeal and love for art."[34] For Zotov, the Russian prima donna represented a victory of culture over nature, in contrast to her Italian counterpart, whose art flowed organically from her natural, physical endowments and originary setting.

The sharp inequity in the financial resources available to Italian and Russian opera troupes during the nineteenth century also made the notion of a "Russian prima donna" seem oxymoronic. For much of the nineteenth century, Russian female vocalists employed by the Imperial Theater directorate were generally young women of limited means who had graduated from the state's Theater Institute. Singers under contract played the roles that the directorate chose for them, often performing in multiple theaters during the course of a single day. Russian female vocalists needed official permission to leave town for brief periods, to marry, or to change their names. A social abyss separated these early female stage professionals from the genteel young ladies who could acquit themselves creditably if asked to sing, play the piano, or pluck a harp before company. As Richard Stites declares: "Few Russian novels about the gentry failed to feature a piano performance or song by a young marriageable girl. . . . Like the ball, home performance was a well-established practice of chaste interaction among the sexes, the compliments and blushes being as much a part of the performance as the movement of the hands or the vocal chords."[35] Performances by amateur female singers also constituted a regular feature of salon culture during the first half of the nineteenth century.

While Russian music critics stressed the social prestige and titled spouses with which Western divas ornamented their public personae, they relentlessly emphasized the humble origins and questionable social poise of their own Russian singers. The histories of actresses and singers contained in the archive of the Russian Imperial Theater directorate trace the modest scope of these lives and careers as reflected in contracts, deferential requests, small incremental raises, and pensions.[36] An account of such a female performer's career serialized in a midcentury theater journal offers a suggestive accompaniment to these archival documents.[37] "Pictures of the Past: Notes of a Russian Female Performer" describes the experiences of singer and dancer Alexandra Asenkova, a village girl who considered herself lucky to have been accepted at the Theater Institute. The heroine undergoes a long apprenticeship period at the institute and becomes a reliable stage professional. The female narrator tells her story not as a series of artistic triumphs or as an ascent to celebrity, but as the tale of how her own unremarkable life intersected with the lives of important and famous figures such as the Imperial family of Tsar Alexander

I, for whom she performed, and major historical events such as the 1811 burning of the Bolshoi Theater and the Napoleonic Wars.

S. V. Taneev's memoirs about the Imperial Theater describe the extensive training provided by the Theater Institute during the period 1825–56. The approximately one hundred students of the institute, both women and men, attended courses in catechism, French, German, Italian, Russian, arithmetic, geography, history, penmanship, ballroom dancing, fencing, singing, drawing and handiwork, rhetoric and declamation, mythology, music theory, piano, and violin.[38] Taneev represents the female stage artist in Russia as the product of a rigorous training process, suggesting that entrants to the institute possessed none of the necessary skills. The Russian female performer also needed to be adept at negotiating the perils of a surrounding aristocratic milieu eager for romantic diversions:

> The young Guards and representatives of the highest elite looked upon the female performing artists as upon a vast gynaeceum, distinguished from a peasant harem only by its brilliance, refinement, and richness of choice. The women pupils of the theater institutes, female dancers, ballet and theater extras, and leading ladies, the "first subjects" in comedy and drama—all of these served as the object of attentions, passions, and innumerable romantic adventures with tangled intrigues, daring abductions and bloody duels.[39]

Female performers represent doubly appropriated narrative objects; they are compelled to perform roles in theatrical productions, as well as in the Romantic social escapades conceived by their patrons.

The best-known Russian female opera singers from the early nineteenth century included Elizaveta Sandunova, a Theater School graduate who performed for Catherine the Great at the Hermitage Theater in 1791, Nimfodora Semenova, sister of the more famous dramatic actress Ekaterina Semenova, and Maria Stepanova, celebrated for her renderings of Glinka soprano roles: Antonida from *A Life for the Tsar* and Ludmila from *Ruslan and Liudmila*. The contralto Anna Vorob'eva-Petrova can be considered the first professional Russian female singer with a distinctly non-Western vocal style. She excelled at singing the Russian art songs (*romansy*) composed by Glinka, Dargomyzhskii, and others. Although Vorob'eva-Petrova was much beloved by her pub-

Figure 13. Elizaveta Lavrovskaia as Ratmir. The mid-century Russian female opera performer often appeared costumed as a man, a function of the excellent mezzo-soprano voices "native" to Russia and the limited parts available for this vocal type.

lic, however, her operatic career played itself out quietly and modestly on the Russian stage. With characteristic bravado, the memoirist Avdot'ia Golovacheva-Panaeva states that, "if she [Vorob'eva-Petrova] had been a foreigner, she would have become a European celebrity and made herself a fortune."[40] Glinka himself trained Vorob'eva-Petrova, who made her name playing mezzo-soprano and contralto cross-dressed roles, both Russian and Western: Vanya in *A Life for the Tsar*, Ratmir in *Ruslan and Ludmila*, Tancredi, and Romeo.

"Breeches parts" or "trouser roles" (*travesti* in French) for women represented the last gasp of a tradition from eighteenth-century opera seria, opera

Figure 14. Evlalia Kadmina as Vanya. Until Pushkin's Tatiana became an operatic heroine in 1879, the role of the heroic young lad Vanya was the best-loved operatic part for Russian female singers.

buffa, and early Romantic opera. Central to early-nineteenth-century operas such as Rossini's *Tancredi* (1813), these roles were soon eclipsed by the rise of the Romantic tenor. The last truly major "trouser role" from Italian opera was Romeo in Bellini's *I Capuleti e i Montecchi* (1830). After that, the female singer specializing in trouser roles had to content herself with playing young boys marginal to the operatic plot, usually shepherds or pages. The two trouser roles from Glinka's operas, the orphan boy Vanya and the poet-prince Ratmir,

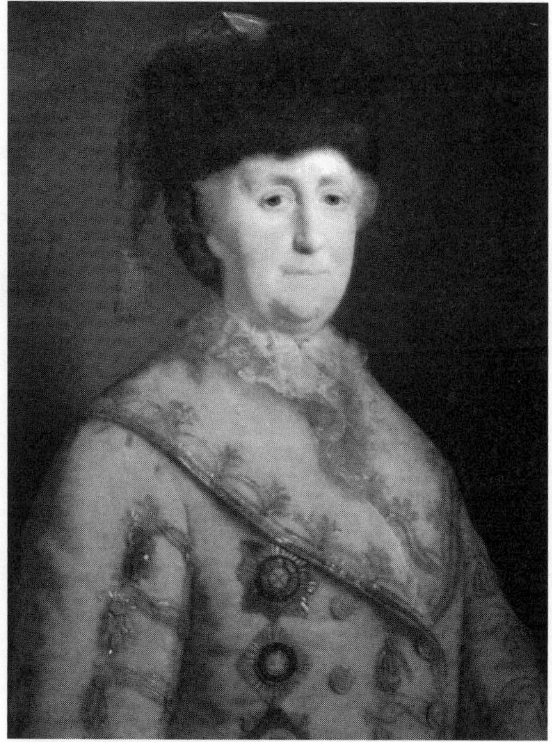

Figure 15. Catherine the Great in male traveling costume. Does this eighteenth-century portrait suggest an affinity with the visual representations of cross-dressed Russian mezzos from the following century?

gave the tradition a longer life, and a more central one, in Russia.[41] Indeed, until Tchaikovskii re-conceived Pushkin's Tatiana Larina as an operatic heroine, Vanya, a youth who heroically gallops to Moscow to warn Russian troops of a threatened attack by Poles in 1612, very possibly represented the best-loved Russian operatic role for women. Perhaps Catherine the Great's fondness for donning male attire when traveling, reviewing military troops, or having her portrait painted retained its imaginative potency for early-nineteenth-century Russia.

In the mid-1830s, Vorob'eva-Petrova began to play women's roles, Adalgisa in *Norma* among them, and moved somewhat awkwardly onto territory more traditional for a female opera singer: "Madame Vorob'eva-Petrova played the role of a *woman* in a major opera for the first time, and, as many people noticed, upon her entrance onto the stage, grew timid; that is why at the beginning of the work, one could detect a shakiness in her voice."[42] Vorob'eva-Petrova also continued to play her trouser roles, since her public and the theater directorate expected her to do so. The directorate's insistence that Vorob'eva-Petrova sing operatic roles ranging from soprano to baritone ruined her voice, causing her to leave the stage in 1846 and rendering her a victim of the times, which were inauspicious ones for Russian opera singers.

Mezzo-soprano and contralto roles remained a defining feature in the careers of nineteenth-century Russian female vocalists such as Daria Leonova and Evlalia Kadmina. The strength of these lower female voice types in Russia can even be said to have skewed the evolution of the Russian prima donna in terms of available roles and heroinic self-definition. Mezzo and contralto female roles tended to be "darker," more thwarted characters than their soprano counterparts; a good example is the role of Naina, the evil enchantress in Glinka's *Ruslan and Ludmila.* Often, mezzo and contralto roles are simply supporting characters such as mothers, sisters, companions, and servants, or comic ones, and they are quite frequently old women.

Lower-voiced Russian female singers had to wait until the second half of the nineteenth century for the advent of roles that would enable them to thrive professionally. Such roles did eventually materialize: the title role in Bizet's *Carmen* (1875), Marina in Musorgskii's *Boris Godunov* (1874), and Marfa in his *Khovanshchina* (1886). But the role of prima donna simply did not fit Russian singers until the very end of the nineteenth century.[43] In a uniquely Russian "spin" on the public nature of their work, these performers put more effort into demonstrating their civic-mindedness than into displaying their capacity for temperament and extravagance. Female opera singers in Russia gave charity performances to benefit indigent students and supported the effort to bring new Russian works to the stage.

If the Western prima donna represented quintessential femininity and grace, her Russian counterpart more often seemed intellectual, outsize, even freakish. This sense of the Russian diva as anomalous persisted throughout the pre-revolutionary period, in spite of the approving notice critics accorded conventional beauties like Evgenia Mravina and Maria Kuznetsova-Benois. The dramatic soprano Felia Litvin, celebrated for her Wagnerian roles, prevailed as an exception in spite of the general prejudice that divas look and act like ballroom belles: "She has such wonderful mastery of the plasticity of movement, in all her gestures there is such a remarkable grace . . . that for moments the imperfection of her external appearance becomes completely insignificant . . . in this beauty, there are no . . . signs of conventional female refinement or salon manneredness. This is the grace of antique statues, always full of great nobility, sometimes of epic greatness . . . alien to the artificiality of the conventional socially refined style.[44] Litvin does not represent a nineteenth-century type, but embodies a universal, mythological femininity linked to the nature of art itself. The Wagnerian heroine, in general, better suited the alternative tradition of the Russian diva than did the heroines of Italian Romantic opera.[45]

Russian divas had to define themselves artistically by mastering roles from both Western and Russian operas. Russian literary works represented the Russian prima donna as a creature with an ambiguous, troubled relationship to the Western tradition against which she shaped her identity. Verbitskaia's *The Abandoned Man*, for example, makes its prima donna heroine's unconventional features proof of her artistic stature:

> This was a stately, well-proportioned, and very tall woman; and, even in a man's costume . . . she was majestic. Her face, of a purely Russian type, could not be called regular; it was even ugly: the forehead was too high, and the chin too small; the nose rather broad, the color of her face wan. . . . But the nervous line of her lips . . . and . . . the large, grey, somehow "radiant" eyes, made one forget all her flaws. . . . This was the face of a true performing artist . . . and it conquered the public.[46]

Verbitskaia's narrator describes Vera's features as "of a purely Russian type," that is, as a series of excesses and inadequacies in height, forehead, chin, and nose, measured against the traditional standard of beauty for a Western female performer. Although Vera lacks conventional beauty, or perhaps because of

Figure 16. Maria Slavina as Wagnerian heroine. Majestic Wagnerian women were played powerfully and effectively by rich-voiced Russian divas from the later nineteenth century.

this lack, her face bears the legible stamp of the "true" artist, a mark visible to every member of the Russian audience. Verbitskaia's novel stages the recognition toward which Russian female singers struggled for decades.

With the increasing prestige accorded to Russian theater professionals toward the end of the nineteenth century, female stage artists began emerging from more diverse social strata. The establishment of music conservatories in both St. Petersburg and Moscow in the 1860s, as well as the later demise of the theater directorate monopoly in 1882, contributed to the changing image of the prima donna in Russia. By the end of the century, conservatories were "overcrowded with young girls, ladies, and widows studying singing, and each one without fail dreams of being a prima donna of the Mariinskii Theater."[47] Nineteenth-century literature often represents the Russian prima donna as a naive dilettante (see chapter 7). And literary history treats these fictions themselves as second rate.

THE PRIMA DONNA AND SOCIETY

Nineteenth-century society celebrated the prima donna, comparing her to royalty and divinity. But the fact that the prima donna was a working professional who received money for her services compromised her status as deity of the arts and even suggested an affinity with servants, shopgirls, and prostitutes. The prima donna's ambiguous social position reflected the separation between society members and the service class. H. Sutherland Edwards describes the institution of the "silken cord" at receptions in England of the early nineteenth century, a physical barrier that prevented stage artists and musicians from mixing freely with their noble hosts:

> It is known that at private parties the singers engaged to contribute to the entertainment of the company used to be separated from the invited guests by a silken cord, which kept them in a fold of their own. Every foreign musician who has published memoirs concerning the England of fifty or sixty years ago . . . has called attention to the insular peculiarity by which singers and musicians of the highest artistic reputation were thus isolated.[48]

This barrier appears in Raphael Zotov's story "Two Prima Donnas" (1842) when a visiting European diva, a guest at the home of a local dignitary, crosses into the separate room where the musicians are playing. Zotov's diva-heroine deliberately reminds the distinguished guests of her origins by drawing attention to the social barrier between patrons and patronized.

Marrying into the nobility offered the prima donna an escape from the "silken cord." The German prima donna Henrietta Sontag left the operatic stage when she married the Italian nobleman Count Rossi. A number of famous nineteenth-century prima donnas, including Pauline Lucca, (in turn the Baroness von Rhaden and the Baroness von Wallhofen) Christine Nilsson (Countess de Miranda), and Adelina Patti (Marquise de Caux), made similar alliances with titled noblemen. The first Russian diva, serf performer Praskovia Zhemchugova, secretly married her owner, Count Sheremetev, in 1801, but died two years later of tuberculosis after giving birth to a son.[49]

Several prima donnas married well-known male vocalists and held court in the theater. The marriage of soprano Giulia Grisi and tenor Giovanni Mario set the tone for this sort of "royal" alliance, which proved a powerful attraction for the St. Petersburg opera-going public: "The hall of the Bol'shoi theater began anew to fill up with the beau monde, once again music lovers, both true and feigned, rushed there to delight their ears with the divine voice of the king of tenors, and to be enraptured by the inspired singing of his life's companion."[50] The theater chronicler Vol'f transfers the suspect nature of the claims Grisi and Mario made to royalty onto those "feigned" (*pritvornye*) music lovers, who flock to the theater to bask in the reflected glory of the operatic couple.

A compelling operatic spectacle transfixed the St. Petersburg public in the late 1870s, when Adelina Patti's affair with the tenor Nicolini and her indifference to her husband, the Marquis de Caux, played itself out as operatic metaphor before a fascinated opera house. The Patti-Nicolini romance unfolded as the two performed love duets in *Il Trovatore*, *Romeo et Juliette*, and *La Traviata*, and strolled conspicuously in the Summer Garden, accompanied by the watchful marquis. A performance of Gounod's *Romeo and Juliette* set up an absorbing triangulation of operatic and extra-operatic plots, as the audience divided their attention between the lovers singing on stage and the marquis fuming in his parterre seat: "He [the marquis] behaved with impropriety, turning his back to the stage when Nicolini appeared on it alone, and rushing from the hall like one possessed before the curtain fell at the end of an act, not wishing to leave Romeo and Juliet alone together."[51] The public responded to the marquis's antics with amusement, and expressed warm support for the lovers on stage. According to Vol'f, the denouement of the affair came when the marquis rushed backstage during a performance of Verdi's *Rigoletto*, an opera rife with seduction and dark curses, and accused Patti of "barefaced public flirting" with Nicolini: "The most stormy scene ensued; the furious diva flung all of her diamonds in her spouse's face, and threw him out of her dressing room, announcing that she did not intend to live with him any longer. The intermission, meanwhile, lasted an extraordinarily long time."[52] Although one might question Vol'f's account of this off-stage confrontation, the appeal of such a scene lies, obviously, in its operatic intensity. Patti's affair with Nicolini allowed the diva to play herself before an adoring Russian public, and to appropriate the sweeping gestures of Romantic opera for her own "private" drama.[53]

In an operatic hyperbolization of the relationship between prima donna and royalty in Russia, Adelina Patti had earlier performed the role of Katerina in Meyerbeer's *L'Étoile du Nord* (1854). In this opera, a village girl becomes a soldier in the Russian army and is crowned Empress of Russia in the final act. Several decades later, Giordano's *Fedora* (1898) cast the prima donna as Princess Fedora Romazov, who lives in Europe and mingles with the international elite. But the historical Russian prima donna encounters many more difficulties in negotiating the territories of her cultural empire. The memoirist Filipp Vigel' recounts the sad story of the Russian singer Daria Bolina's marriage to the nobleman Markov during the early part of the nineteenth century. According to Vigel', the theater directorate refused the eighteen-year-old singer permission to marry, compelling her to break her contract and leave the stage forever. Vigel' believes that the match with Markov deprived Bolina of what might have been a long and prosperous career, and instead forced her into a social role for which she was unprepared. Once Bolina's incurable awkwardness became apparent, her embarrassed husband tried to keep her quietly at home, the result being that, "Not having received in school the proper training for her future rank, nor a social education later, she turned into something completely vulgar."[54] Twenty years after the elopement, Vigel' visited Markov and his wife, and observed with distress: "I found something worse than a country miss, a simple cook, awkward and timid, who did not know how to walk, sit, or curtsy, and who seemed not to dare even to speak." Markov later became a governor, and Vigel' speculates that Bolina's new role as a governor's wife must have been more difficult than all of her past stage roles. The rigorous education Bolina received in the Theater Institute did not train her to live in a privileged social milieu, only to pretend to this status on stage. The nascent stage queen treated to public acclaim was unmasked as a member of the servant class who had mistakenly found her way into the drawing room.

Even a well-established Western prima donna could find herself in a situation that underscored her ambiguous social status. Prince A. V. Meshcherskii describes an encounter with Pauline Viardot at a ball held by the Countess Rostopchina in 1844. The countess noticed with some concern that Viardot was the only woman not dancing, and asked Meshcherskii to come to her guest's rescue. While dancing a quadrille with Viardot, Meshcherskii became uncomfortably aware of the attention he and his partner were exciting: "I noticed a great agitation among the mamas sitting along the wall of the ballroom: they were somehow thrown into a flutter and began to whisper something among themselves, pointing in my direction. . . . I found out that I was the reason for this commotion, because the mamas found it too ticklish for their daughters to be dancing together with an actress, and found my act bold and improper."[55] Viardot, a respectably married woman, reigned over the audience in the Bolshoi Theater, but could not comfortably share a ballroom floor with marriageable Russian maidens. The gallant Meshcherskii notes as an aside that Viardot "danced a bit jumpingly, as all Frenchwomen do." Meshcherskii's comment recasts the immortal Viardot as a slightly ridiculous figure, suddenly vulnerable to critical scrutiny in terms of social position and graces.

The money that the prima donna received for her performances provided a source of fascination and anxiety for her public. Memoirs and periodical literature detailed the sums a prima donna received for single opera performances, as well as the terms of her "benefit" concerts, performances for which the featured singer received a percentage of the box-office revenues.[56] Russian female vocalists received very small salaries in comparison with the Western singers under contract to the directorate. A female chorus member (*khoristka*) in the Russian opera troupe during the middle of the century earned 240–400 rubles per year. Solo performers such as the contralto Daria Leonova received an annual salary of between 750 and 1,200 rubles.[57] In contrast, Pauline Viardot had commanded 50,000 rubles in bills (*assignatsii*), or upwards of 14,000 silver rubles, for her season contract twenty years earlier in 1843. It was not until the 1890s that Russian prima donnas like Evgenia Mravina and Medea Figner began to receive more comparable salaries of 10,000 to 15,000 rubles a season.

A prima donna who displayed too avid an interest in financial gain became the object of public disapproval in Russia. Vigel' criticizes the soprano Angelica Catalani for staging only as many public appearances as would be profitable and for charging 25 rubles per ticket, a considerable sum for the early nineteenth century. Vigel' twice went to hear Catalani, but declared, "I did not have even fifty kopecks worth of pleasure."[58] He turns Catalani's calculations against her, assigning a monetary value to his pleasure, the real product of her art. The memoirist Ivanskaia similarly characterizes the Swedish prima donna Nilsson as excessively thrifty, casting her as a small-minded housewife: "in Paris, already receiving a large salary, she lived on the third floor, nearer to the opera, so as not to spend money on carriages; she went to the market for provisions herself and strictly managed the butcher's bill; . . . she always bargained hard over the payment for an engagement and never sang anywhere for free."[59] Ivanskaia's relish in reporting these details makes it clear that, as a deity of art, the prima donna was meant to occupy herself with loftier matters. Yet the theme of money serves as a constant refrain in prima donna lore, emphasizing the inseparability of the female performing artist from her value in cultural, social, and monetary currency. Patti, for example, drew huge crowds in the late 1860s and early 1870s, a circumstance that enabled the theater directorate to eliminate its staggering long-term deficit for the Italian opera troupe. Patti's presence in St. Petersburg also offered an opportunity for society women to take part in the brisk market for opera tickets; noblewomen could make a tidy profit by buying up seats and boxes and reselling them at inflated prices.[60] Public acclaim, too, had its price. Novels such as Verbitskaia's *The Abandoned Man* and Nemirovich-Danchenko's *Stage Wings* stress the impossibility of a successful debut without donations to influential reviewers and audience claques who would be primed to applaud.

SELF-REPRESENTATION: THE PRIMA DONNA AS COLLECTIBLE

The nineteenth-century prima donna provided a rich source of cultural lore that circulated throughout Western Europe, Russia, and America in the form of legends, anecdotes, and gossip. The prima donna also served as a subject for proliferating visual images that were created, published, reproduced, bought, sold, traded, and then treasured, exhibited, and archived. During the early part of the nineteenth century, lithographs depicted female performing artists such as Giuditta Pasta, Maria Malibran, and Erminia Frezzolini in the flowing draperies of antiquity, holding a lyre or a scroll of music. As the conventions of lithographic representations evolved, the prima donna-as-represented became less a deity of art, and increasingly, a woman of fashion. Lithographs began to feature their female subjects in fashionable dresses, with elaborate hairstyles and quantities of jewelry. Small, reproducible busts of prima donnas were sold in city shops. During the second half of the nineteenth century, theaters produced studio photographs of their female opera singers, posed against theatrical backdrops or intimate interior settings. Images of these divas in recognizable roles became especially popular. As the century drew to a close, female stage artists dispersed their images even more widely via small, postcard-sized photographs, often bearing an autograph or brief personal message. The prima donna's ceremonial presentation of her autographed photograph, as in Patti's gesture to Davydov, recalled the romantic convention of offering a small portrait to a male admirer: a standard heroinic gesture in eighteenth- and nineteenth-century literature. The multiplicity of self-representations the prima donna inspired altered the context for this convention, however, making these images into reproducible, transferable commodities.[61] The advent of these images-for-purchase transformed the recipient of the prima donna's likenesses from a lover into a consumer. The prima donna herself, no longer simply an otherwordly personification of art, became a contemporary cultural icon.[62]

It is tempting to assume that the trade in representations of the prima donna catered to a female audience that took a great interest in details of toilette. Female collectors of prima donna images could treat these visual representations like fashion plates in illustrated journals, and study the prima donna's skill in creating her self-portrait.[63] But as the novels of Henry James attest, the figure of the collector in the nineteenth century was male-gendered, and male opera-goers did indeed collect pictures of female opera singers. The air of connoisseurship in consumption lent the necessary respectable tone to such a collection. An 1861 satirical cartoon from the journal *The Spark* mocks this practice, depicting two gentlemen in conversation. One asks the other, "Why did you buy a portrait of Frezzolini?" The second gentleman replies complacently "It's easy to see that you haven't been abroad. From London, I brought portraits of almost all of the horses from Count Derby's stable. Now I am collecting portraits of female singers and dancers. . . . In London, every respectable man has these portraits."[64] The portraits of nineteenth-century prima donnas that this Russian gentleman collects actually function as a composite portrait of *himself*, a man of requisite, Western-oriented taste in sport and art.

In an era that predated the audio recording, visual representations and written accounts were all that remained of a prima donna's performances. Early attempts to advertise the availability of memorabilia, such as portraits or busts, assert an equivalence between the experience of hearing the prima donna sing and that of gazing upon her image. An 1845 newspaper urged opera lovers to buy a statuette of Viardot as a replacement for the prima donna herself, who would eventually leave St. Petersburg: "The marvelous voice of Madame Viardot still resounds, we still delight in the wonderful outpourings of the truly Rossinian songstress; but there will come a time when only memories will resurrect [*voskresiat*] the minutes of enjoyment—then a statuette of

ВОЗВРАТИВШІЙСЯ НА РОДИНУ ТУРИСТЪ.

(Ан. Красильникова.)

Грав. П. Куренковъ.

— Зачѣмъ ты купилъ портретъ Фреццолини?

— Вотъ и видно, что ты за границей не бывалъ. Изъ Лондона я привезъ портреты почти всѣхъ лошадей конюшни графа Дерби. Теперь собираю коллекцію портретовъ пѣвицъ и танцовщицъ... Въ Лондонѣ всякій порядочный человѣкъ имѣетъ эти портреты.

Figure 17. Frezzolini cartoon from "The Spark." This cartoon, entitled "A Tourist Returned to his Native Land," mocks the fashion among Russian gentlemen for collecting opera diva lithographs. A portrait of Frezzolini is implicitly compared to a portrait of Count Derby's prize horses.

Pauline Viardot-Garcia will be . . . a treasure, and every person with pleasure will stock up on lovely sculpture, faithfully depicting the features so dear to every music lover."[65]

This exhortation speaks to the fleeting nature of pleasure, and offers the statuette of Viardot as a reserve commodity to protect the purchaser against a future moment of aesthetic deprivation. The notice characterizes the statuette, a reproducible object, as a treasure, which faithfully (*verno*) duplicates Viardot's features just as Viardot herself truly (*istinno*) renders Rossini's musical phrases. By means of the memories that the statuette evokes, past operatic experiences, with their overtones of religious ecstasy, can be brought back to life, or literally resurrected, as the Russian verb *voskresiat'* indicates. Viardot's image offers a figure for memory itself, evoking the remembered details of personal experience and its pleasure. In this sense, the statuette of Viardot represents the spectator and his experience.

The writer Ivan Turgenev would continue this tradition with his prose poem "Be Still!" (1879), which expresses his wish to memorialize Viardot's image at the final moment of her song:

> Be still! Remain forever in my memory as I see you now!
>
> The final inspired note has escaped from your lips. Your eyes no longer shine and sparkle. They grow dim, overcome by happiness, by blissful consciousness of the beauty you succeeded in expressing, toward which you seem to extend your triumphant, exhausted arms!
>
> What light, more subtle and pure than the light of the sun, has flowed over your entire form, over the smallest fold of your clothing?
>
> What god has thrown back your scattered curls with his caressing breath?
>
> His kiss burns on your brow, grown pale as marble!
>
> Behold—the secret revealed, the secret of poetry, life, love! Behold, behold, immortality! There is no other immortality, no need for any other. At this moment, you are immortal.
>
> This moment will pass—and you will again be a pinch of ash, a woman, a child . . . But what does it matter to you? At this moment, you are higher than everything transient, temporary. *Your* moment will never end.
>
> Be still! And let me share your immortality. Let fall into my soul a reflection of your eternal beauty![66]

The circumstances behind Turgenev's lyrical statement underscore the power of memory to rewrite the very moment so celebrated in "Be Still!" The immortalized moment in 1879 occurred long after Viardot's artistic prime. According to the reminiscences of others present, Viardot's flawed rendition of a Tchaikovskii romance awakened memories of the diva in her glory, causing Turgenev to call out "What a magnificent old woman!" (*Zamechatel'naia starukha kakaia!*).[67] Clearly, "this" moment is itself only a figure for other perfect, albeit imperfectly recollected artistic moments.

Visual representations of opera artists could also stand for a rewritten or re-remembered past. A matched set of oil paintings of tenor Giovanni Mario and soprano Giulia Grisi, costumed as Don Giovanni and Donna Anna, still hang in the St. Petersburg Conservatory of Music, fulfilling just such a function. According to the memoirist A. A. Stakhovich, Mario sent the portraits as a gift to the "President of the 'Mariistes' Club" after retiring from the stage.[68] The portraits' presence at the top of the grand old staircase provides a silent reminder that the conservatory incorporated into its architectural structure the shell of the old Bolshoi Theater, the scene of St. Petersburg opera-going, until the city had the theater demolished in the 1880s. And yet, the portraits effect a rewriting of cultural history, and of Mario's role in this history. Mario and Grisi reigned in St. Petersburg during the 1849–50 season and performed often at the Bolshoi. But Mario never performed the role of Don Giovanni in St. Petersburg; he had the baritone part specially transposed for his tenor voice in London later, at the request of the British royal family. Grisi *did* distinguish herself with her interpretation of Mozart's Donna Anna during her brief tenure at the St. Petersburg Italian Opera, but neither her stay in Russia nor her marriage to Mario were of significant duration. The portraits cast Mario and Grisi as the characters from Mozart's opera, mythologizing their personal and artistic relationship, and reshaping the past. Don Giovanni and Donna Anna represent an odd choice of roles to embody for posterity, since the operatic repertoire offers many less ambiguously connected lovers.

Echoing the acts of re-rememberings that the Viardot statuette and the oil paintings of Mario and Grisi evoke, period lithographs depict stage scenes

Figure 18. Viardot, Rubini, and Tamburini. Although framed by theatrical drapery and set structures, this operatic scene quite literally provides a window on the world. Such representations asserted a particular sort of "reality" for the operatic experience.

from opera culture, but alter them to represent the *cultural memory*, not the literal reality, of these events. A famous lithograph of Viardot, Rubini, and Tamburini performing in Alexei L'vov's opera *Bianca and Gualtiero* shows the trio on stage, posed on an impossibly elaborate theater stage set, whose windows look out onto a convincing natural landscape. This lithograph presents the operatic experience as a transparent window on reality, confounding the relationship between nature and culture. A lithograph of Grisi performing the role of Norma similarly depicts the costumed prima donna and her Druid

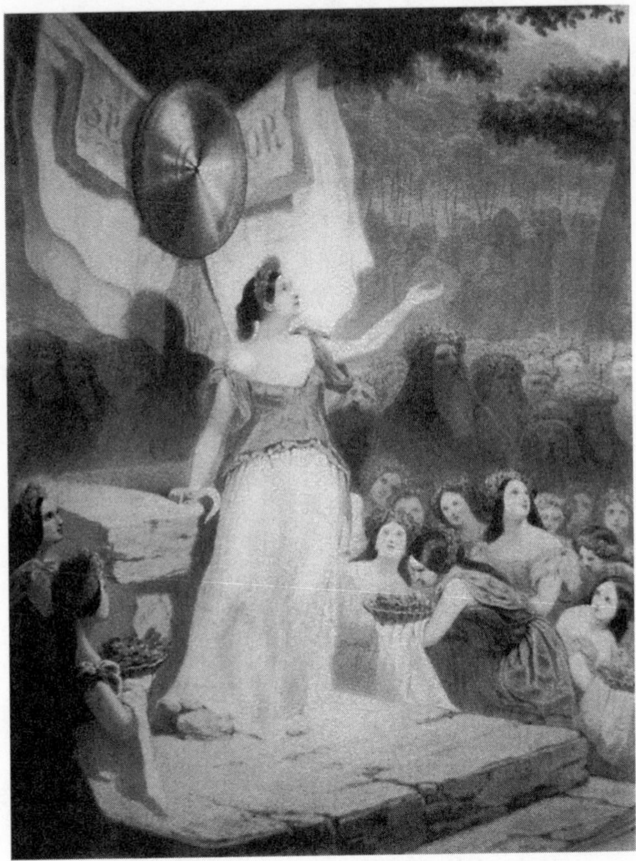

Figure 19. Giulia Grisi as Norma. Grisi sings her aria in a composite of stage and natural setting that defies the limitations of realist representation for opera.

handmaidens standing in a most realistically rendered forest. These lithographs recontextualize the operatic experience, claiming for it an ontological authority that transcends the conventions and requirements of realist representation.

Collectors and memoirists invest the images of a vanished opera culture with the power to re-animate and speak its history. The spotted lithographs and photographs that have survived reveal a love for visual detail on the part

Figure 20. Maria Dolina playing a Russian operatic heroine. Despite their bejeweled robes and headdresses, nineteenth-century Russian operatic heroines had an almost generic aspect, seeming trapped by the accoutrements of "Russianness."

of performers and viewers alike, analogous to a love for the perfectly turned musical phrase or stage gesture. But, no matter how detailed, these images never fully satisfy the viewer's curiosity. Even Russia's expert theater historians cannot identify all of the performers and roles they represent.

Certain roles give themselves away by details of costuming and setting: Carmen with her tambourine, Amneris in her Egyptian headdress, and Juliet on the balcony. But the lack of opera-specific details or props make it difficult

Figure 21. Adelina Patti and Pauline Lucca. How can two divas occupy the same representational space?

to tell one Russian folktale or fairy-tale operatic heroine from another. The princess from *Rusalka* is gorgeously attired, but the opera gives her remarkably little to do and no way to distinguish herself from other heroines. The same is true of Glinka's Ludmila, who sits and waits to be rescued. The viewer can most often pick out the ubiquitous Vanya from *A Life for the Tsar* in breeches and fur hat. The visual images of Russian female singers reveal a strange lack of definition, almost a generic quality to the slowly evolving tradition of Russian operatic heroine. Street-dress portraits of Russian divas tend toward the dignified, rather than the glamorous; Daria Leonova never smiles, Elizaveta Lavrovskaia's dresses lack even the simplest ornament; and, when not in costume as a passionate Eastern heroine, Maria Slavina cuts a portly figure. Evgenia Mravina offers a rare exception to this disdain for feminine excess, posing in ermine with huge puffed sleeves and a becoming hat. The Russian diva could not help but define herself against or in relation to the Western operatic tradition and its practices.

Visual representations regularly show a Western or Russian diva seated pensively at a writing desk, bent over a book or document. What are these female opera performers playing at?[69] They resemble society women, reading the latest novels and keeping up with their correspondence. Another favorite pose captures the female singer standing in profile in a domestic interior, supporting herself by holding onto the back of a chair. The diva is always alone in these "scenes," shown outside of a real personal or social context. An 1869 lithograph of Adelina Patti and Pauline Lucca extends the existential isolation of the prima donna's image by representing the two divas as disembodied heads. Clearly taken from two different sources, the images of the two artists face one another, each enclosed in its own flowered border. This double representation offers the two prima donnas suggestively as rivals and alternatives to one another, or perhaps as mirror images. Some images dramatize the prima donna in non-operatic ways, depicting her in riding costume or as a hostess awaiting her guests in a richly appointed salon. In the most striking visual representation of all, the prima donna herself appears only as a portrait, or, more accurately, as an absence. A photograph of a table overflowing with gifts, flowers, wreaths, and jewelry, as well as a small portrait of the artist, commemorates the 25-year anniversary of Maria Slavina's stage career in 1903. Slavina's anniversary photograph represents the prima donna as the sum total of the gifts that refer to her artistic achievements. The prima donna does not take human form; instead she is evoked by the tangible symbols of a cultural institution.

The visual representations of the prima donna produced during the nineteenth century asserted her authenticity both as a woman and as a performing artist. In response to this visual proliferation, Petr Tchaikovskii characterized the singer Carlotta Patti, sister of the famous Adelina, as a sinister, lifeless doll:

> When Madame Carlotta Patti came out onto the stage, gleaming . . . with her expensive ornaments, her coiffure as if poured from bronze, and with a bright rouged spot on the artificially whitish background of her face, when she fixed herself motionlessly in place, and I fixed my opera-glasses upon her,—it seemed to me that I was seeing one of those wax figures that appear in the windows of hair-

> dressers' shops . . . and . . . this lifelessly pretty wax woman began to sing an aria from *Lucia*. . . . Her voice was probably set into her throat by some clever craftsman; the movements of her head are also the result of a wittily invented mechanism.[70]

Carlotta Patti exists here only as the sham construction of a male collaboration: the work of the "master" who designed her, and the critical gaze of Tchaikovskii himself, channeled through his opera glasses and his role as musical critic. This male viewer evokes the authors who transformed the prima donna into a literary heroine, a different kind of doll, making her act out a story of artistic triumph and personal decline according to the generic conventions of the day.[71]

The nineteenth-century prima donna was perceived by her public as a being who asserted the transcendent nature of art, and possessed a power balanced by the diva's pragmatic interest in professional identity, social origin, and money. The prima donna personified art; her presence was dispersed by innumerable visual representations and written tributes. And yet, the diva's multiple operatic roles caused her public much concern regarding the provisional nature of her identity. But despite the inherently contradictory nature of a woman who could not publicly age, a consummate professional who could not visibly worry about money, and public adoration that brought social isolation, the prima donna offered all Russian citizens intimate access to her image. A paradoxical overarching unity balances the internal contradictions that structure this cultural icon.

Chapter Four

Representing Opera
Scene and Self

Literary representations of operatic scenes deploy the mimetic properties of language within a multi-level narrative context. What is the real represented subject of such scenes: the performers, the artistic work, or the experience of the spectator? In fact, retellings of the operatic experience explore the mechanics of representation itself. Opera's ability to convey an "objective" reality has long been in question, owing to the largely nonrepresentational nature of music.[1] Literary works circumvent this problem by presenting an opera performance as the creation of a fictional spectator, who "co-produces" the experience in aesthetic and narrative terms.[2] The fictional spectator mediates between operatic and extra-operatic experience in the literary work, which is to say that the spectator's experience suggests these connections to the reader. In some cases, a literary narrator provides an ideological or ironic frame for the spectator's perspective.

Operatic scenes in fictional literature often emphasize the idiosyncratic nature of reception, and nowhere is this truer than in Tolstoi's famous opera-house scene from *War and Peace.* Tolstoi's heroine, Natasha Rostova, takes in the details of the opera performance as though studying the rites of an alien culture. Natasha's estranged perspective, known as *ostranenie* according to the Russian Formalist Viktor Shklovskii's famous formulation, combines a stagy, ingenuous wonder with a pronounced awareness of theatrical artifice.[3]

> The floor of the stage consisted of smooth boards, at the sides was some painted cardboard representing trees, and at the back was a cloth stretched over boards. In the center of the stage sat some girls in red bodices and white skirts. One very fat girl in a white silk dress sat apart on a low bench, to the back of which a piece of

> green cardboard was glued. They all sang something. When they had finished their song the girl in white went up to the prompter's box and a man with tight silk trousers over his stout legs, and holding a plume and a dagger, went up to her and began singing, waving his arms about. First the man in the tight trousers sang alone, then she sang, then they both paused while the orchestra played and the man fingered the hand of the girl in white, obviously awaiting the beat to start singing with her.[4]

Tolstoi's third-person narration draws attention to the underpinnings of operatic illusion so insistently that the reader cannot help but wonder at Natasha's keen powers of observation. Natasha notes that the singing heroine advances to the "prompter's box," and the male soloist counts the beats before beginning a duet; she later perceives that shades have been put over the footlights for a midnight scene, that the king is nervous and sings badly, and that a dancer adjusts her bodice before executing a difficult set of steps. Natasha is also acutely aware of the planks, painted cardboard, and canvas used to create the scenic effects. Tolstoi's point is that opera represents a depraved, cultivated taste, and that Natasha has not yet learned to appreciate its conventions. But Natasha's acuity in noting the mechanisms underlying the spectacle suggests that she has the makings of an excellent opera critic. The narration's ingenuousness only partially masks Tolstoi's purposes, since Natasha's estrangement seems as *staged* as the opera performance itself. Tolstoi specifically intended Natasha's confrontation of opera to play a critical part in *War and Peace*, and placed this scene at the end of Book 2, the very center of the novel. Tolstoi declared in a letter to P. I. Bartenev that the meeting between Anatol and Natasha at the opera was "the most difficult place and the central knot of the entire novel."[5]

It is Tolstoi's *narrator* who directs the reader's attention to the strangeness that attends the profound conventionality of the operatic spectacle. As the opera unfolds, Natasha herself slips into a state of intoxication (*op'ianenie*) that causes operatic and social practices to seem natural. But the narrator's eagle eye never falters. The flat, childlike sentences that ostensibly represent her thought processes provide the reader with all of the information needed to respond "properly" to the opera-house scene, that is, to condemn it.

Natasha thus serves as a kind of painted cardboard set, from behind which Tolstoi's narrator prompts the reader's response. The reader becomes the *true* performer in this scene, the character who enacts the requisite dawning of understanding in place of Tolstoi's distracted heroine.[6]

The very nature of the operatic interlude in *War and Peace* makes it clear that Tolstoi's contemporary reader is the real spectator. The estranging effects rely on the reader's familiarity with nineteenth-century operatic convention. But the French operas of Grétry and Isouard that dominated the opera stage during the early nineteenth century could hardly have served as a source of recognizable operatic motifs for Tolstoi's 1860s reading public. In order to justify a description of a Western opera performance in the style of the 1850s–60s in *War and Peace*, a novel set during the Napoleonic wars, Tolstoi composed his own literary opera using a synthesis of unattributed motifs from works by Meyerbeer, Gounod, and Verdi.[7] Tolstoi's operatic hash provides a translating filter through which his reader can appropriate the social and artistic experiences of a literary character.

Theater semiotician Marco de Marinis proposes the notion of the "performance text," an ephemeral, theoretical object produced during an actual performance. The performance text comprises multiple, partial texts that call upon the spectator to process their codes according to acoustic, visual, and interpretive conventions.[8] Pragmatic approaches to theater "read" performances in terms of production and reception.[9] De Marinis suggests that every performance posits a model spectator, akin to an ideal reader, who is able to process all the codes. In Tolstoi's case, the primordial semiotic innocence that the opera-house scene stages sets up a pragmatic mode for the reader to master.

Fictional accounts of performances deliberately emphasize the idiosyncracies of a spectator in order to underscore departures from the ideal model, or sometimes to define this ideal. Memoiristic first-person accounts, in contrast, render autobiographical spectators the unwitting objects of reception studies. The complex nature of operatic art, highly conventionalized and encompassing multiple generic forms, makes opera an ideal subject for examining the pragmatics of performance.

RENARRATION AND PERFORMANCE: KUKOL'NIK, GRIGOR'EV, HOFFMANN, AND BAUER

The act of narration, which presupposes a narratee and a motive for narrating, is inherently performative. When a narrator describes a stage performance, the defining theatricality of all narrated events renders the attempt to translate theater into story doubly complex. Fictional first-person accounts of nineteenth-century opera capitalize upon this circumstance to stage collisions between Romantic "operatic" notions and realist literary forms. But the tension between overwrought operatic epiphanies and deflating parodic accounts of these experiences often remains unresolved. Fictional exercises in operatic pragmatics offer a critique of *both* all-devouring Romantic subjectivity and distanced realist methods. Opera actually lies somewhere in the middle.

Nestor Kukol'nik's story "Three Operas" (1841) treats the representation of operatic scenes from Bellini's *Norma*, Rossini's *Semiramide*, and Donizetti's *Anne Boleyn* during the soprano Giuditta Pasta's visit to St. Petersburg that same year. "Three Operas" follows upon and extends Kukol'nik's literary works of the 1830s: Russian historical plays and dramatic fantasies treating the lives of artists. "Three Operas" transforms this latter sort of meditation itself into a performative spectacle, and surrounds the whole with a comic-feuilletonistic frame. In this way, Kukol'nik's story points to a longstanding relationship between the grand pretensions of operatic art and the accompanying supporting or lampooning presence of nineteenth-century journalists and newspaper critics. "Three Operas" implicitly poses the question of whether opera depicted in prosaic forms must always be out of place.

Kukol'nik's contrastive framing also suggests inadvertent self-satire. Kukol'nik's suffering, unappreciated artist characters of the 1830s, with their interminable verse monologues, give way in "Three Operas" to a long-winded hero rendered in light prose. Over the course of the story, Kukol'nik's hero Klenov struggles to describe Pasta's dramatic skill and to grasp the nature of artistic genius. Kukol'nik's ironic first-person narrator, a St. Petersburg journalist, in turn chronicles Klenov's agonized deliberations over whether he should become an actor. The hero's artistic dilemma, indeed the literary work itself in the form of Kukol'nik's story, appears so parodically reduced in stature that it is in danger of disappearing altogether.

Klenov attempts to describe Pasta's art with recourse to a grammar of theatrical art, but Pasta's performance escapes his classificatory schemes.[10] Klenov's narration instead maps Pasta's artistic decisions onto her rendering of Norma's deliberations: "The time for her prayer arrives—it is not easy for this heart to pray, but she must lead the chorus of supplicants; here she needs coquettishness, pretence, art, brilliance of singing; otherwise, the Gauls will not believe her sincerity."[11] Pasta's physical self represents the true site of knowledge: "artists still come to admire every pose of Pasta's, every turn of her head, every movement of her wise hands, to study, as if at the Academy. They find in her a complete study of the ancients, they find what is new, but always true, faithful, and natural." Pasta's art of mime, Klenov declares, is "a play of physiognomy . . . a complete school, a book, volumes, a library of dramatic art." Klenov characterizes the prima donna as a living text, an animated inscription of dramatic art.[12] Pasta embodies the history of representation through art, a story she tells with her body during each opera performance.

In the final section of "Three Operas," Klenov visits the narrator at a dacha and announces his plan to go abroad, since he has given up hope of becoming an actor. Klenov explains his decision with recourse to the dramatic perfection of Pasta's art: "in Anne Boleyn there are two actresses: one is a court lady, not born to the purple; the other perceptibly tries to hide her origins by means of the purple, to play the role of the queen. Here there is none of Semiramis's ease; in contrast, every gesture seems learned, repeated before the mirror and enacted deliberately in the presence of the court."[13] Klenov's account of Pasta represents a critique of his anatomical project, which aimed to translate dramatic precepts into instructional prose. Instead, Klenov describes Donizetti's opera in terms of the procedure by which Pasta creates her role and imbues it with the appearance of reality. And in dramatizing Norma, Semiramis, and Anne Boleyn, doomed queens all, Pasta allegorizes her declining career.

But Klenov cannot do likewise without becoming a figure of fun, intoning Anne Boleyn's lines, almost as though reviling the remote greatness of Pasta, to the narrator's great amazement: "You! My rival! You! You!" (*Tu! Mia rivale! Tu! Tu!*). The dacha scene functions as a mini-version of the literary treatment that the narrator applies to Klenov. Prosaic setting and ironic detachment demote operatic pretense to satire, and even to farce. The feuilletonistic frame makes opera strange, and the narrator's closing remarks do the same to its inconsequential hero: "'Wait a moment,' I thought, 'I make you, with all your ravings, dreams, prejudices, and delusions, with your domestic secrets, a sacrifice to my journal!' I fulfill my word—here he is, Aleksei Semenovich Klenov. Take him. I pass the offender from my hands to yours. Read and judge!"[14] Klenov does end up as art, but instead of achieving dramatic stature, he becomes a literary caricature.

Apollon Grigor'ev, critic, poet, and memoirist, translated the libretti of numerous Western operas into Russian, and treated operatic form in several of his literary works. Despite his Slavophilic convictions, Grigor'ev evolved into something of a literary centrist in his critical prose about authors such as Pushkin, Gogol, Turgenev, Goncharov, and Ostrovskii. Grigor'ev's story "Robert le Diable" (1846), with reference to Meyerbeer's opera by the same name, reflects its author's struggle to write about art in a post-Romantic cultural climate.

Grigor'ev's "Robert le Diable" begins with the narrator-hero's assertion, "I was still living in Moscow, I was young, I was in love."[15] The narrator has become a journalist since the events the story describes, which suggests that Grigor'ev's "Robert" might be read through the same ironic-feuilletonistic lens as that through which I discussed Kukol'nik's "Three Operas." The narrator delivers a rhetorical cadenza on the subject of his beloved, a proper Russian maiden, underscoring the conventionality of his behavior and the narrow range of his gestures:

> I loved. . . . O! how I loved then, gracious sirs,—ideally, frantically, fantastically, eccentrically—so boldly that I even—O horror!—permitted myself, against parental instructions, to sit [with her] an entire extra quarter of an hour after midnight, that I even—O depravity!—heroically preached, in verse, of course, contempt for society's opinion, that I even—O height of dishonor!—wrote poems at the place where I worked.[16]

The operatic exclamations of Grigor'ev's older narrator ("O height of dishonor!"), bracketed off from the rest of his speech, signal his distance from the Romantic conventions of his youth and from generic hyperbole itself.

Grigor'ev wrote "Robert le Diable" when he was only 24 years old, hardly a world-weary old man recalling a younger self. The story followed on the heels of his overheated poetry of the period 1843–45, during which he was suffering from unrequited love. He moved from Moscow to St. Petersburg in 1844, where he began to publish actively in the theatrical journal *Repertoire and Pantheon*. The unhealthy and misguided individualism of Romanticism became one of his pet themes.

"Robert le Diable" depicts its first-person fictional spectator as co-producer of the opera performance; the hero's self-presentation at the opera theater effects an aesthetic reconception of Meyerbeer's opera.[17] As a result of the protagonist's subjective foregrounding and discarding of its elements, Meyerbeer's opera undergoes a radical transformation. The new version of *Robert le Diable* pays little attention to its conventional tenor protagonist, Robert, instead emphasizing Robert's demonic father Bertram, a rather out-of-date Romantic anti-hero.[18] The narrator is drawn to Bertram almost to the exclusion of all else, as he imitates Robert's struggle against the demon's fatal appeal: "I myself was trembling as if in a fever—I was riveted to this colossal, terrible, irresistibly attractive image. And in the scene of the game, I did not see the raging Robert. I saw only him."[19] By the end of the story, Romantic opera seems almost a product of the hero's aesthetic adolescence, an external projection of his cherished but immature self-image.[20] With Bertram's despairing cries echoing in his ears, the narrator rushes from the theater: "I did not want to listen to the rather vulgar ending of this greatest of tragedies." The narrator usurps the final moment of the story, superimposing his own overdramatic exit from the theater onto Bertram's final plunge into the abyss. Grigor'ev's story, much like Kukol'nik's "Three Operas," links the projection of an operatic role with the generally problematic creation of a public self. Self-representation inevitably makes itself vulnerable to ironic reframing. Bertram's fall proves the fragility of an operatically and Romantically overdrawn self.

E. T. A. Hoffmann's "Don Juan" (1812) may be considered the Western antecedent to both Kukol'nik's "Three Operas" and Grigor'ev's "Robert le Diable."[21] In "Don Juan," the narrator describes a dreamlike performance of Mozart's *Don Giovanni*, to which he appends his own analysis of the opera, rereading the Don Juan legend according to the conventions of Romanticism.[22] Hoffmann's sketch describes the narrator's mystical communion with Mozart's characters, as he conceives them. The story emphasizes the relationship between spectator and operatic experience, and takes the form of a letter from the narrator to "Dear Theodore" that articulates the experience of re-visioning.

The letter that is Hoffmann's "Don Juan" opens with a bell announcing the raising of the opera curtain, which wakes the narrator from his deep sleep in a hotel room, making his letter itself resemble a performance. Upon inquiring about the sounds of nearby orchestral instruments, the narrator learns that a concealed door in his hotel room leads to a box in the adjoining opera theater. This spatial juxtaposition in Hoffmann's story re-conceives the literary device of the dream sequence. The opera theater, a realm that gives rein to the individual imagination, represents a literal extension of the borrowed, temporarily "private" space of the narrator's hotel room. The narrator's consciousness that someone has entered his opera box during the first act therefore distresses him: "I had been so happy to have the loge to myself, and to be able to absorb with every nervous fibre of my being . . . this perfect version of the masterpiece, that I felt a single spoken word (inevitably a banal one!) would wrench me painfully out of this glorious mood of poetic and musical enchantment!"[23] The visitor reveals herself as a composite of the operatic character Donna Anna and the prima donna who plays her. The female visitor recognizes the narrator as a composer, declaring, "I have sung you. I am your melodies."[24] The visitor does not threaten the narrator's communion with his creative self, since she herself embodies that self.

That evening, the narrator decides to return through the hidden door into the dark and deserted opera theater. He explicitly links his experience of watching the opera with his literary efforts when he muses, "How easy it would be to carry in the small table, two lamps, and writing materials!"[25] He then embarks upon an interpretive retelling of *Don Giovanni*, which complements his earlier imaginative vision. The fact that the narrator returns to the opera theater to revisit his experience of *Don Giovanni* suggests that he can stage such a private reenactment whenever he chooses. Each time the spectator watches Mozart's opera, he re-conceives it anew.

At the story's conclusion, the narrator learns that the prima donna has died, evidently undone by her passionate rendering of Donna Anna. The prima donna seems to represent an emanation of the narrator-composer's own artistic consciousness; she reveals the inner workings of the opera to him, and confirms their transcendental communion with a kiss in the form of "a long note, held as though in an eternal thirst of longing," a kind of pre-Wagnerian death-from-love, or *Liebestod*.[26] The narrator's vision subsumes all reality.

Hoffmann prefigures Kukol'nik and Grigor'ev in locating the represented operatic scene explicitly within the spectator's experience, and challenging literary language to convey the spectator's "creation." But his self-contained Romantic vision represents an ideal theater of the self that Kukol'nik and Grigor'ev cannot inhabit without reference to an incompatible external artistic or social space.[27] Kukol'nik and Grigor'ev display a distrust of Romantically inspired operatic fantasies, the very fantasies that would return in the form of a memoir-and-memorabilia craze during the last part of the nineteenth century.

By the early twentieth century, operatically conceived nostalgia took on a decadent aspect, becoming linked to madness and delusion. The director Evgenii Bauer's silent film *Daydreams* (1915) plots a juxtaposition of operatic spectacle and sexual seduction within the hero's disordered mind, culminating, as does Hoffmann's story, in the death of the female performing artist.[28] Bauer explores the hero's culpability, particularly in aesthetic terms.

At the film's opening, Bauer's hero Nedelin grieves obsessively for his dead wife, Elena. He stands at his wife's flower-covered funeral bier, kisses her forehead, and cuts off her braid. At home, Nedelin gazes at Elena's portraits and caresses the long, thick braid, which he keeps in a glass box in the drawing room. While out walking, Nedelin notices a woman who resembles Elena enter a theater by the side door. He hurriedly buys a ticket, and finds a seat in the opera theater in time to watch the famous cloister scene from act three of Meyerbeer's *Robert le Diable.* The young woman he saw plays Helene (Elena!), queen of the spectral nuns, who captivates the hero Robert with her dancing. This section of Bauer's film recalls Grigor'ev's "Robert le Diable," in which the "Petersburg Elena" wins over the Moscow audience with her seductive dancing: "O look, look how beautiful she is, how naked she is, how loftily shameless she is, how her every breath emanates sweet bliss and languor! Yes! This is art, this is art . . . this is the apotheosis of passion, the apotheosis of languor—with madness in her eyes, desire in every movement. . . . O yes! This is art! Honor and glory to art!"[29] In fact, Nedelin allows himself to be seduced by art. During this scene in the Bauer film, the camera alternates between closeup shots of the stage and longer-range segments from the back of the auditorium that show the audience. The conductor's baton waves in the lower part of the screen, reminding the viewer that the performance is an illusion. At intervals, the camera also reflects Elena's view from the stage, showing us an agitated Nedelin stretching his arms out toward the stage, and attracting the disapproving notice of other audience members. Nedelin is no less fascinated by Elena than is Robert, the operatic hero. At the end of the cloister scene, Elena is the last spirit to return reluctantly to her tomb, as if responding to Nedelin. In the camera's view, Nedelin writes himself into the operatic drama. Backstage, he introduces himself to the performing artist, Tina Viarskaia, who gives him her card. This token would seem to prove her identity, but actually provides Nedelin with a ticket to further self-delusion.

Nedelin visits Tina, whom he finds lying motionless upon a chaise in a pose that recalls his dead wife's funeral. "A living portrait of Elena!" he exclaims, pulling her long dark hair across her throat and kissing her passionately. He commissions Sol'skii, an artist friend, to paint a portrait of Tina dressed in Elena's clothes and jewelry, but becomes distraught when Tina begins to caper and pose with these "props."

As Nedelin sits at home brooding, he recalls his married life, summoning up a vision of himself and Elena in a park. When he pulls the imagined Elena's hair across her throat, the viewer recognizes the gesture he made earlier with Tina. Nedelin also replays the memory of himself severing Elena's braid as she lay in funereal state. This repeated scene makes it clear that Nedelin's consciousness with its ritual repetitions represents the shaping force behind the affinities that the film proposes to the viewer. Perhaps Nedelin's memory of his wife in a white dress unconsciously contradicts his recognition of "Elena" in the dancing Helene, who is, after all, doomed to eternal torment for breaking her nun's vows. Bauer's film meditates on the nature of "likeness" by evoking multiple representations of Elena in portraiture and in life, as well as in memory. Nedelin seeks to recreate Tina as a living image of Elena, and to use her as the source of new animated likenesses. But Tina is a performing artist, and cannot assume a fixed identity.

During the final scene of *Daydreams*, Tina visits Nedelin to see whether he has tired of pining for Elena. When she realizes that he is still depressed, she seizes the braid from its box and taunts him. She coils the braid about her own neck, and Nedelin has a brief vision of Elena that superimposes itself over Tina, whom he strangles with the braid. In bringing together the tantalizing images of his departed wife, Nedelin succeeds in creating a static portrait of her, but, paradoxically, loses her forever.[30] Like the diva in Hoffmann's "Don Juan," Tina perishes in the service of an "artist's" larger vision. Bauer's film suggests the influences of multiple generic traditions—opera, literature, stage melodrama, portraiture—on the cinema's capacity to represent experience. Human consciousness presents itself explicitly as a *theater*. In this, Bauer's film resembles "theatricalist" stage works such as Nikolai Evreinov's monodrama "Theater of the Soul" (1912), in which a divided Self literally and physically constitutes the entire production.

The fictional spectator reframes the performance according to the central purpose the theatrical event serves in the text: as an illustration of the ways in which framing determines genre (Kukol'nik), as a metaphor for the process of maturation, expressed as the progression from Romantic to post-Romantic aesthetics (Grigor'ev), as a perfect representation of opera in language (Hoffmann), and as a form of mimesis that mediates between animating memory and the static forms of portraiture (Bauer). The operatic scene in literature always represents something other than itself. The narrative-of-opera makes problematic the very possibility of representation, a likeness that is not identity.

ALCHEVSKAIA'S TRIP TO THE OPERA: TEACHING CULTURE

The fictional opera spectator is an authorial invention, a medium for the representation of the fictional operatic event. But when a *nonfictional* spectator describes an *actual* opera performance in memoir, letter, or diary, the account may take on a similarly prescriptive character, as in Christina Alchevskaia's (1843–1920) response to an October 1892 performance of Tchaikovskii's *Eugene Onegin* (1879) at the Mariinskii Theater. Alchevskaia, a populist pedagogy specialist from Khar'kov, visited St. Petersburg in connection with the planned publication of a reader for adults. Alchevskaia is best known as the author of three compendia of popular reading material, published in 1884, 1887, and 1906, all entitled *What The People Should Read*.[31] In contrast to Grigor'ev's story "Robert le Diable," Alchevskaia's diary fragment took shape as a truly private document instead of as a literary stylization of one. Alchevskaia's description of *Eugene Onegin* shapes her imagined reader's response to the operatic event according to ideological-pedagogical, rather than aesthetic, considerations.[32]

Alchevskaia's description of the opera performance directs itself at an unidentified addressee, a composite of the like-minded intelligentsia she rallied to her pedagogical cause. As interpreter, intermediary, and instructor, Alchevskaia incorporates Tchaikovskii's opera and Pushkin's novel-in-verse into the pet project of an activist private citizen: promoting and disseminating a set of common values. For her, opera shares literature's traditional mission in Russia as the carrier of life's lessons.

Alchevskaia's written rendering of opera provides one of the most sustained accounts of an opera performance in the memoirs from imperial Russia. Alchevskaia's diary fragment also establishes a context for the operatic event, preceding it with details about her work and following the performance with a quasi-fantastical dream sequence composed of Russian cultural motifs. Her fragment moreover reveals her response to Tchaikovskii's opera in private, emotional terms. As an independent-minded woman of middle age who experiences opera as conveying essential truths about life, Alchevskaia resem-

Figure 22. Christina Alchevskaia. Even a devoted public servant like Alchevskaia could find time to attend the opera. In fact, she felt that operas like Tchaikovskii's *Eugene Onegin* helped to create a cultural community of like-minded Russian citizens.

bles a reverse image of Tolstoi's Natasha Rostova. Alchevskaia permits herself an evening of operatic intoxication as a restorative tonic in a life dominated by duty. As did Tchaikovskii, to say nothing of Dostoevskii in his 1880 Pushkin speech, Alchevskaia makes Tatiana the focus of Pushkin's novel, and identifies with her. Tatiana publicly voices her private yearnings during the famous letter scene, while Alchevskaia amplifies her own girlishly sentimental response to the opera. Alchevskaia, like Tatiana, seems to long for an interlocutor.

Alchevskaia's description of her trip to the Mariinskii Theater begins with her customary role as tireless missionary: "'No, today I cannot send out my notes of invitation, I cannot gather about me the council of pedagogues, I cannot talk about the book as I should!' I thought. . . . And then they told me about the opera *Eugene Onegin*. . . . 'I'll go to the opera!' I decided, and at 7:30 I was already driving up to the Mariinskii Theater."[33] Alchevskaia makes a mini-drama of her decision to attend the opera performance. Being a spectator offers a departure from her professional role, which places her at the center of a working group. And yet, Alchevskaia evokes the theater in metaphorical connection with her life work in her earlier writings. In an address to a meeting of Khar'kov school teachers in 1889, she made the following remarks about a trip to St. Petersburg in connection with the 1887 volume of *What The People Should Read*:

> As usual, Petersburg greeted me with the warmth and cordiality that many people do not recognize in it, which seems to me a definite error. As the focus of intelligentsia strengths and gifts, this enormous and enlightened city always represents for me a stern and fair appraiser of intellectual labor. . . . While the provinces gossip and rudely ransack your soul, trying to find in it the petty instincts of pride and self-importance, and poisoning your life with small stings and plots,—Petersburg . . . loudly and authoritatively applauds you, approving your honest strivings and rousing your boldness of spirit.[34]

Alchevskaia saw herself as a sort of prima donna of public life, and she characterized St. Petersburg as the judge who conferred upon her the mantle of cultural authority.

Alchevskaia attended a performance of *Eugene Onegin* featuring Medea and Nikolai Figner as Tatiana and Lenskii. The Italian soprano Medea Figner married Mariinskii tenor Nikolai Figner and sang in St. Petersburg from the late 1880s until the 1910s. Medea Figner became one of the most popular Tatianas in the entire performance history of Tchaikovskii's opera, and later created the role of Liza in Tchaikovskii's *Queen of Spades* (1890). She represents one of the very few Western opera artists to succeed in surmounting

Figure 23. Evgenia Mravina as Tatiana. Mravina appears here as the tender, naïve Tatiana from the opera's early scenes.

Russian cultural barriers.[35] Western prima donnas rarely attempted Russian roles, especially those, like Tatiana, so integrally connected with Russia's most cherished literary images. The heroine whom Alchevskaia characterizes as "a pale, dreamy brunette with an expressive face" constituted one of the quintessential Russian female operatic roles of this period.[36]

Alchevskaia's description of the performance begins telegraphically, not unlike a set of stage directions: "The curtain goes up. To the left is the manor house with columns; to the right at the front of the stage, in the garden, the lady of the manor, Larina, and the nurse are making jam and carrying on an

Figure 24. Medea Figner as Tatiana. Figner, a truly "naturalized" opera singer in Russia, delighted audiences with her portrayal of the mature, sophisticated Tatiana, who turns away the man she loves in order to remain faithful to her older husband.

insignificant conversation."[37] Alchevskaia's initial reportage quickly shifts to a set of instructions for the viewer: "You pay little attention to their mediocre singing, your gaze is riveted on the open window with the sharply delineated silhouettes of Olga and Tatiana there." This strategy continues throughout Alchevskaia's narration of the opera performance; the Mariinskii's staging of *Eugene Onegin* encodes her imagined viewer's response to a spectacle she characterizes as Pushkin's masterwork brought to life. While listening to the tightly constructed duet between the two sisters, Alchevskaia is certain she can distinguish Olga's voice, which rings with "childlike, buoyant notes," from Tatiana's, in which she hears "a kind of pensiveness, a kind of presentiment of life, with its anxieties and passions." Alchevskaia awaits Tatiana's appearance on stage, fearing that the performance cannot sustain its perfect identity with Pushkin's novel. Tchaikovskii's opera must answer to her dearly held preconceptions, the accumulation of a lifetime spent reading Pushkin's novel.[38]

Alchevskaia feels reassured by Tatiana's appearance ("Yes, she is exactly as your imagination depicted her!"), but begins to fret over the arrival of Onegin ("you are afraid that reality might depart from the dream"). Alchevskaia immediately detects signs of Onegin's spiritual malaise: "In spite of the power of his figure, you catch signs of exhaustion and sadness in it." She goes so far as to deny the influence of Pushkin's novel, stressing that the power of this scene transcends preconceptions: "when he looks from afar through his lorgnette at Tatiana with his deep, analytical, sadly demonic gaze, and she raises her expressive eyes to him, you feel without words, without the book, this moment of passion's conception, which promises her much grief and tears." Alchevskaia's denial of the text behind the performance contradicts her liberal use of quotations from Pushkin. She even cites passages from *Eugene Onegin* that do not appear in Tchaikovskii's libretto, suggesting that these passages implicitly accompany the operatic spectacle. When Onegin and Tatiana stroll through the garden, Alchevskaia assumes that the audience will silently declaim the lines in the well-known initial stanza absent in Tchaikovskii's libretto: "You . . . cannot help declaiming to yourself: 'What vile perfidiousness,' and so on." Alchevskaia actually misquotes Pushkin here, substituting the word "vile" (*gnusnoe*) for the less emphatic "low" (*nizkoe*). Her error speaks to the richness of Pushkin's *Eugene Onegin* as a source of misquotings and distortions, and to the reader's role in the continued life of this central Russian text. As Lotman points out, Pushkin's novel inspired a magnificent and diverse novelistic tradition, but the novel itself stands outside of this tradition, which continually appropriated and transformed its constituent elements.[39] Misreadings constitute an essential part of a text's relationship to its cultural context.

Alchevskaia claims that she has witnessed not a representation of life, but *life itself* on the Mariinskii stage, possibly referring to Pushkin's own characterization of *Eugene Onegin* as "life's novel": "Before me passed life in marvelous sounds and musical combinations. The form into which this story of life was cast attuned and raised my nerves to an even greater sensitivity, but there were no separate arias, songs, and melodies: everything—words, tunes, orchestra—merged into something whole, extraordinarily harmonious, well-proportioned, beautiful. Probably this strange sensation is called 'ensemble,' I thought later."

By "ensemble," Alchevskaia means opera itself, the transcendent, all-encompassing art form. She suggests that opera is better equipped than the written word to represent artistic truth, indeed to represent truth itself. Perhaps this is why she radically alters her narrative strategy after concluding her description of the first scene. She concedes that it is difficult for her to "repeat in consecutive order and in detail the entire progression of the opera on stage," and declares, "In my imagination, only individual pictures are drawn." To compensate for the shortcomings of the written word, she takes Tchaikovskii's treatment of Pushkin's text even further, transforming his "lyrical scenes" into a series of vignettes: "I see Tatiana with her hair let down. . . . Then I see Tatiana at her desk. . . . Later I see the scene, when Tatiana . . . meets with Onegin in the garden, after the letter." Alchevskaia's inability to transcribe the entire performance influences her decision to re-conceive Pushkin's text as a portrait gallery of cultural archetypes. She justifies her narrative compression of the opera performance, or rather, its conversion into the anti-narrative mode of description, with reference to the dramatic skill of Medea Figner. The prima donna shows the audience what it can never see in life: "how the years gradually go by and what influence they exert on the heroine." The narrative connecting the visual images exists as a product of the performer's genius and the audience's matching capacity to fill in the spaces, analogous to the work of opera.

The opera theater in which all participate in producing *Eugene Onegin* offers a metaphor for Russian culture. Alchevskaia uses the opera's duel scene as a reference to Pushkin's own death, reading the scene before her as a reenactment of a central, shared Russian "scene": "You are terrified, you can't breathe, and sobs choke you. . . . Lenskii and Pushkin merge in your imagination into something inseparable, whole: the same situation, the same conditions, the same duel, the same field, to which you traveled on the day of the fiftieth anniversary of Pushkin's death." Alchevskaia superimposes Pushkin's death onto Lenskii's, and then adds another layer to this narrative site with her reference to the 1887 Pushkin anniversary celebration. She rereads *Eugene Onegin* as a symbolic retelling of Russia's loss.

During Onegin's final scene with Tatiana, Alchevskaia identifies with both male hero and imagined reader: "You, somehow unnoticed by yourself, are penetrated by Onegin's feelings." How curious that the famously unreadable Onegin should be an open book to Alchevskaia! She imitates Onegin by bowing down before Tatiana, the cultural icon: "You want to fall before her on your knees and entreat her not to destroy her own happiness, which is so close, so possible." Alchevskaia here adopts the incongruous stance of pleading with Tatiana to break her marriage vows. She also incorporates Tatiana's famous words into her own retelling of Onegin's experience ("happiness, which is so close, so possible"). Alchevskaia's memory fails her once again, since Tatiana actually expresses this sentiment in the past tense, "Happiness was so possible. So close, so close!" (*Schast'e bylo tak vozmozhno. Tak blizko, tak blizko!*). Alchevskaia streamlines Tchaikovskii's version, according to which Onegin and Tatiana sing these lines as a duet. Tchaikovskii's elaboration on Pushkin's text mimetically reflects the shared emotions of the protagonists. But Alchevskaia's rendering suggests that Onegin (mis)reads Tatiana's mind.

Alchevskaia changes the most important feature of Tatiana's utterance, its emphasis on the *past* nature of these possibilities, and offers instead a still-present alternative resolution to the archetypal confrontation between Pushkin's characters. Alchevskaia also *reverses* the order of Tatiana's assertions, implying that happiness is possible because the two protagonists have been unexpectedly reunited, and not, as Pushkin's Tatiana intends, that happiness had been close for having once been possible, through socially sanctioned legal marriage.[40] Tatiana's final words to Onegin strike Alchevskaia, "like a hammer," and the end of the performance finds her in a state of agitation: "'Alone again!' pronounces someone in a hollow, demonic voice, and in your head Onegin, Pushkin, the demon, and Lermontov somehow intermingle. . . . No, this is not a performance, this is life! You have lived through something inexpressibly sad, you have lost something, buried someone: you want to cry, sob, wring your hands in despair." To Onegin's mourning for his lost love, Alchevskaia adds her own grief at the passing of Pushkin and Lermontov. And in the ritualized repetition of Pushkin's death and Tatiana's refusal of Onegin, Alchevskaia's account perpetuates her own beloved vision of Russian culture. The story of *Eugene Onegin*, as Alchevskaia tells it, represents a primary lesson to be learned. Alchevskaia's view of Pushkin's novel as the text of texts follows the tradition of Dostoevskii's 1880 Pushkin speech, which "treated *Eugene Onegin* as scripture."[41] And in the 1890s, Pushkin's novel becomes a widespread standard text in the curriculum of Russian schools.

After the performance, Alchevskaia extends her encounter with Pushkin and his oeuvre beyond the theater walls, transforming the city of St. Petersburg into a broader venue for her communion with the Russian cultural legacy:

> The carriage quickly rolls along the even roadway of a street in the capital . . . in the square . . . it is almost dark, but I distinctly see the bronze statue of Pushkin in full figure. He stands, his genius's head lowered, and thinks deep thoughts. . . . I was told later that apparently that monument is in Moscow, apparently I passed by Emperor Nikolai Pavlovich, galloping on a horse. No, this is not true: I saw Pushkin, the poet Pushkin with brow lowered.

Alchevskaia experiences a sort of wishful hallucination, mistaking the mounted statue of Tsar Nicholas I in the Mariinskaia (now Isaac) Square in St. Petersburg for the famous Pushkin monument in Moscow. She does not make the more aesthetically pleasing error of confusing the Pushkin statue with the nearby monument to Peter the Great, which figures so prominently in Pushkin's long poem "The Bronze Horseman" and on the map of literary St. Petersburg. Instead, Alchevskaia associates Pushkin with the poet's own Tsar Nicholas I, while preserving recognizably Pushkinian overtones in the confrontation between a human being and one of the city's best-known statues. Alchevskaia's unconscious linking of Tsar Nicholas with Pushkin also reminds the reader of the connection she envisions between state and culture, a republic of literate adults attuned to the nuances of Pushkin's text.

In the preceding passage, Alchevskaia evokes a number of Pushkin's lyrics with a phrase, "with brow lowered" (*s pokinuvshim chelom*) ostensibly of her own invention. The phrase evokes Pushkin's poem "Poet" (1827): "He does not bow his proud head" (*Ne klonit gordoi golovy*). This phrase also echoes two separate lines describing Cleopatra from Pushkin's unfinished story "Egyptian Nights" (1835): "Lowered her marvelous head" (*Ponikla divnoiu glavoi*), and "But once again she lifts her brow" (*No vnov' ona chelo podemlet*). Alchevskaia's eagerness to see Pushkin's influence as an integral part of her very consciousness ironically results in her misquoting and re-appropriating the poet's words.

Alchevskaia's fancies during her carriage ride imperceptibly blur into a dream sequence, in which she sees Pushkin with a doubled countenance. One of the poet's faces is "harsh, with curly black hair, ugly, as it is customary for people to define him," the other "with the dreamy gaze of deep, expressive eyes and with those antique outlines that are generally called beauty." Alchevskaia's two-faced Pushkin once more evokes the lyric "Poet," which describes the two states of the poet's existence: his low, everyday condition, and his flights of inspiration. Alchevskaia creates her *own* Janus-like Pushkin monument, superimposing this creation over her previous description of the Moscow Pushkin monument.

The prima donna then appears in the dream, and Alchevskaia marvels at Medea Figner's mastery of the Russian language and artistic tradition. Like Alchevskaia's semi-literate adult pupils, Figner came to Russian literature later in life. Alchevskaia claims that Figner has succeeded in realizing Pushkin's Tatiana, "as no Russian singer has created her." Alchevskaia asks the dream Medea Figner whether the company can repeat the entire performance of *Eugene Onegin*. Medea Figner protests: "No, that is impossible! . . . You cannot imagine how much emotional force we put into our singing." The prima donna instead offers to have the company simply repeat Alchevskaia's favorite passages. Medea Figner changes instantly into Tatiana, strikes an attitude, and sings the opening of the letter scene. She gestures to the baritone Iakovlev, who steps forward, assumes a pose, and sings a fragment from Onegin's lecture to Tatiana. Alchevskaia's dream, like her description of the opera performance, transforms the characters from *Eugene Onegin* into cultural monuments, freezing them in characteristic poses and selecting moments from the opera that stand for the whole. "By what miracle are you guessing my favorite passages?" Alchevskaia asks in amazement. Medea Figner answers with a smile, "It is not a miracle at all. . . . These are the favorite passages of our entire public." But Alchevskaia's own considerable effort to capture her response to Tchaikovskii's opera contradicts her fond assumption that shared cultural referents circulate naturally. This contradiction signals Alchevskaia's return to the problem of the adult reader, and to the dissemination of the cultural referents she has so lovingly invoked.

Once awake, Alchevskaia puts aside her operatic fancies, and reminds herself that the goal of her trip is a book for adult classroom reading. She must see people, enter into negotiations, listen to conflicting views, and write everything down. She finds a few spare moments to visit Nevskii Prospect, where she gazes at photograph displays of the Mariinskii artists. Having purchased a series of photographs and a suitable album for them, she muses, "all of this seems to me some kind of inviolable little corner of my personal life, into which even the question of the classroom book for adult reading would not dare to burst." She transforms Tchaikovskii's opera based on a book into a new sort of book, an album that usurps the place of the planned adult reader in her heart and that constitutes a kind of ultimate reader. The represented operatic scenes in her diary translate the hard work of a pedagogy specialist into an evening of pleasure, making pedagogy and opera serve a common cultural project.[42] Alchevskaia used opera to instruct her imagined reader in the art of being Russian.

TCHAIKOVSKII'S *EUGENE ONEGIN*: OPERA AS LITERATURE

Tchaikovskii's opera had not always been as "transparent" as Alchevskaia claimed. In adapting Pushkin's novel to opera, Tchaikovskii trusted his audience to continue performing their readerly tasks: actively filling in the gaps that Pushkin's narrator creates, imagining scenes only hinted at by the narrative, and transforming Pushkin's literary doodles into human characters with histories and emotional lives. But the first audiences for Tchaikovskii's *Eugene Onegin* had trouble processing the opera's artistic codes, particularly in terms of psychological realism and historical verisimilitude. A survey of the reception history of Tchaikovskii's opera provides a context for Alchevskaia's diary fragment, locating her seemingly idiosyncratic account within an evolving process of interpretation.

It has long been a premise of twentieth-century Russian opera scholarship that Tchaikovskii's opera *Eugene Onegin* draws extensively on the Russian realist novel for its rendering of Pushkin's novel in verse. Musicologist Boris Asaf'ev expressed the relationship as follows:

> Chaikovskii's "lyrical scenes," that is, *Eugene Onegin*—are chains of monologues ("alone with him/herself") and dialogues ("conversations," "interviews"), so interlaced with one another and so psychologically motivated, that "the operatic" with its rhetoric and "demonstrativeness," with its "masks and buskins," is decisively overcome. By the realism of all its inner nature and its entire aural effect, *Eugene Onegin* was a remarkable event, equal to the finest achievements of Russian realistic literature.[43]

Or, as succinctly stated by music historian Abram Gozenpud, "in Chaikovskii's *Eugene Onegin*, the Pushkinian tradition merges with the Turgenevian."[44] Western scholars, in contrast, have tended to see Tchaikovskii's opera as anything but realist, regretting that Pushkin's delicate ironies are swept away in a sudsy torrent of lyricism. Western criticism treats Tchaikovskii and his opera much the way that Pushkin's narrator treats Lenskii. This is to say that Western critics do not dispute Tchaikovskii's claims to emotional authenticity, but find these claims ridiculous in aesthetic terms. Vladimir Nabokov, in his voluminous commentary to *Eugene Onegin*, simply dismisses Tchaikovskii's realization of Pushkin's novel with glancing references to Tchaikovskii's "silly" and "slapdash" opera.[45]

A brief survey of the relationship between operatic and prose forms in Russia provides a clue to the basis for linking Tchaikovskii's opera with the techniques of literary realism. Beginning with Mozart and Beethoven, as is well known, music became more psychologically complex, depicting human emotion through techniques of transition, modulation, preparation and resolution.[46] Opera began to free itself from its traditional formal framework of recitatives, arias, and ensembles and departed from imposed structure and pacing.[47] As a result of these developments, opera became more like the symphony, whose continuous musical form evokes human psychological processes, and by extension, more like the realist novel.[48] Opera's increasing emphasis on human psychological processes, rather than on external action as such, evoked the novelistic form, extending opera's more obvious affinities with stage drama.

The relationship between opera and prose fiction was transformed most radically in Russia during nineteenth-century opera's evolution from verse to prose forms. Musorgskii's unfinished version of Gogol's play *The Marriage* in 1868 represents the earliest known operatic setting of a prose text, emphasizing the changes of intonation that occur in conversation.[49] Musical prose made possible the joining together of phrases of irregular length, in contrast to musical verse, with its symmetrical four-bar phrases. Musical dialogue then compensated for the loss of formal structure caused by the use of a prose libretto.

But Tchaikovskii's opera did not model itself after these Russian experiments in operatic form. First of all, Pushkin wrote his novel in verse, not prose. Moreover, Tchaikovskii substantially reworked Pushkin's text to fit his own operatic conception. And yet, Gary Schmidgall's essay on Tchaikovskii's *Eugene Onegin* suggests that the opera nevertheless adopts the conventions of realist prose fiction by "dialogizing" Pushkin's literary text. In this way, Tchaikovskii blends Onegin's confessional letter and Tatiana's rejection of his suit into a dialogue, which the two characters enact in a scene together.[50] The changes made to Pushkin's narrative presentation of his characters radically affect possible interpretations of this scene. According to this new dialogic structure, as Nicholas Zhekulin observes, "Tatiana's admission of her continuing love for him thus appears to be more a consequence of Onegin's pleading than the almost incidental statement that is found in Pushkin."[51] As brilliantly described by the music scholar Richard Taruskin, the women's quartet in the opera's opening scene exemplifies this new dialogization, staging an artistic and psychological collision of the domestic romance (*romans*) sung by Tatiana and Olga with the recitative reflections on aging by Madame Larina and the old nurse.[52] In this context, the collisions of verse form and conversational intonation that Formalist Yurii Tynianov found so remarkable in Pushkin's novel might be said to characterize Tchaikovskii's opera as well.[53] Interpretations of Tchaikovskii's *Eugene Onegin* such as Taruskin's represent a major revision of the opera's critical history in the West, and offer the possibility of reconciling the separate traditions of Western and Russian reception.

The reconciliation is made possible when realism becomes more than a function of mimesis and reproduction, and represents an *inner* reality, not a merely formal one. As Taruskin observes, although Tchaikovskii admitted that operatic form was based on falsehood (*lozh'*), that is, on stylized illusion, the composer declared himself to be a realist in a specifically Russian sense: "It seems to me that I am truly gifted with the ability to express *truthfully*, *sincerely* and *simply*, in music, those feelings, moods, and images toward which the text aims. In this sense *I am a realist* and fundamentally a Russian."[54] As it happens, novelist Fedor Dostoevskii made much the same claim for his own art: "They call me a psychologist: not true: I am only a realist in a higher sense, i.e., I depict all the depths of the human soul."[55] Structuralist theoretician Roman Jakobson canonized Dostoevskii's views on realism in his famous 1921 article "On Realism in Art," reminding readers what a subjective and temporally relative concept realism had always been: "Exaggeration in art is unavoidable, wrote Dostoevskii; in order to show an object, it is necessary to deform the shape it used to have."[56]

Realism might also consist of showing how thoroughly a character's consciousness is permeated by artistic tropes and motifs. Taruskin links Tchaikovskii's specifically *musical* realism with the techniques of Pushkin's narrator, arguing that Tchaikovskii created his opera "in an idiom intensely redolent of the domestic, theatrical, and ballroom music of its time and place—its, not his—and in so doing he situates it, just as Pushkin situates the literary prototype, in the years 1819–25." Tchaikovskii's characters express their feelings "through a finely calculated filter of musical genres and conventions."[57] Similarly, Zhekulin provides a musical analysis of the opera's final scene that focuses on Tchaikovskii's references to musical material from earlier scenes, evoked to represent a character's consciousness. The protagonists part because Tatiana cannot rid herself of the memory of Lenskii's death. The audience knows this from the duel scene motifs that recur throughout the final scene. Musical motifs from Onegin's earlier, sterile self further establish the fact that his emotional range has not really expanded. In this way, Taruskin and Zhekulin make a case against the oft-repeated criticism that Tchaikovskii's opera lacks the narrative sophistication of Pushkin's novel in verse. In providing these framing retrospective repetitions on earlier selves, Tchaikovskii's opera may, in fact, offer what amounts to an ironic, realist critique of operatic lyricism.

Tchaikovskii's opera was particularly troubling to audiences of his time precisely as concerns realism in operatic art. The audience at the initial performances of *Eugene Onegin* in 1879 was shocked to see, in the words of the composer's brother Modest, "landowners, nannies, provincial young ladies, generals, and gentlemen in frock coats, singing arias and duets."[58] Critics of *Eugene Onegin* thought that operatic works depicting a more or less contemporary reality violated established generic norms. One critic insisted that opera as "a conventional form of art" dictates that "the story . . . be pushed into a sufficiently distant past, which we cannot imagine completely clearly."[59] Opera should properly treat historical or mythological subjects, peopled with lofty, mythic, or exotic characters. Such characters appropriately reveal themselves to the audience by means of the selfsame conventional operatic devices that seemed incongruous in Tchaikovskii's opera: "Larina's daughters come out onto the balcony: Tatiana, with a book in her hands, immediately declares that she loves to daydream, and Olga, in a lengthy aria, provides a complete analysis of her character, treating herself completely objectively and displaying her talents for reflection. How natural and plausible it all is!"[60] Critical and popular response to Tchaikovskii's opera continued in this vein, as the opera only very gradually evolved from an anomaly into a masterwork. A Moscow production of *Eugene Onegin* in 1889, only three years before Alchevskaia's visit to the Mariinskii Theater, inspired a fresh round of critical pronouncements on the work's inappropriateness for the operatic stage:

> to take stories from the contemporary life of the cultured class, to transform a contemporary society drawing room into opera, is impossibly risky, I think. The prosaic frock coat and dress coat—on the opera stage; the empty swell, surfeited by life, who has polished all his feelings to an external gloss, transformed into an operatic baritone; a general in full dress uniform, invited to the footlights to sing a tender aria in bass voice—to all this I cannot be reconciled.[61]

Tchaikovskii's contemporary critics neglected to consider stage convention, much less their own responses, in a historical context. This was odd, considering that Russian authors, foremost among them Pushkin, had been radically transforming established literary forms for the better part of the century. Instead, the modern setting influenced critics to view Tchaikovskii's opera in terms of real-life drawing-room mores. The reviewer of the 1889 Moscow production pointed out that Onegin must certainly have hesitated upon his first meeting with Tatiana to make the cynical observation, "My uncle, man of firm convictions . . . / By falling gravely ill, he's won / A due respect for his afflictions— / The only clever thing he's done." And surely a provincial mama like Madame Larina would never leave her marriageable young daughters alone with two young men, one of them a complete stranger.[62] Another critic regretted that the chorus of guests grouped about Onegin during the ball scene produced an unpleasant effect on viewers "by its extreme unnaturalness."[63]

Subtitling the opera "Lyrical Scenes" gave Tchaikovskii some measure of freedom from traditional operatic structures. But even the term "lyrical" was problematic for Tchaikovskii's critics, who found scenes such as the social introductions and light conversation of the opera's opening scene anything but lyrical.[64] Tchaikovskii also sought to evade operatic norms with his extensive use of recitative technique, especially in Onegin's solo part.[65] But critics were nearly unanimous in their view that Onegin was simply not a suitable character for the operatic stage: "Eugene himself— . . . is the hero of a novel, but not an operatic hero; there are no grounds for music in him, until . . . he becomes a person who is capable of loving passionately and strongly."[66] Tchaikovskii's critics failed to consider Onegin's recitative-structured dryness and reserve as a specifically operatic way of expressing character. Critics *did* consider Tatiana an essentially lyrical operatic heroine, and several of them suggested that Tchaikovskii's opera should have been titled *Tatiana Larina* to reflect the actual nature of the changes Tchaikovskii effected in setting Pushkin's novel. The shift in emphasis from Onegin to Tatiana reflects Tchaikovskii's own preference for female heroine over male protagonist in Pushkin's work. But this shift also mirrors the evolving reception of the novel *Eugene Onegin*.

Although the critic Vissarion Belinskii declared in 1844 that Onegin and Tatiana could both be considered the heroes of Pushkin's novel, Belinskii clearly privileged Onegin in his interpretive commentary, reconceiving Onegin's actions in a sympathetic light.[67] The elevation of Tatiana to a more privileged position in the novel dates from Dostoevskii's Pushkin speech of 1880, which made Tatiana the patron saint of the Russian nation. Tchaikovskii, Dostoevskii, and Alchevskaia all take part in one of the major critical shifts in the novel's interpretive history, recasting Pushkin's work in generic terms, by turns as opera, scripture, and diary entry. These generic re-visionings of Pushkin's text also provided an early indication of the coming shift in emphasis from the novel's "content," that is, moral and social significance, to its expressly literary form on the part of twentieth-century scholars like Shklovskii, Tynianov, Bakhtin, and Lotman.[68] Meanwhile, Russian opera audiences grew ever more historically distanced from Pushkin's characters, as well as from the principles of nineteenth-century literary verisimilitude. Reading *Eugene Onegin* on the opera stage in terms of its "inner" reality no longer posed much difficulty.

In contrast, nineteenth-century critics of Tchaikovskii's *Eugene Onegin* had objected to the opera in generic terms, from beginning to end. Of the opening scene, one critic declared, "The first scene of the opera is not distinguished by any special poetry; Larina is prosaically making jam."[69] Another critic objected to the opera's final scene, claiming that the lovers' embrace recalled the dream sequence in Offenbach's operetta *La Belle Hélène*: "and had Prince Gremin not appeared at that minute, opportunely or not, and shown Onegin the door, it is doubtful whether Tatiana would have remained faithful to her duty, and whether the general would have remained without an unpleasant ornament on his high forehead."[70]

Tchaikovskii's opera seemed to critics in danger of slipping out of the generic realm of opera into the mundane stretches of prose fiction (jam) or the frivolous space of operetta (cuckolded husbands). Critics found no poetry in the territory staked out between the two, but only a "rather vulgar" operatic overstatement, typified by Tatiana's shrill, abruptly broken-off cadenza: "Goodbye forever!"[71] They objected to the composer's violations of literary verisimilitude in the service of operatic convention, but also condemned Tchaikovskii's departure from operatic norms in his attempt to dramatize novelistic themes. It is ironic that Tchaikovskii was cast by his contemporaries as an operatic iconoclast. The composer attempted no bold structural innovations such as those of Musorgskii. In fact, in Taruskin's view, "Everything about Chaikovsky, from his political views to his social deportment and attitudes to his musical tastes, was conservative and conventional."[72]

The initial reception of Tchaikovskii's *Eugene Onegin* differed markedly from the opera's final canonization by the Soviet critical establishment. In a 1940s study, Boris Asaf'ev claimed that Tchaikovskii displayed a Balzac-like talent for combining psycho-realistic observations with classical rhythms and forms, marred by only occasional outbreaks of distracting romanticism.[73] Tchaikovskii, in Asaf'ev's view, reworked recitative "into coherent speech tissue, into conversation, with subtle intonational-thematic content."[74] Asaf'ev believed that Tchaikovskii's opera derived its realist elements from Russian romances (*romansy*), art songs whose fragments had made their way "into the intonational dictionary of the epoch," much in the way that new words enter a spoken language.[75] Asaf'ev's analysis of Tchaikovskii's *Eugene Onegin* characterizes the opera as an evolutionary link between early- and late-nineteenth-century Russian art, both musical *and* literary.[76] The Russian art song, performed in domestic settings, private salons, and small concert halls, provided the building blocks for a new sort of opera, joining poetry and music to tell stories on an intimate human scale. Asaf'ev believed that Tchaikovskii's opera asserted a shared social context for such stories, as well as a set of common artistic conventions for telling them.

Asaf'ev's reading of romance song influences in Tchaikovskii's opera as artistically progressive has been countered by Taruskin's recent claim that Tchaikovskii's use of romance motifs is, in fact, intentionally retrogressive. But, more important, musico-historical studies such as Asaf'ev's smooth over the troubled early history of Tchaikovskii's opera, and make the canonization of his *Eugene Onegin* seem the result of the work's intrinsic qualities. Tchaikovskii's *Eugene Onegin* ultimately became a standard work in the Russian operatic repertoire, celebrated for both lyricism *and* psychological realism. The credit for this transformation belongs to Russian opera spectators, whose observing consciousnesses provided the real theater for restaging Pushkin.

Chapter Five

Naturalizing Opera
The Case of La Traviata *in Russia*

The history of Verdi's opera *La Traviata* (1853) in imperial Russia exemplifies the transformative potential the Western operatic repertoire acquired within the Russian cultural context. In the wake of soprano Angiolina Bosio's artistic rehabilitation of Violetta in the 1850s, Russian literature recast Verdi's heroine as an embattled actress or singer, rather than as a prostitute. This reconception allowed the opera diva, not merely the heroines she played, to serve as a carrier of artistic and moral meaning. In this context, Violetta's self-sacrifice for the well-being of her lover and his family parallels the diva's devotion to public service in the name of art. In Russia, Violetta the operatic character became diva-like, a manifestation of spiritualized expressivity. Russian literary works thus re-imagined *La Traviata*'s courtesan heroine, Violetta Valery, as well as her literary counterpart, Alexandre Dumas's "camellia" Marguerite Gautier, as a Western cousin to the redeemed fallen women of the Russian realist novel.

Russian critics considered Verdi's opera itself in need of moral rehabilitation. The case of *La Traviata* allegorizes nineteenth-century Russia's ongoing attempt to justify the ubiquitous presence of Western opera in an increasingly nationalistic cultural climate. The principal motifs of Verdi's *La Traviata*—disease and taintedness—signaled a contagion of threatening Western social values best "treated" with infusions of high-mindedness and creative reinterpretation.[1] Still, *La Traviata* seemed in constant danger of slipping back into cultural disrepute, not because of its heroine's ambiguous social standing, but owing to the opera's explicit commodification of love and happiness. *La Traviata*'s thematic emphasis on the financial underpinnings of bourgeois life uncomfortably evoked the fabulous sums the Russian state donated to support the resident Italian opera troupe in St. Petersburg. In order that Russian audiences might continue to enjoy *La Traviata*, critics evoked "pure" feeling and unmediated emotional expression as the opera's most notable characteristics.

La Traviata occupied a problematic social and aesthetic middle ground for Russian critics, depicting the demimonde with an unnerving blend of Romantic and Realist convention. The doomed love affair between a Parisian courtesan and the scion of a bourgeois family seemed a far cry from the mid-nineteenth-century Russian social context, with its notoriously undeveloped middle estate.[2] Furthermore, as a work of late bel canto opera, *La Traviata* was out of step with midcentury experiments in operatic form by Russian composers such as Alexander Dargomyzhskii and Modest Musorgskii, who sought to redefine the connection between words and music. *La Traviata* appeared initially caught "in the middle" in Russia, confronting traditional cultural mores and progressive aesthetic praxes. But *La Traviata*'s surprising malleability within its new interpretive context illuminates the process by which Western cultural tropes permeated Russian social life, becoming transformed in the bargain.

RUSSIAN CRITICS TAKE STOCK

La Traviata received its Russian premiere during the coronation week of Tsar Alexander II in September 1856, when the Imperial Theater directorate commissioned the St. Petersburg Italian opera troupe for three performances.[3] If *La Traviata* seems an odd choice for such an important national occasion, the explanation appears simple enough: the directorate wanted to stage a new opera by a popular composer and to showcase its investment in the Italian troupe. Following the opera's premiere in Russia came two waves of critical pronouncements on *La Traviata*: the judgments rendered on the opera's initial performances (1856–60), and commentary offered when *La Traviata* first became part of the Russian opera troupe's repertoire (1868).

Reviewers of *La Traviata*'s first performances in Russia regarded the opera skeptically. Rostislav (the pseudonym of F. M. Tolstoi) cited Verdi's monotonous reliance on waltzes.[4] The critic Rappaport felt that the story, while "entertaining" in Dumas's novel, *La Dame aux camélias* (1848), provided "a most scanty ground for opera."[5] The composer and critic Alexander Serov concurred: "a declaration of love at a ball—insult—death from consumption—there you have the *entire* plot!"[6] Serov dourly predicted that *La Traviata* would meet an early death, much like its consumptive heroine. Only critics from Odessa defended *La Traviata*, calling the opera "an important page in the *physiologie* of Woman" and a "musical masterpiece."[7] The Odessan audience liked everything about *La Traviata*, going so far as to applaud the furniture for the third act.[8]

Verdi's opera again came under stern scrutiny when it threatened to sully the Russian opera troupe's repertoire. During the spring of 1868, the opera elicited critical reviews of an almost comic ferocity. The nationalistic critic Rappaport declared bluntly that "the *national* stage should serve completely different goals, and *La Traviata* on the Russian stage is no more than an anomaly."[9] Critic and composer Cesar Cui used vivid imagery to make a similar point:

> In order to characterize *La Traviata* in a single word, I will say that it's a *minced beef cutlet*. Maestro Verdi needed to prepare an edible dish, but he didn't wish to buy new provisions. He had left over from past meals a piece of soup meat here, a piece of cooked meat there; he carefully chopped everything up, made cutlets, and offered them to his customers. And what of it? My comparison goes even further: just as an inedible, stale, and unhealthy dish is eaten with avidity and eagerness in various boarding schools and educational establishments, the public relishes and savors [*gutiruet i savuriruet*] *La Traviata*.[10]

This scathing critique illustrates the principal considerations according to which Russian critics found *La Traviata* suspect. Cui's image of a stale cutlet evokes the famous passage in *La Dame aux camélias* in which Armand Duval has the malodorous remains of his mistress exhumed. The "stale cutlet" also suggests the arrangements by which the demi-mondaine heroine passes from one male patron to another. While expressing disapproval over recycled motifs and ill-combined musical elements, Cui's cutlet metaphor protests the cultural contamination that Russian critics feared as a result of excessive Western influences. Cui's use of the French verbs *gouter* and *savourer*, which he conjugates in the original Russian according to the model for foreign borrowings, characterizes the public's taste for *La Traviata* as an appetite for fashionable French vice. Cui's reference to "boarding schools and educational establishments" underscores the pedagogical role that he and many other Russian critics envisioned for art. Cui's cutlet metaphor argues for cooking up a more nourishing "meat and potatoes" realism, instead of relying on an appealing musical context to make a sordid reality palatable.

These critical objections aside, a case can be made for the redeeming structural transformations that Verdi's opera worked upon Dumas's novel. To be sure, Verdi's opera smoothed over the original content of *La Dame aux camélias* to such an extent that, as one opera historian noted sardonically, "'Violetta's' stage business with the champagne in the opening scene is really all that remains to stamp her as a 'transgressor' of a particular kind; and, without fastidiousness, it might be wished that 'Violetta' not throw her champagne about the stage, which, besides being a little unbecoming, would in actual life be imprudent, as some of it might fall on her dress."[11]

But numerous critics have also asserted that in Verdi's opera, the original heroine Marguerite Gautier, whose true nature represents the enigma posed by Dumas's novel, becomes more accessible and sympathetic to the audience.[12] As opera scholar Joseph Kerman points out, Verdi re-conceived his heroine by radically adapting the conventions of bel canto opera, "a theatrical style whose very life was hyperbole."[13] While still requiring the prima donna to possess the technical skill for the contrasting *cantabile* and *cabaletta* sections typical of bel canto style, Verdi's opera used these familiar forms to trace the movements of human consciousness in a manner reminiscent of the psychological novel.[14]

In nineteenth-century Russia, a rhetoric of moral and artistic redemption often accompanied evaluations of *La Traviata*'s aesthetic worth. The Western-oriented critic G. A. Larosh declared, for example, that Verdi had transformed Dumas's novel from a women's "weepie" to an artistic work of deeper significance:

> . . . Verdi's opera, in everyone's opinion, turned out to be not only worthy of the novel, over which so many female readers have shed tears of sympathy and tender emotion, but even seemed to impart to the novel a new sympathetic warmth, peculiar to the world of sound, as though memories of the unfortunate Marguerite Gautier were augmented by memories of the affecting melodies that Verdi placed on her lips.[15]

If Verdi's opera could retroactively rehabilitate Dumas's novel, perhaps a mediating genre or literary form could translate the troublesome Traviata plot into Russian social terms. A feuilleton from 1856 playfully attempted to transpose the story of *La Traviata* into the Russian cultural context, anticipating many such attempts during the second half of the nineteenth century. In this "Russian Traviata," the modest heroine Parasha goes on the stage to support her sick father. A wealthy young count courts her and assures her of his constancy, even though "in private he, of course, acknowledged the inequality of a match with an actress, and planned to forsake her."[16] The Russian *Traviata* transforms the heroine from a pampered courtesan who supports the hero with her tainted earnings to a penniless actress whose defining trait is filial devotion.

The count's mother scripts the likely end of the love affair in order to convince Parasha to save the count from himself: "You will distract him from society . . . from his family, confine him to the close circle of his own home. . . . He loves you, and at first, he will be happy, but sooner or later he will feel that he is missing a great deal. He will begin to pine, and, perhaps, will cease to love you. And he will certainly reproach you."

Parasha uses her dramatic arts to feign interest in a fat tax farmer (*tolstyi otkupshchik*) and nobly rejects the count. During the last act of "Russian Traviata," Parasha, like her Western counterpart, suffers the final stages of consumption. The count hurries to her side, having learned of her sacrifice and secured his mother's blessing, but it is too late. In both the Russian and the Western *Traviata*, the heroine is willing to play the *part* of a woman who chooses her own material self-interest over love. This magnificent performance represents the heroine's last, precious gift to the hero; it is analogous to the portrait of herself that Violetta bequeaths Alfredo during their last meeting.

"Russian Traviata" ends as the fictional "young writer" asks the narrator of the feuilleton for his opinion. "Old hat!" answers the narrator. "Everything is old, there is nothing new under the sun: the point is not in the novelty of the idea, but in the ability to find new sides to it." With this rejoinder, the half-serious reworking of *La Traviata* invites the Russian reader to reflect on the possibility of mapping Verdi's opera onto the Russian social terrain. The inelegant name "Parasha" offers its own form of a response, evoking the heroine of Alexander Pushkin's narrative poem "The Bronze Horseman" (1833), an insubstantial love object literally swept away by the forces of history and nature.

"Russian Traviata" is mercifully brief on the subject of the heroine's demise, informing the reader simply that "Parasha dies." In contrast, the fourth act of Verdi's *La Traviata*—which takes place at Violetta's deathbed—posed great difficulty for Russian reviewers with the questions it raised about verisimilitude on the operatic stage. Violetta does not die by poison, strangling, the sword, or public execution, as do many operatic heroines. Instead, Verdi's heroine expires of consumption, a malady that might well be expected to interfere with a soprano's rendering of her solo part. Audiences found *La Traviata*'s deathbed scene touching in its intimate simplicity, without chorus or grand-scale final number. But reviewers objected strenuously. Serov asserted that the deathbed scene created "an effect not dramatic, but pathological; a picture not operatic, not theatrical, but hospital-like [*gospital'naia*]."[17] Serov deplored what he called "the incomprehensible movement away from the laws of the exquisite," and saw as the result of this tendency some future opera, in which "we will be taken, probably, into a clinic and made to be witnesses of amputations or the dissection of corpses!" Like Cui's metaphor of the minced beef cutlet, Serov's invocation of corpses signals a distaste for the opera's sexual themes.

Russian reviewers were also troubled by the fits of coughing that nineteenth-century Violettas staged between sung phrases. This realistic touch made listeners all too aware that the characters before them were singing and not speaking, a persistent problem for opera as a genre: "the very fictional situation is extremely poor. Is it possible to depict truly and naturally a woman who is dying of consumption in a transport of despair, while producing . . .

sounds that demand first and foremost that her lungs be absolutely healthy?"[18] This objection to *La Traviata* as performed in Russia extended through the reign of Adelina Patti, whom one reviewer chastised for interspersing wrenching coughs and groans between her legendary trills. This reviewer objected to the anti-musical effect of Patti's verisimilitudinous technique as "especially inappropriate in *La Traviata*, where no one would dream of looking for musical-dramatic truth."[19]

Offenbach's opera *The Tales of Hoffmann* (1881) resolves this incongruity in *La Traviata* by making the soprano's respiratory ailment both literal and metaphorical. Opera itself seduces and destroys Offenbach's young heroine Antonia, when singing proves too much for her weak lungs. A fatal operatic compulsion foils Antonia's anticipated bourgeois union with her fiancé Hoffmann. Also in this opera, the Venetian prostitute Giulietta, who gives parties like Violetta's, betrays Hoffmann by stealing his soul's reflection after making a pact with the Devil. *La Traviata* explores the intersections of art, illness, and identity without recourse to multiple narratives, split personalities, and magical effects. But it also remains distant from verisimo-inspired "big city" operas such as Giordano's *Mala Vita* (1892) and Puccini's *La Bohème* (1896), which survey social worlds quite different from that in *La Traviata.*

In rejecting verisimilitudinous effects and gritty social realism, Russian reviewers refused to allow *La Traviata* to be anything but pretty and pleasing, but they despised Verdi's opera for being too light. The sole performer to succeed in unifying *La Traviata*'s disparate effects was soprano Angiolina Bosio, who brilliantly re-conceived the role of Violetta both on and off the stage. Bosio's interpretation of Violetta became an ideal of aesthetic and spiritual beauty for nineteenth-century St. Petersburg and for Russian literature. And Bosio herself became associated with a kind of cultural martyrdom whose effects also accrued to Verdi's opera. Bosio's life and the plot of *La Traviata* merged to form a single Russian cultural text.

ANGIOLINA BOSIO: LIVING AND DYING AS VIOLETTA

Italian-born Angiolina Bosio spent the most important years of her career (1855–59) as an opera singer in St. Petersburg. During this period, the tsar awarded her the title "His Majesty's Soloist," granting her honorary Russian citizenship. Angiolina Bosio was, in cultural terms, a "naturalized" artist in Russia. Her Russian public felt she belonged to St. Petersburg, and critics referred to her as "*our* prima donna." As Rappaport asserted, "No other singer here has ever enjoyed such unanimous love from the public as Madame Bosio."[20] The city's students, whose cause she supported with benefit concerts, all but worshipped her. Aristocratic opera-goers claimed her somewhat more ambiguously as their own:

> Bosio in *La Traviata*, they now talk only of Bosio in *La Traviata* during a morning visit in yellow gloves, over an iced bottle after lunch, *entre la poire et le fromage* . . . before the fireplace, and over dinner at Dusseau or Borelle. Matchless! Marvelous! say our lionesses in French; diva! diva! the lions answer them in Italian. Truly, this Angiolina is a diva, diva in Italian, and a marvel [*divo*] in Russian. What a voice, what singing![21]

This multilingual duet that takes place between Bosio's admirers stages a spectacle of admiration in which female and male choruses exchange rapturous exclamations. The evocation of pleasures such as French cuisine, elegant gloves, morning calls, and Bosio's singing characterizes the feuilleton's subjects as a sophisticated, Western-oriented elite. But despite the aristocratic patronage clearly extended to Bosio, the soprano also seems an item for consumption by her surfeited sponsors.

Bosio's ambiguous social standing in St. Petersburg often surfaced at the stylistic level in written accounts of her performances. Her reviewers awkwardly attempted to situate her in social terms, their alternately condescending and fawning phrases creating curious tonal hybrids: "Her facial features are not sufficiently regular; her nose is a little to one side. But her mouth is very sweet, her teeth magnificent, her eyes splendid, and her hair very luxurious. . . . She costumes herself superbly and in all roles is a truly upstanding woman."[22] The cited reviewer veers wildly from a disrespectful evaluation of Bosio's charms to fervent adulation. Another reviewer refers to the singer with a formal humility that itself seems performed: "but enough . . . my pen is too weak to express the gratitude that the incomparable singer has earned for the pleasure we have obtained."[23] It was perhaps less socially fraught for reviewers to transfer their approval of Bosio to the operatic heroines she played.[24] After all, like a courtesan, the opera prima donna merely impersonated a lady.

Critics often preferred to treat Bosio as a saint rather than as a real woman. The prevailing critical line asserted that she was not suited to play powerful and cruel heroines like Norma, Lucrezia Borgia, and Semiramis, since "she could be graceful, tender, touching, but not tragic."[25] H. Sutherland Edwards compares Bosio to Raphael's St. Cecilia, and claims that the soprano made "poetry" out of every part she undertook: "No one ever saw her assume a theatrical pose, or play to the audience, or make any kind of 'point.'"[26] Russian critics agreed, claiming that Bosio transformed Dumas's vulgar subject matter through her ability to "poeticize the far-from-attractive character of Violetta."[27] With a little help from Verdi, Bosio re-conceived Dumas's melodrama of Parisian bourgeois mores to emphasize the spiritual sufferings of a female social outcast. According to the critics, Bosio accomplished this revisionist interpretation with recourse to the Romantic evocation of the opera diva through poetry, rather than through prosaic forms.

In March of 1859, Bosio traveled by train to Moscow, where she gave several coolly received performances. She fell ill on the return trip and convalesced for some days at her apartment on Nevsky Prospect. She died on 1 April at the age of 29. Her death gave rise to an outpouring of public grief in St. Petersburg and to a slew of unconfirmed rumors and stories. Many of these stories later appeared in accounts of the city's operatic "Golden Age," and thereby attained a retrospective legitimacy. Bosio also made cameo appearances in well-known Russian literary works by Nekraskov, Chernyshevskii, Turgenev, and Mandelshtam, among others.

Memoiristic accounts characterizied Bosio's death in terms of Verdi's *La Traviata*, linking the soprano's final moments with Violetta's deathbed scene: "poor Bosio preferred this role, in which she was magnificent, natural, even too natural, as they say her demise was identical to the death of Traviata; . . . she, too, could speak the fateful words upon her death, 'Gran dio! morir si giovane! (Dear God! To die so young!)'"[28] Turgenev himself helped associate Bosio's death with the demise of Verdi's heroine. In a letter to writer Ivan Goncharov, Turgenev writes, "I saw her on the day of her last performance:

she played 'Traviata'; she did not think then, playing the dying woman, that she would soon have to perform this role in earnest."[29] Turgenev would later write the story "Klara Milich" (1882), in which an opera singer commits suicide, possibly in response to the tragic romances she performs (see Chapter 7).

The press reporting on Bosio's funeral dramatized her fatal trip to Moscow, hinting that the soprano was already ill, and that the city's negative reception hastened her demise: "Don't you know that in the life of an artist there are minutes . . . when death is in their soul and heart, when the pallor from emotional suffering is concealed by rouge, hidden under a studied smile."[30] This "description" of Bosio resembles nothing so much as that of Violetta in the third act of *La Traviata*, where, with breaking heart, she plays the callous courtesan to drive Alfredo from her. The reviewer casts Moscow as the cruel society of Verdi's opera, a deliberate challenge to the Moscow-Petersburg mythos, in which Petersburg figured as the chillier cultural environment.

According to various sources, Bosio was touched by the outpouring of public concern, and declared on her deathbed: "My illness is my most beautiful triumph." It is difficult not to read a deliberate irony into Bosio's alleged remark about her artistic career, which was a decidedly modest one during the pre-Russia years. Whether or not Bosio herself made a connection between her final illness and *La Traviata*, her audience began to reframe their memories of her performing the role of Violetta. Count Valuev's recollections posit the diva's unconscious but perceptible awareness of her own impending end:

> I did not know her personally, but I feel as though in her I lost someone dear, close to my heart. . . . I cannot remember without tender emotion her first and last scenes in *Traviata*. Never, nowhere, did anyone make such an impression on me in that opera. It was as if she sensed with her spirit that she was fated to die of an illness like the one from which Marguerite Gautier died.[31]

Valuev shifts from admitting that he did not actually know Bosio, to claiming a special, sympathetic access to the soprano's interior life. The diary of Minister Mikhail Dmitrievich Voedvodskii goes even further, reporting a premonitory vision from Bosio's dreams without citing a source for this knowledge: "a month before her demise, the deceased dreamed that all of the singers of our Italian opera were singing the Requiem,—she alone was only listening, felt amazement at this, wanted to sing, but was unable to."[32] Voevodskii's Bosio legend links the prima donna with the legends around Mozart's death, which have it that a mysterious visitor commissioned the composer to write his own Requiem Mass. Voevodskii allots Bosio a place in the pantheon of musical prodigies who died before fulfilling their artistic promise, thus making her life more artlike.[33]

Not all of the apocrypha concerning Bosio was adulatory. The opera memoirist N. I. Raevskii re-narrated Bosio's fatal concert trip to Moscow, making the soprano responsible for her own misfortune. According to Raevskii's version, Bosio quarreled with one of the other female singers, then pettishly moved to an unheated train car to sulk, and caught a chill.[34] This story appeared in the theater directorate's annual anthology of articles; the slander's presence in an official cultural publication guaranteed its survival into the twentieth century.

According to Avdotia Golovacheva-Panaeva's memoirs, Bosio "paid with her life for her miserliness."[35] The memoirist claims that Bosio traveled to Moscow during Lent, when the Imperial Theaters were closed, so as not to sacrifice any concert fees. Golovacheva-Panaeva also writes spitefully of an elderly gentleman besotted with Bosio, a married woman. Nearly every morning, he sent Bosio "a large box of candies, beneath which lay a quantity of gold, a string of pearls, or diamonds." This story transforms the respectably married Bosio into Dumas's literary heroine, Marguerite Gautier, a woman whose economic independence came from the financial support of her male patrons.[36] Golovacheva-Panaeva concludes her account by describing a public sale of the prima donna's private effects, arranged by Bosio's bereaved husband: "Bosio's admirers eagerly bought up her personal belongings, and one of my acquaintances . . . bought a broken comb of Bosio's for ten rubles, and became very angry when I contended that the swindler, Bosio's husband, had sold him one of his own broken combs or one belonging to Bosio's maid." There is no description of this sale anywhere in the literature documenting the aftermath of Bosio's death in Petersburg. The cited passage does, however, recall the opening chapter from Dumas's novel, which describes the sale of the deceased Marguerite's apartment furnishings and luxurious personal effects. The comb—a broken, personal article—is an obvious synecdoche for Bosio-Violetta herself. Still, attempts to besmirch Bosio's character through association with Marguerite proved less successful overall than did the project of rehabilitating Violetta with recourse to Bosio.

Some accounts used the soprano's death as an excuse to attack the Italian opera as an institution, treating this cultural event much like a fashionable new work. Tickets to Bosio's funeral in Petersburg were difficult to obtain, and only a select few gained entrance to the church for the funeral service. Serov claimed that 200,000 people accompanied Bosio's coffin to the Catholic cemetery: "O, fashion!" he commented ruefully.[37] Serov's laconic response was echoed by a contemporary journal that printed the following "overhead" conversation:

> "Did you hear? What a misfortune . . . "
> "What?"
> "Gizo, that Italian singer that was here not long ago . . . "
> "Well?"
> "She's died!"
> "What? Gizo has died? Oh my God! What a shame! And she sang so splendidly!"[38]

The news of "Gizo's" death acts as the signal for a bit of warbling on the part of her admirers, a comment both on the conventional phrasing of these regrets, and on the cadences of Italian opera itself.

Most accounts of Bosio's funeral assumed a personal, passionate, even overwrought tone, as if their authors were playing the role of Alfredo. But most Petersburg periodicals emphasized a personal rather than an official connection with the diva. I. Kokorev, in a letter of 7 April 1859, describes the demonstration that resulted when Petersburg's students demanded the privilege of carrying Bosio's coffin, and were unceremoniously quelled by the city police. According to Kokorev's account, the central part of the city, Nevsky Prospect in particular, was taken up with this event: "its entire width was flooded with people, [standing] in windows, on balconies, in Gostinnyi Dvor—everywhere there were people and more people—you couldn't get through on foot or in a vehicle, for at least an hour carriages had to go around by adjoining streets. Such a spectacle of unselfish regard is worth something!"[39] Oddly enough, Kokorev's account evoked the very discourse of commodification that complicated *La Traviata*'s reception in Russia (the spectacle being "worth something"). One journalist professed himself so personally overcome with grief at the prima donna's death that he had to defer writing a full account of her career to a future article.[40]

The literary genre most conventionally appropriate to Bosio's death was the memorial lyric, a number of which appeared in newspapers and journals. The most famous verse tribute to Bosio occurs in a passage from Nikolai Nekrasov's long poem "About the Weather" (1865):

> We will remember—Bosio. Presumptuous Petropolis
> Spared nothing for her.
> But in vain you wrapped up
> Your nightingale's throat in sable,
> Daughter of Italy!
> It is difficult for Southern roses to get along with the Russian frost.
>
> Before its fatal force
> You bowed your ideal brow,
> And you lie in a foreign land
> In an empty and mournful cemetery.
> An alien people forgot you
> On the very day they laid you in the ground,
> And another has now been singing for a long time,
> Where they used to shower you with flowers.
> There it is light, there the double-bass drones,
> There as usual the kettledrums are loud.
> Yes! It is sad here in the North.
> Money comes hard and laurels dear!

This address to Bosio is a favorite with Russian poetry lovers, who delight in quoting it by heart. Nekrasov's paean to Bosio, with its high-style phrases, contrasts with a preceding section in the poem concerning members of a rural tribe, who arrive from the North to wonder innocently at the city dwellers. The hardy Northern folk seem better equipped to withstand Peterburg's cruel climate than the city's "rich-voiced Southern guests." In "About the Weather," Nekrasov asserts that Western culture cannot take root in the inhospitable environment of Russia. He makes the moral and aesthetic indifference of the city's populace responsible for Bosio's death and for the fading of her memory. But he was incorrect in declaring Bosio forgotten. Ironically, his well-known verse fragment about forgetting became instrumental in the preservation of Bosio's name as a Russian cultural referent.

Following Nekrasov's example, the twentieth-century poet Osip Mandelshtam was drawn to the image of Bosio and her relationship to the city of Petersburg. Mandelshtam planned a story called "Bosio's Death," which he never wrote. References to the diva do appear in his story of cultural ephemera, "The Egyptian Stamp," and in "Fourth Prose" (1930), where the narrator declares that Bosio will sing at his trial. For Mandelshtam, Bosio represented a point of intersection for key cultural concepts, identified by music scholar Boris Kats as "South, North, Europe, Russia, Italy, Petersburg, music, opera, voice, Russian and Italian speech, nineteenth century, Catholicism, artistry, motherland, foreign land, wandering, beauty, fragility, defenselessness, death, forgetting."[41] Mandelshtam's Bosio is a time traveler, a messenger from the past who emphasizes Russians' complex, ambivalent relationship with their own culture.

Although writers like Nekrasov and Mandelshtam stressed the elusive quality of Bosio's legacy in Russia, attempts were made to render her memory permanent and material. After Bosio's death, the citizens of Petersburg commissioned a sculpture from the Florentine artist Pietro Costa and in 1860 erected a monument to the soprano.[42] A black cast-iron bust of Bosio stands upon a column, at the base of which appear a lyre with broken strings, a reed pipe, and an open music notebook. A full-figure personification of Music rests her head against Bosio's right shoulder, embracing the prima donna and holding a laurel wreath and a scroll of music. The iconic language of this monument asserts the complete identification of Bosio with her art. The personification of Music suggests the legend of Saint Cecilia, whose musical gifts caused an angel to fall in love with her and pay her visits from heaven. The monument's memorial verses underscore this affinity, referring to Bosio's

Figure 25. Bosio monument, Masters of Art Cemetery. This monument still stands in the "Masters of Art" Cemetery in St. Petersburg. Its presence is a continuing reminder of the unexpected ways in which Western opera took root in Russian culture.

departure to join the celestial choir.[43] Images from antiquity and the arts evoke Bosio's Italian origins. Petersburg's monument to her variously communicates the combined sense of belonging and otherness that characterized the prima donna's career in Russia, as did the monument's original location in the now-defunct Catholic cemetery of Saint Catherine. Following an official resolution passed in 1939, Stalin liquidated this Roman Catholic cemetery and closed its small church. City officials transferred Bosio's monument and ashes to the Cemetery of the Masters of Art (*Nekropol' masterov iskusstv*) in the Alexander Nevskii monastery complex, where they remain to this day.[44] Bosio's presence in the Masters of Art cemetery, a particularly important

Petersburg cultural "text," marks her complete naturalization as a Russian artist.

In addition to the monument, a memorial lithograph to Bosio appeared in an illustrated journal, which circulated among her public along with the accompanying text of a funeral speech:

> her friends . . . lost in her a feeling heart, a tender soul and a developed mind, which, in combination with a merry and sweet disposition, awakened a sympathy for this woman perhaps even livelier and deeper than the respect accorded her talent. . . . She was the embodiment of honor and the consciousness of moral obligation. She was pious, and art for her was a second religion. No necessary work frightened her; she was afraid to allow herself the smallest whim that might bring with it fatigue, and from which the public might suffer a loss. For her this was a question of honor and personal dignity.[45]

The tribute goes on to declare that Bosio's many acts of secret charity became known only after her death, and hints at life episodes unknown to her public. The speaker regrets that Bosio died "at the very moment when she could finally dream of her own happiness, after long service in the name of our pleasure." Like Violetta, Bosio died just as the final obstacles to her happiness had been removed. What is more, Bosio too lived for "our pleasure." But the insistent evocation of piety, honor, duty and moral obligation in the funeral speech balance any hint of impropriety. Violetta herself turns to religion at the end of *La Traviata*, declaring it to be the only balm to those who suffer ("*Religione è sollievo a' sofferenti*").[46]

The memorial lithograph relates its own version of the soprano's life and career. At the center of the lithograph is a likeness of Bosio, and, encircling this portrait, a garland displaying the names of the operatic heroines she created. The name of "Violetta" graces the top of the garland, as Bosio's supreme artistic achievement, with Luisa, Gilda, Zerlina, Elvira, Desdemona, Leonora, Norina, Martha, and Rosina forming the rest of the circle. Below the garland lies a drawing of Bosio's gravesite, and a replica of her signature. Bosio's memorial lithograph presents the story of her life and career differently from the later gravesite monument, fragmenting her identity into a series of gentle operatic heroines, while privileging her identification with

Figure 26. Bosio memorial lithograph. Bosio's life story is told here in the form of a succession of operatic heroines, culminating in a quiet grave far from her native Italy.

the role of Violetta. Bosio's signature is a telling detail, as it refers to her professional identity, and most particularly to her binding signature on the contracts she made with the Imperial Theater directorate. The signature credits Bosio with the creation of her operatic "impersonations," something like an artist's signature on a painting.

Nekrasov's contentions notwithstanding, Petersburg's music critics long mourned the passing of Bosio, the Violetta they termed "unforgettable" (*nezabvennaia*). Well into the 1870s, Russian critics found new Violettas wanting in comparison with their memories of Bosio. Without Bosio's ennobling presence, one critic asserted, Violetta became merely "a vulgar miss [*lorette]* of mediocre music, incapable of inspiring passionate feeling."[47] The Parisian lorette of the 1850s and 1860s was typically a would-be singer or actress, who accepted money from her admirers in return for sexual favors, and this image explicitly conflated stage performers and prostitutes. Bosio's Violetta had to be renewed and re-appropriated within the Russian context in order to remain in the Russian cultural canon.

But Russian female opera singers did not begin to specialize in Italian bel canto operatic roles until well into the second part of the nineteenth century. This repertorial lacuna was partly due to cultural politics, but also to the absence of Russian soprano voices of the bel canto type. Russian performers learned the classical repertoire, especially Mozart and Rossini, the small repertoire of Russian operas by composers such as Glinka and Verstovskii, and light favorites by European composers Flotow, Auber, and others. From the late 1860s onward, however, the Russian opera troupe began to compete in earnest with the cultural usurper, the Italian opera troupe. Roles in operas such as *La Traviata* allowed Russian sopranos to display their mastery of Western operatic techniques and dramatic conventions. By the 1870s, Verdi's Violetta had become a set of familiar gestures and attitudes staged in parallel by both Russian and Western sopranos. This composite Violetta merged cultural myths of the prima donna in Russia with subtextual references to Verdi and Dumas.

When the Russian opera troupe first performed *La Traviata* in 1868, Russian music critics declared Verdi's opera unsuitable for Russian sopranos. Cesar Cui wrote of Adelaida Biudel', the Russian troupe's first Violetta: "Mademoiselle Biudel' sings her last aria very nicely, but it is a great pity that she sings it."[48] Two seasons later, the critic Rappaport reacted similarly to the Russian soprano Polina Levitskaia: "It is a pity that for her benefit concert she had to perform *La Traviata*, which has no place at all on the Russian stage, but what is one to do?"[49] Rappaport maligned *La Traviata* for its perceived lack of dramatic seriousness, but partially redeemed the opera with a strategy borrowed from Bosio's time. Levitskaia, he claimed, created a "new type" of

Violetta, who experiences true love as a flood of new, nobler emotions, as a result of which "her sorry past instantly disappears." In this way, Rappaport continued Russian critics' old habit of making Verdi's heroine morally and personally sympathetic by erasing the most disturbing aspects of her story.

Petersburg of the 1870s saw some of the most famous Western sopranos, including Adelina Patti, Christine Nilsson, and Desirée Artôt, in the role of Violetta. Reviewers claimed that each soprano held the key to specific aspects of the role. Patti excelled at the technical challenges of the role, particularly in the early scenes, when Violetta is gay and coquettish. Reviews invariably emphasized Patti's showy toilette: "Madame Patti's dresses were distinguished by a remarkable taste and splendor, and worthily competed with the dazzling brilliance of the diamonds that ornamented them."[50] The memoirist Ivanskaia described Nilsson, in contrast to Patti, as weak in the first act, where she had to depict "the lively, but nevertheless exquisite 'camellia.'"[51] But the ethereal Nilsson could smooth over any troublesome realistic touches in the final act. She perfected dying gracefully on stage. The corpulent Artôt was strongest at expressing Violetta's passionate side, but reviewers declared her ill suited for the melancholy death scene or for death by consumption, since "an apoplectic stroke would be more likely."[52] The physical and social realities of Verdi's *La Traviata* had become a matter for light irony instead of outrage on the critics' part. Recollections of various Violettas formed a kind of operatic scrapbook, a collage of favorite operatic moments.

By the 1870s, *La Traviata* had become an uncontroversial favorite, a showcase for divine vocal prowess. But the Russian public still associated it with the period of the Italian opera troupe's greatest glory, and looked upon Violetta herself as a diva-like creature, a rare being of extraordinary expressivity. While Russian sopranos appropriated the role of Violetta, Russian literature juxtaposed literary heroines with Verdi's Violetta, continuing the project of rehabilitating Dumas's notorious heroine.

LA TRAVIATA AS RUSSIAN LITERATURE

The "fallen woman" descends below the watermark of respectable society's norms. In both Western and Russian literature, she has received her due from literary scholars.[53] The fallen woman exhibits her degradation in aesthetic and generic terms, since she often seems "both hyperdetermined and disturbingly 'false' (painted, melodramatic, histrionic)."[54] The nineteenth-century female stage performer was at risk of being condemned socially according to this conflated conception of fallenness, particularly because she seemed an active transgressor rather than a passive victim, plying her trade in public for money.

Sexually compromised literary women such as Emma Bovary, Isabel Vane, and Anna Karenina are spectacularly punished or punish themselves for their sins. To be sure, adulteresses and loose women receive harsher literary treatment than do prostitutes from the poorer classes or despoiled maidens. One of the earliest models for the redeemed fallen woman in literature is Abbé Prévost's Manon Lescaut, from his novel *L'Histoire du chevalier des Grieux et de Manon Lescaut* (1731), later treated in operas by Auber, Massenet, and Puccini. The lowborn Manon nearly ruins her brilliant young lover, who gambles, steals, and lies to keep her happy. Dumas's novel explicitly stages this affinity by having the narrator buy Marguerite's copy of *Manon Lescaut* at the auction of her personal possessions. But the fact that Marguerite's choices protect rather than imperil her young lover's social standing points to the rich nineteenth-century potential for rereadings and respinnings of the literary fallen woman.

The Russian literary tradition enlists the fallen woman in a particularly broad range of social, moral, and spiritual projects: Chernyshevskii's Nastasia leaves the streets and goes to work as a seamstress in a women's arstel, and Dostoevskii's Sonia redeems the murderer Raskolnikov's lost soul. The fallen woman in Russian literature also serves as a foil for her would-be male rehabilitator, who finds himself variously ennobled, undone, or parodied for his pains. George Siegel points out that by reducing the narrator to self-abasement before the prostitute Liza in *Notes from the Underground* (1864), Dostoevskii prepared the ground for transforming the fallen woman into a redeemer in *Crime and Punishment* (1866).[55] Olga Matich traces this pattern of redemption back to Dumas's *La Dame aux camélias*, in which "Armand tries to save Marguerite, who in turn makes an even grander gesture by selflessly relinquishing him to prevent his social ruin."[56] The incarnations of Verdi's *La*

Traviata and Dumas's novel as Russian literary subtext foreground the explicitly performative aspects of the fallen woman's role, while enlisting Violetta as an activist in Russian social reform. Russian literature re-conceived the Romantic tropes and topoi found in the Traviata plot by remaking these conventions in meta-theatrical terms, resetting the story in an actual theatrical milieu. Works by Leskov, Krestovskaia, Turgenev, Chernyshevskii, Dostoevskii, Tolstoi, the Koval'skie siblings, Bauer, Paustovskii, and Inber illustrate Russian cultural appropriations and transformations of Verdi's opera. Many of these works attempt to redeem the insistently middlebrow *La Traviata* not simply in moral terms, but as high art. *La Traviata* lies at the very core of conception for Tolstoi's *Anna Karenina* (see Chapter 6).

Piamma, the provincial heroine of Nikolai Leskov's laconic story "A Theatrical Nature" (1884), is possessed of an "exalted" (*eksal'tirovannyi*) nature. She runs away from home to go on the stage, but encounters difficulties when she refuses to grant sexual favors to patrons. Piamma is unwilling to play the part of a Violetta on stage or in life. She yearns to perform tragic drama, but is compelled by provincial theatrical life to work within a lower generic spectrum that includes operetta. Leskov, like Verdi, establishes his heroine as rejecting traditional social norms, while she upholds standard moral *and* aesthetic principles. Piamma aspires to raise herself generically, not socially.

In Leskov's story, a young hussar takes the part of Alfredo, fighting a duel in Piamma's honor and winning her love.[57] Piamma sacrifices her career to nurse her wounded hussar in the country, much as *La Traviata*'s Violetta Valery breaks her Paris ties and depletes her financial resources to pay for her country idyll with Alfredo. Piamma receives a visit from her hussar's mother, in a direct parallel with Germont's visit in the second act of *La Traviata*. But the hussar's mother is stunned by the young couple's chaste love, and marvels at the narrow cot upon which Piamma sleeps. Leskov's departure from *La Traviata* in sexual/moral terms makes an obvious bid for the reader's sympathy. As in the feuilleton "Russian Traviata," Leskov's heroine is an actress, a woman whose occupation in life only *appears* suspect.

Piamma resolves to safeguard her lover's social well-being, and leaves to join a distant theater troupe. In contrast to a series of callow and forgetful literary Alfredos, her hussar does not return to his pleasant life of privilege, but dies by his own hand. Piamma responds to the news by shooting herself ("theatrically," as the narrative notes). Piamma's suicide represents a far more decisive resolution to the loss of her beloved than does the expected consumptive decline, and is an uncharacteristic form of female death in nineteenth-century art. Leskov's deadpan version of *La Traviata* suggests that Piamma creates her life plot by reconceiving familiar texts, exalting her choices through theater, aiming upward into the generic stratosphere.

Maria Krestovskaia's novel *Artistka* (1891) similarly invokes *La Traviata* to shape the literary treatment of a theatrical milieu, implying that life is most appropriately allegorized as theater. Krestovskaia's heroine, Olga Leont'eva, is an actress whose commitment to personal and artistic freedom infuriates her bureaucrat-husband Chemezov. Unlike Violetta Valery, Olga does not win an honorary membership in bourgeois society as compensation for losing everything else, but rejects the social order herself. Olga's connection with her Russian public proves to be her only enduring relationship. Her earlier romance with Leo, an Italian tenor, makes this point with reference to Verdi's opera, positing *La Traviata* as a fantasy world that the Russian actress must ultimately renounce, much as Violetta gives up Alfredo.

In Venice, Olga attends a performance of *La Traviata* at a small theater, where the tenor attracts her notice. "Alfredo" sings while gazing out into the audience at Olga, who fancies she is living out the events of the opera.[58] Later that evening, Leo appears beneath Olga's hotel window in a gondola, and speaks to her of love, just as Alfredo woos Violetta at the end of the first act. The two lovers (mis)understand one another perfectly, even though Olga speaks little Italian. As Olga tells Chemezov, "that which in Russian perhaps would have sounded silly and sentimental, in Italian came out so simply, prettily, and harmoniously, that it seemed like a kind of marvelous music."[59] Here, Krestovskaia has her heroine ingenuously echo the negative characterizations of Italian opera often made by Russian critics.

Olga and Leo remain on opposite sides of their cultural divide. Even when they play scenes together, she speaks her part in Russian, while he performs in Italian. The lovers make a single, unsuccessful attempt to become characters in the same opera, appearing together as the doomed lovers in a performance of Gounod's opera *Faust*. But Olga realizes that she is a Russian actress, not a Western opera singer. She rejects both the Western artistic forms and the bourgeois mores associated with *La Traviata*. She returns to Russia, and soon learns that Leo has been killed in a duel. Krestovskaia's novel reverses the roles of the principals in Verdi's opera: Leo represents merely an instructive episode for Olga, the hard-nosed professional.[60]

Krestovskaia's Olga is a *traviata*, literally a "wayward one," in claiming her primary identity as a female performing artist. Olga revels in her departure from generic constraints, including those of the marriage plot. Russian critics were not kind to *Artistka*, however, disagreeing with Krestovskaia's vision of her heroine as a high-minded national artist. Critic Alexander Skabichevskii, for example, considered Krestovskaia the darling of oversurfeited middle-class readers, and Olga a silly character with absurd pretensions. For Skabichevskii, Krestovskaia's references to *La Traviata* confirm her heroine's affinity with mediocre art as both literary character and dramatic actress.[61]

But Russian literature also casts *La Traviata* in more serious cultural projects. In Turgenev's novel *On the Eve* (1860), the protagonists Elena and Insarov attend *La Traviata* together in Venice, an experience that renews the couple's sense of their shared purpose in life: uncomplaining service to a higher social cause.[62] Herbert Lindenberger sees the conception of heroic sacrifice in Verdi's opera as representing a "higher narrative" within Turgenev's novel, which "clearly comes to show up the inadequacy of the lower narrative, in fact to dominate it."[63] It is striking, however, that Turgenev chose *La Traviata* to underscore his characters' determination to serve Bulgarian national liberation. The author might have selected in *La Traviata*'s place one of Rossini's operas, such as *Tancredi*, with its freedom-fighting subtext. But perhaps the personal, not abstract, heroism that Violetta manifests in her renunciation of Alfredo led Turgenev to make this choice. Turgenev equates Violetta's quiet, uncelebrated sacrifice with Insarov's premature death and with the final chapters of Elena's life, which are not revealed to the reader. In this way, Turgenev argues for a heroism that is generically distinct from its habitual associations with public life. For him, heroism finds a place in both lyric opera and psychological novel, two notably middle-range generic forms.[64] In a most un-Turgenevian manner, the performance of *La Traviata* that Insarov and Elena witness seems crudely staged, but all the more moving and artistically true for that.

Although Turgenev does not mention Bosio by name, scholars concur that she is the unpolished young soprano he describes in the opera scene. It was Bosio, after all, who succeeded in reinterpreting what had been the merely virtuosic role of Violetta and in transforming Verdi's flighty demi-mondaine into a paragon of noble self-abnegation. In the dual contexts of *La Traviata* and the soprano's own dignified public life, Bosio allowed Turgenev to reconcile his characters' yearning to serve a heroic cause with the limited human scale of their influence. *La Traviata* echoes this principle in its structure; the opera begins in the public arena, at Violetta's soiree, but ends in the privacy of her bedroom, where a few intimates witness her final, heroic moments. Violetta dies in a house stripped by creditors, in an operatic setting devoid of customary final-act grandeur. Turgenev's implicit suggestion that Insarov dies Violetta's death seems a bold one, asserting an equal value for the ways in which these two lives—one emphatically male, the other insistently female—are spent.[65]

Up until the interlude in Venice, Turgenev's novel posits music, writing, and the plastic arts as inadequate to express the depths of human feeling. Shubin jokingly assumes the poses of famous statues. Elena finds reading unsatisfying, and doesn't care for poetry. In Venice, she and Insarov immerse themselves uncharacteristically in art, rowing along the Grand Canal to admire the old palaces and churches, viewing Tintoretto and Titian paintings at the Academy, and attending the opera. Ultimately, Venice becomes a personal place for Turgenev's characters, not a public one, artistically speaking. During the final scenes, Turgenev deploys a compressed system of aestheticizing effects to convey his heroine's consciousness: Elena makes the flight path of a white seagull into an omen of Insarov's fate, and dreams of freeing him from a monastery cell. As in *La Traviata*, art is the only real consolation for death. The coloratura's vocal flight makes Violetta's last breaths count. The awful beauty Elena senses in life's design redeems the final disappointed hopes of Verdi's opera and Turgenev's novel alike. In this additional sense, Violetta as re-conceived by Turgenev seems truly heroic.

Chernyshevskii's novel *What Is to Be Done?* (1863) also uses *La Traviata* as counterpoint to a radically reconceived romantic relationship in a Russian context. While Violetta's love for Alfredo violates the precepts of bourgeois family life, Vera Pavlovna's incipient love for Kirsanov receives the active support of her husband, Lopukhov. When Lopukhov urges Kirsanov to take Vera Pavlovna to a performance of *La Traviata*, he implicitly grants Kirsanov permission to court Vera Pavlovna. Like Turgenev, Chernyshevskii chooses *La Traviata*, an opera that emphasizes personal rather than political, historical, or mythological concerns, to emphasize the political and expressive potential of private life. Chernyshevskii found a higher metaphysical meaning in the social and aesthetic transgressions that hypocritical bourgeois mores condemned.

Chernyshevskii distributes attributes of the Traviata persona among his female characters. The French courtesan Julie with her requisite heart of gold; the reformed prostitute Nastasia Kriukova; Vera Pavlovna, who is ready and willing to subvert bourgeois marital norms; and Vera's double, the dream goddess, all represent aspects of Violetta. The *Traviata* subtext has its origin in Chernyshevskii's own biography, since his marriage to Olga Vasil'eva "rehabilitated" a girl with a questionable reputation. Chernyshevskii's Olga adored staging social revels and placing herself, Violetta-like, at the center of every event.[66]

In Chernyshevskii's novel, an explicitly composite emanation of Bosio and the French diva Josephine de Méric appears to Vera Pavlovna during the third in a series of utopian dreams. The dream-diva's gesturing hand causes the declarations of Vera Pavlovna's soul to appear in her diary as a narrative of reluctant admission about her marriage to Lopukhov: "Is it possible that I love him because he leads me from the cellar? That I love not him, but my deliverance from the cellar?"[67] The diva's hand points to the diary's pages and commands Vera Pavlovna to author a new understanding of her own inner life. Except for her gesturing hand and compelling voice, the diva emanation never comes into view in this scene. She serves as an ideal of Chernyshevskian rational egoism, her singing a means to her own pleasure as well as her audience's, her assertions carrying the weight of spiritual and moral authority.

Strikingly, Chernyshevskii's dream Bosio sings in Russian, not in Italian, misquoting a verse from Pushkin's early lyric "Adeli" (1822): "The hour of pleasure / Seize it, seize it! / Youth's years / Give to love."[68] The cited verse, like Violetta's famous aria "Sempre libera," celebrates pleasure and love, but recasts this assertation for the Russian literary context by evoking Alexander Pushkin, the Russian national poet who, like Bosio and Violetta, died too early. Once again, *La Traviata* is naturalized in Russia.

Dostoevskii's novel *Idiot* (1868) emphasizes the commodification of the fallen woman by evoking the Dumas-Verdi subtext. Dostoevskii transforms the famous scene in the third act of *La Traviata*, when Alfredo contemptuously hurls bank notes at Violetta, by having Nastasia Filippovna throw the bank notes from Rogozhin on the fire.[69] Nastasia Filippovna's gesture rejects the bourgeois values that Violetta Valery goes to such lengths to uphold, casting aside filial obedience and respect for financial security. But the ultimate outcome in Dostoevskii for the heroine of dubious social standing resembles that in Dumas. As Donald Rayfield declares, "the heroine must be disposed of because she stands in the way of a good, bourgeois marriage. Epanchin as father and Totskii as both suitor and false-father have to distance Nastasia Filippovna from the pure and unsullied Aglaia, Adelaida and Aleksandra." Dostoevskii's novel transforms Dumas's unsullied bourgeois maiden (Armand's sister, appropriately named Blanche) into multiple maidens, rendering the subtext parodic. The well-intentioned Myshkin and the murderously jealous Rogozhin cannot help destroying Nastasia Filippovna, whose fate seems subtextually predetermined.

Critics have noted the essential staginess of the long opening sequences of Dostoevskii's novel, in which members of the cast assemble for dramatic confrontations, enter and exit conspicuously, and perform striking gestures and revelations. Conflicts between potential male sponsors for the possibly tainted Nastasia Filippovna form the essential spectacle of this sequence, which resembles a kind of referendum on Violetta. In the opening chapter of Dostoevskii's novel, the gossip of railway car travelers links Nastasia's unclear social standing with the eponymous courtesan of Stendhal's 1827 novel and the practices of theatergoing: "No, she is not an Armance. There's only Totskii. And in the evenings she sits in her own box at the Bol'shoi or the French theater. The officers there may say anything about her among themselves, but even they can't prove anything."[70] Nastasia signals her connection to the *La Traviata* subtext meta-theatrically, with the social legitimization inherent in having her own opera box. But the system of social semiotics ultimately proves unreadable in Dostoevskii's novel. Nastasia's identity as fallen or redeemed is never satisfactorily resolved by these inadequate Western categories.[71] Dostoevskii does not radicalize *La Traviata* as Turgenev and Chernyshevskii do, but makes Dumas's bourgeois fable morally and aesthetically problematic without turning his heroine into an angel.

Tolstoi's late novel *Resurrection* (1899) also uses the Verdi-Dumas subtext for a purpose that is at odds with the heroicizing, radicalizing strategies of both Turgenev and Chernyshevskii. In the novel's second part, Tolstoi's protagonist Nekhliudov attends a performance of Dumas's play, which he views as an annoying interruption of his intercessions on Katusha Maslova's behalf. In his dissipated youth, Nekhliudov seduced Katusha, then his aunts' ward, and thereby set her on the path to ruin. Katusha has been falsely convicted of murder, and Nekhliudov feels responsible.

The theater scene in *Resurrection* associates three different women—apart from the absent Katusha—with the dramatic character of Marguerite Gautier: the general's wife, Mariette, who has seductively summoned Nekhliudov to the theater; the actress playing the part of Marguerite; and a prostitute Nekhliudov sees on the street after he leaves the theater. Tolstoi equates the false spectacle of the play "in which . . . the actress in a novel fashion showed how consumptive women die" with Mariette's exposed neck and shoulders, and their disturbing effect on Nekhliudov.[72] Nekhliudov thinks to himself that the openly inviting air of the street prostitute seems more honest than the titillating games played at the theater. But this response begs the question of his own behavior during his seduction of Maslova. Nekhliudov neither forced himself upon Maslova, nor treated her respectfully as a woman, but coerced her psychologically and then offered her money as if she were a prostitute. Nekhliudov doesn't see the theatrics that transpire under his very nose.

Nekhliudov's response to the theater-house spectacle feels suspect to the reader because he fails to make the connection between *La Dame aux camélias* and his own circumstances. His self-sacrificing attempts to rehabilitate Maslova seem largely for his own benefit, at least until the final part of the novel. And Maslova shows little interest in playing the hackneyed role of the redeemed fallen woman in order to assuage Nekhliudov's guilt. At the same time, she is Tolstoi's only major female character who is not of aristocratic birth. Tolstoi's novel makes *all* of its characters bear collective guilt for his heroine's suffering. Tolstoi's treatment of Dumas suggests a retrogressive, morally stern reading of a too-familiar text, already fifty years old at the writing of *Resurrection*. But this reading of Dumas eludes Tolstoi's hero, who cannot recognize his own contribution to the Traviata plot.

In fact, the sexually pernicious powers of Dumas and Verdi are not often invoked by Russian literature. The only other example whereby the seduction plot itself risks becoming seductive is the story "Debut" (1912) by Kazimir and Olga Koval'skie, in which Lenochka, a star-struck ingenue, joins a provincial theater troupe. The director Kobylianskii schemes to extract payment for arranging Lenochka's debut, and takes the girl for a stroll in a public garden, where a military orchestra plays tunes from *La Traviata*. Lenochka remains oblivious to Kobylianskii's evil intentions; even the music, further degraded by setting and instrumentation, fails to alert her. Lenochka is caught off guard by Kobylianskii's advances, and her theatrical aspirations come to nothing. The Koval'skie's story invokes *La Traviata* to comment ironically on the heroine's inability to perceive the real role for which she is being prepared. Tolstoi's *Resurrection* stages a fifty-year-old play to show that a corrupt society's essential tastes and preoccupations do not change. The Koval'skies go further, suggesting that *La Traviata* may have outlived its usefulness as a cultural subtext.

But *La Traviata* showed renewed capacity to adapt to a rapidly changing Russian context in the twentieth century. In Evgenii Bauer's silent film "The Twilight of a Woman's Soul" (1913), the aristocratic Vera becomes an opera singer after two related tragedies in her personal life. As a young girl, she is raped by a worker whom she had made the beneficiary of charitable attentions. She kills her rapist with a trowel while he is sleeping, and escapes unseen. Vera shares this painful part of her past with her husband on their wedding day, and interprets his conflicted response as a rejection of her tainted self. She leaves rather than endure this humiliation. When the prince finally locates Vera, she is performing as Violetta in *La Traviata*.[73] Vera sends the prince away when he tries to make amends, and, in despair, he shoots himself. *La Traviata* offers a part that Vera-Violetta assumes defiantly, playing it out to the hilt in both art and life. In emphasizing the reductive view of Vera's history that *La Traviata* suggests, Bauer's film encourages its viewers to view the opera and its heroine more creatively. The role of Violetta represents a sort of "hair shirt" for Vera in the form of a painful self-parody.

After 1917, *La Traviata* offered material upon which the new revolutionary aesthetic could work. Konstantin Paustovskii's short story "Verdi's Music" (1935) stages the opera aboard a Soviet naval cruiser. Its heroine is an upright citizen in a backstage tearjerker that serves as a socialist-realist parable. During intermission, the soprano playing Violetta receives a telegram about her younger brother's impending operation, and is unable to concentrate on her performance. The innocent love of an older sister overmasters operatic grand passion and purifies the prima donna of troublesome sexuality: "When Alfredo knelt before her feet, she bent over and kissed his youthful forehead. A thin blue vein showed through at the temple, just as it did on her brother."[74] The soprano Solntseva sings bravely, as tears roll down her face, and in sympathy, the ship's crew lower the curtain and cut short the performance. The commander sends Solntseva to her brother's side in Moscow in recognition for her willingness to choose service over personal considerations. The story rewrites Verdi's story of passion and renunciation as a recontextualization of nineteenth-century art forms within the demands of the new socialist society. Both the opera performance and Solntseva's devotion to her brother require the commander's authorization. Ironically, in this Soviet setting, *La Traviata* insists on the needs of society over the feelings of the individual, just as the opera had in its initial nineteenth-century Western bourgeois context.[75]

When Solntseva returns to perform *La Traviata* again for the sailors, she receives a standing ovation and a rain of flowers that assert the subordination of operatic convention to the more vivid truths of life: "Simple field flowers fell at Solntseva's feet and intermingled with the antique silks and dark-blue velvet of the Venetian costumes."[76] The commander observes to himself that nothing helps talent develop more than "friendship and simple comradely attention." The drama of the opera pales by comparison with the valiant efforts of Solntseva, a good comrade who does her job.

One of the most sophisticated treatments of *La Traviata* in Soviet Russia, the poet Vera Inber's libretto, was written on commission for the Nemirovich-Danchenko Theater in the mid-1930s. Inber's treatment rendered *La Traviata*'s theatricality both explicit and tangible as a meta-operatic work that fuses nineteenth- and twentieth-century stage conventions. Her libretto shifts the action of Verdi's opera to Venice of the 1870s, and transforms Violetta from a courtesan into an actress, within an actual dramatic context. The stage action occurs on a small platform encircled by opera boxes, from which a fictional audience offers commentary on the events.[77] This "frame" audience in effect represents itself, since one of the premises of Inber's libretto is that Violetta transgresses society's laws in entering into a relationship with Alfredo, a student from a good family in Inber's version. The spectators in these surrounding boxes gradually depart in the course of the performance. During the final act, the frame audience's opera boxes stand empty. Alone, Violetta takes poison. Without an audience, her story is over.

Inber's framing device does double duty during Violetta's evening party in the first act, at which a group of her actor friends dress up and perform a miniature drama "from the life of an actress." Inber's libretto locates the source of theatricality in the personal sphere through the use of formal dramatic convention. As Inber conceived *La Traviata*, the opera's artistic structure mirrors the physical structure of its staging in a series of self-referential rings. Inber's vision of a new *Traviata* harks back to the experiments of the 1920s in redefining theater convention using "outmoded" forms such as melodrama and bel canto opera. *La Traviata* had become entirely self-reflective, its cultural assimilation in Russia complete.

Russian literature showed an affinity for Verdi's opera by exhibiting its own wayward tendencies, transforming *La Traviata* into a Russian text through acts of creative self-assertion. In tossing bank notes into the fire, Dostoevskii's Nastasia performs a symbolic gesture that sums up the history of *La Traviata* in Russia. Russian literature rejects the conventional Western bourgeois values that Verdi's characters revere. In the Russian tradition, social transgression does not taint a heroine who remains morally pure. Instead, the aristocratic or bourgeois society that passes judgment upon such a heroine is itself morally suspect. Society's censure creates opportunities for a suffering heroine to face the "eternal questions" so beloved by Russian literature.

Chapter Six

Reading Opera
The Theater of Psychological Prose

The relationship between prose fiction and opera has historically been one of perceived contrast and incompatibility. This opposition derives in part from the longstanding unsuitability of "low" subject matter from realist novels for expression on the operatic stage. But the traditional lack of affinity between prose fiction and opera also stems from tensions internal to the operatic form, which is a mixture of music and drama. Some theorists of operatic form privilege the written text and treat the musical score as accompaniment and enhancement, while others deem opera primarily a musical art and consider the libretto of little literary or dramatic interest.[1] To cite two relatively recent voices in this debate, Joseph Kerman believes that opera's "integral existence is determined . . . in the whole by musical articulation,"[2] while Catherine Clément asserts that music obscures the "real" meaning of the operatic work, that is, the violent and authoritarian stories that operas tell.[3] The history of opera records the struggle for primacy between music and text that obscures the *affinities* between operatic and literary forms.[4]

Certain nineteenth-century operas—Verdi's *La Traviata* and Tchaikovskii's *Eugene Onegin* among them—looked to the novel for new ways of treating psychological processes in musical drama. But what response did the novel evince toward opera? In the essay "Epic and Novel," Bakhtin characterizes the novel as the most plastic of genres, one that is always "examining itself and subjecting its established forms to review" through its relationship to other kinds of art.[5] The theatricality that pervades the domestic space of many nineteenth-century novels, for example, points toward the repressed presence of drama in everyday life.[6] Theatrical metaphors inform the Romantic tropes in

Lermontov's prose, Gogol's written narratives make extensive use of performative effects, and Dostoevskii's prose strikes readers as inherently dramatic in its structures and multi-voicedness. Opera, as a highly conventionalized generic form, offered a rich source of artistic strategies for nineteenth-century prose fiction to explore. In this way, the novel evoked opera to define itself as a form, not simply *against* operatic convention, but *through* operatic convention invoked in a novelistic context.

OBLOMOV: CASTING THE DIVA

Bellini's opera *Norma* (1831) includes the famous aria "Casta diva," in which the druid priestess Norma sings to the moon and prays for peace with the Romans. Bellini's aria represents a programmatic anti-narrative statement, "a declaration of peace in the midst of demands for action, a victory of passivity:"[7]

> Chaste goddess, as you silver
> these sacred ancient trees,
> turn toward us your lovely face,
> unclouded, without veil.
>
> Temper, o goddess,
> the ardent hearts' zeal.
> Spread over the earth
> the peace you create in heaven.

But this dreamy interlude cannot even sustain itself through the end of the aria. The second part of "Casta diva" sets Norma's reflections about her forbidden love for the Roman Pollione against the chorus urging her to war.

In Ivan Goncharov's novel *Oblomov* (1859), the dreamy part of Bellini's "Casta diva" possesses the incongruous power to rouse the drowsy hero Oblomov to activism in love and life. But the contrast between the peace that the aria "Casta diva" invokes and the activity it produces in *Oblomov* dissolves at a deeper structural level. The internal conflict between stasis and movement enacted within "Casta diva" finds its perfect mirror in Goncharov's novel. Just as Norma's prayer cannot protect the aria's spell of enchantment from the chorus's call to action, so Olga's hopes are dashed, and the happy interlude when

Oblomov becomes her energetic partner gives way to storyless somnolence. *Norma* reluctantly allows non-narrative suspension to be overwhelmed by the opera's events, whereas *Oblomov* cannot maintain its narrative impetus in the face of its hero's urge to lie down. Goncharov's "novel," an ever-potential narrative, represents the dream; Oblomov's couch is the true reality, one that is, in its own way, operatic. *Oblomov*, a quintessentially Russian text about how one should live, ultimately proves incapable of depicting the interior operatic landscape that lies at the heart of the novel. *Oblomov* points toward this landscape in its special status as a kind of anti-novel, "a book in which the main protagonist spends most of his time asleep, thus mocking the very notions of plot, suspense, and character development that were the cornerstones of many other nineteenth-century Russian and European novels."[8] *Oblomov* as a novel exhibits affinities with operatic form precisely in those elements that seem least likely to manifest such a connection.

Near the end of *Oblomov*, the action-oriented Stolz explains away his wife Olga's persistent melancholy as "doubts and questionings" that "represent the *surfeit* [emphasis mine], the luxury of life . . . on the summits of happiness, when there are no coarse desires."[9] But this explanation feels unsatisfactory. The reader never again "hears" Olga sing after her love affair with Oblomov ends. Her questions and unfulfilled longings remain a kind of surplus of the text, much like opera, which is repeatedly evoked but never actually staged as such in Goncharov's novel. The most notable surplus of the text in *Oblomov* is, of course, the portly Oblomov himself, with whom nothing novelistically useful can be done.

Olga herself falls *short* of the text, short of being the novel's heroine.[10] Olga represents a sort of reverse Galatea, as well as a would-be Pygmalion to Oblomov.[11] The end of her relationship with Oblomov transforms Olga into a pale, silent creature, "as calm and immobile as a stone statue."[12] In narrative terms, she remains so throughout the rest of the novel. Her married life with Stolz transpires in compressed summary form, as curiously unfulfilling for the reader as it appears to be for Olga herself. Olga has apparently been infected by a strain of the dread malaise "oblomovitis" (*oblomovshchina*), which leaves her yearning beyond the satisfactions granted to characters in novels.[13]

Oblomov is a novel full of ghosts and unmaterialized possibilities. The city of St. Petersburg itself represents a ghost of the text, appearing only fleetingly and in fragments. The chatter of Oblomov's visitors in the opening sequences evokes the social and geographical spaces of St. Petersburg, but Oblomov refuses his guests' invitations to venture out into this territory of narrative potential.[14] The city hovers somewhere proximate to the story of Oblomov, just outside the confines of his rooms on Gorokhovaia Street, visible in the distance from the summer dacha community, and serving as the destination of his tedious carriage rides from Vyborg. Oblomov's inability to negotiate the frozen Neva, which separates his living quarters in Vyborg from Theater Square, means that he will not be able to join Olga in the world. Like opera and Oblomov, St. Petersburg is a vague, marginal presence in Goncharov's novel that nevertheless turns out to be a central one. The novel most tangibly evokes the Vyborg section of St. Petersburg, with its dirt lanes and chickens, where Oblomov takes up residence at the end of his summer idyll with Olga. But even Vyborg offers a potential site for eerie, supernatural occurrences, when Oblomov declares that wolves roam the streets in winter. The supernatural and the operatic represent a kind of longed-for alternative to the realist novel and the traditional images of St. Petersburg as a cold, formal city. In a most subversive manner, Goncharov's novel finds its alternative satisfactions in the largely hidden interstices of its characters' detailed realist milieu.

Just as *Oblomov* chooses the most prosaic settings in which to evoke the supernatural, the novel stages Bellini's "Casta Diva" in exclusively domestic, drawing-room settings. Goncharov's novel similarly confines its hero's passionate longings to his interior world, a literary space of an unexpectedly theatrical nature. Oblomov lives the greater part of his life in a single room, which serves as bedroom, study, and parlor. The first 150 pages of *Oblomov* transpire in this setting, suggesting an ideal structure for a play. Oblomov's room itself suggests a stage set with furnishings that create an initial impression of luxurious splendor, but resemble shoddy theatrical props upon closer examination. The opening chapters present a sequence of set pieces, as Oblomov's acquaintances drop in and perform song-and-dance-like "arias." As if to emphasize the theatrical quality of this sequence, Oblomov's first visitor is Volkov, who babbles about ballet dancers, tossing bouquets, *tableaux vivants*, French and Russian actresses, and the opera season. The entrance of Oblomov's childhood friend Stolz is anticipated throughout Part I, and delayed theatrically to build up suspense. Stolz finally enters the novel at the very end of Part I, having just witnessed a ridiculous "scene" between Oblomov and his servant Zakhar. The theatrical aspects of *Oblomov* occur within paradoxically private physical and narrative spaces.

"Casta diva" offers the key to the novel's closet theatricality. Although readers of *Oblomov* typically associate Bellini's aria with Olga, who sings it for Oblomov, the novel complicates this affinity. Oblomov doesn't really want Olga to sing Bellini's aria when her performance is first proposed by Stolz. "What if you sing badly? I'd feel awful afterwards," Oblomov declares "ingenuously," and points to Stolz. "It's he who wants you to."[15] It is actually Oblomov who plays the part of Norma, the central suffering consciousness of the work. Oblomov himself makes the first mention of "Casta diva" in the novel, through a chain of associations that begins with homely culinary delights:

> "In the house, lights are already burning; knives are clattering in the kitchen; a frying-pan full of mushrooms, cutlets, berries—music in the drawing-room—*Casta diva, Casta diva!* . . ." Oblomov burst into song. "I can't think of *Casta diva* without wishing to sing it," he said, singing the beginning of the cavatina. "How that woman cried her heart out! How full of sadness those sounds are! And no one around her knows anything. . . . She is alone. . . . Her secret oppresses her; she entrusts it to the moon."[16]

Oblomov's creative powers link the kitchen with the drawing room, the site of domestic musical activity.[17] "Casta diva" lets him have his cake and eat it, too. In his fantasy, unseen hands in the kitchen attend to his needs, while he savors the sweet, solitary laceration of his spirit. The loving presence in his life remains unobtrusively off stage, and he remains ever the potential singer.

Oblomov is the sole character in the novel capable of true flights of imagination, as evidenced by his dense improvisatory descriptions of a fantasy world that represents the aim of all earthly striving. These flights give rise to artistic creations quite separate from Oblomov's famous Dream, which is authored by the novel's narrator. When Oblomov elaborates his lyrical vision of a Russian Eden with its lovely garden, charming wife, and bountiful kitchen, his friend Stolz exclaims, "Why, you're a poet, Ilya!"[18] Oblomov replies, "Yes, a poet in life, because life is poetry." Oblomov's tastes in music are eclectic and nondoctrinaire; he appreciates barrel-organ music and bargemen's songs no less than he does Meyerbeer or Mozart. He can create art from the material at hand, whatever he has in his room.

"Casta diva" only *seems* to point toward an active life for mind, body, and spirit, toward Olga's power to raise Oblomov temporarily from a supine position. Significantly, the aria represents an address by the diva playing Norma to a chaste ("casta") diva-deity, goddess of the heavens. While Oblomov rejects the operatic when it merely graces a conventional social occasion at the theater or in a drawing room, he invokes the aria as a sacred communion with self and imagination. The singer of "Casta diva" gazes at the moon goddess who alone disdains earth's nocturnal veil. Wordly pursuits such as marrying a nice girl and getting one's estate in order represent the "veil" that covers the beautiful, nonutilitarian aspects of human life. *Oblomov* ultimately asserts that lying in bed can be a deeply creative, self-affirming act. He remains chaste, aesthetically speaking.

For Oblomov, the accepted conception of opera signals the absence of creativity or individuality. After their return to the city at the end of the summer, Olga urges him to purchase a stall for the opera season. Propriety forbids him from sharing a box with Olga before he has publicly declared himself. She promises him, "when you have finished your business, you will take your place in our box by right." Oblomov yawns through the performances "as though he were going to swallow the stage,"[19] and chafes at his role of "lovesick boy," with its obligatory swain's visit to his beloved's box during intermissions. He is uncomfortable when Olga fixes her opera glasses upon him from her own highly visible seat in the theater. Olga proposes the theater as an appropriate place for them to meet during this interim period precisely because of the public, formal nature of a relationship conducted there. She also favors the Summer Garden, another stagy setting for a lovers' rendezvous. But Oblomov resists these theatrical manifestations of his commitment to her. He rejects

Olga's notion of opera's place in life in favor of his own, more idiosyncratic envisioning.

When Stolz pays a call to Oblomov after a long absence, he finds his friend living in squalid conditions. Oblomov does not want to be roused to memories of Olga, but instead sets to drinking currant vodka and sucking on a mutton bone. "Olga Sergeyevna won't make you any vodka like this," declares Oblomov. "She can sing *Casta diva* but doesn't know how to make such vodka! Nor how to make a chicken-and-mushroom pie!"[20] Oblomov makes the first and last mentions of Bellini's aria in the novel, in both cases linking "Casta diva" with gustatory pleasures. Oblomov does not reject "Casta diva" as irrelevant to what is truly nourishing in life. He argues for a different, no less worthy virtuosity in Agafya Matveevna's housekeeping arts. Oblomov's notion of the operatic strives to transcend the modes of conventional existence that he finds so boring. Goncharov's novel suggests that its slow-moving hero is its most original, creative presence.

Reading and writing pervade the text of *Oblomov* as activities with the potential to negotiate the divide between private and public life, for its hero perhaps most of all. Words might offer a way to let opera in to the novel, to manifest the inner landscape that Goncharov's characters don't know how to inhabit. *Oblomov* opens with a parodic vision of a feminine boudoir, as its pale-complexioned hero reposes in an Eastern-style robe. Oblomov in his Persian dressing gown seems akin to Pushkin's closet writer Charskii, and to Gogol's shut-in Pliushkin surrounded by his dusty papers.[21] Oblomov's environment resembles a kind of writing graveyard, with its yellowed books on stands and fly-ridden inkwells. The mirrors recall "tablets which might be used for writing memoranda on in the dust."[22] Oblomov's plan for improving the management of his estate represents his master oeuvre, a major creative undertaking that spans many years. According to this project, Oblomov would literally re-conceive his personal world, would reconstruct his reality. But public displays of literacy interest Oblomov no more than public manifestations of opera do. This is made clear during the first part of the novel, when he receives a visit from Penkin, a Russian graphomaniac who unceasingly composes articles, reviews, and fictional works. Oblomov feels wearied by his friend's endless preoccupation with consuming and producing words. For Oblomov, the creative act remains a private matter.

One of Oblomov's moments of greatest happiness comes at the dacha, as he sits alone at his writing table, composing a long letter to Olga: "Oblomov was writing with inspiration; his pen was flying over the pages. His eyes shone and his cheeks were flushed."[23] The gist of the letter is that Olga has erred in her estimation of Oblomov, and should find a better man to love. Oblomov is unbearably curious about Olga's reaction to his letter, and hides in the bushes in hopes of witnessing what artists rarely see—the private communion of an individual with their work. When Olga discovers his presence, Oblomov's furtive desire to watch Olga read his words embarrasses them both. But the letter eventually becomes Oblomov's enduring legacy to his friends. Olga shows the document to Stolz, who convinces her of the essential truth in Oblomov's "reading" of their summer love affair. In this sense, Oblomov authors Goncharov's novel. But *Oblomov* insists to the end on slight forms and oblique, sideways approaches to the heart of meaning.

The novel closes as Stolz strolls through Vyborg with a writer acquaintance, revealed as the narrator himself, who muses upon the fate of beggars. Stolz asks why the writer wants to know their stories. "Not going to write *Mystères de Petersbourg*, are you?"[24] Stolz inquires, referring to Eugène Sue's colorful sketches of Paris from the early 1840s. Sue's work inspired the sketches of non-aristocratic city dwellers that Russian writers such as Nekrasov and Grigorovich began to produce in the 1840s. Appropriately, an old beggar whom Stolz encounters turns out to be Oblomov's servant Zakhar, who tells of his sad decline into homelessness since his master's death. Goncharov's novel transforms itself into a sketch (*ocherk*) in its final sentences, writing itself out into the fringes both in geographic and literary terms. *Oblomov* ends by gesturing toward the margins, a literary space that holds the potential to expand into a full-length novel. Opera does not offer itself as a flamboyant center in *Oblomov*, but hovers at the novel's periphery, the true site of privacy and artistic freedom. The end of the novel issues a challenge to the writer-narrator to re-conceive and renew established generic forms.

ANNA KARENINA: THE SINGING DECANTERS

In *Anna Karenina*, Tolstoi explores the relationships between theatrical genre and social convention.[25] Opera, which the novel links with its heroine, represents the upper ranges of the available generic hierarchy, as well as a kind of generic reference point.[26] But Tolstoi's novel also makes abundant references to contemporary drama, melodrama, operetta, and comic farce, showing how theatrical genre shapes the experience of the literary protagonists. *Anna Karenina* depicts a permeation of the narrative space of the novel by seemingly antithetical forms like opera precisely because its literary characters model their behavior after works of art. This is why Anna, Vronsky, and Karenin seek logistically *and* aesthetically satisfying resolutions to their personal dilemmas. Tolstoi's novel stages "spectacular" public events such as the Moscow ball, the steeplechase, Levin's wedding to Kitty, and the provincial Nobility elections, but also asserts that more intimate episodes are no less theatrical in their underlying dramatic structure.

Anna Karenina responds to the tradition of juxtaposing operatic performance with novelistic narrative in nineteenth-century fictions, which characterize opera as a false, dangerously compelling alternative reality. Emma Bovary embarks upon an adulterous affair after attending Donizetti's opera *Lucia di Lammermoor*, and Natasha Rostova's defamiliarizing gaze confronts operatic artifice, only to succumb to its lure. But Tolstoi's relationship with opera during the 1860s and 1870s was more flexible than his later treatise "What is Art?" (1898) suggests. Tolstoi's emphatic denunciations of opera, which he describes as "an artificial form, which had and has success only amongst the higher classes," retrospectively obscure the nuances of operatic subtext in both *War and Peace* and *Anna Karenina*.[27] Before his religious crisis, Tolstoi enjoyed the operas of Mozart, Rossini, Weber, and Glinka, and was not immune to the appeal of lighter dramatic genres.[28] Although Tolstoi ultimately condemned opera, he never denied the power of this definitively public art form to influence the ways that people, including literary characters, respond to seemingly "stock" situations. Tolstoi's realism does not preclude showing how art structures life.

Tolstoi's conception of theatrical realism may offer a productive complement to Amy Mandelker's articulation of the "iconic," which she sees as a way for Tolstoi to heal the split between the sublime and the beautiful in Western aesthetics and to suggest a new, spiritualized way of responding to visual images.[29] Tolstoi does not offer theater as a means of mediating between the carnate and the spiritual. Instead, he points to theater as a part of the aesthetic structuring mechanisms with which his characters try to make sense of their lives and his readers to process his novel. In *Anna Karenina*, theater serves as a cognitive, hermeneutic tool and a metaphor for human consciousness, not simply as an immoral distraction from the real business of life. Gary Saul Morson points out this productive ambiguity in Tolstoi's novel when he observes that, although the author "deeply distrusted not only conventional plots but also plotting per se, because they impose closure and structure on a world that is fundamentally innocent of both," Tolstoi resolved the need to plot his novel coherently by giving "the structuring impulse" to his characters.[30]

In the very movement of characters between theaters, Tolstoi's novel emphasizes the relationship between artistic and social categories. Vronskii leaves the opera at the St. Petersburg Bolshoi for the French Theater, where he must hush up a scandal involving two officers in his squadron. He pays little attention to either performance. Betsy leaves the opera before the end of the final act to prepare for guests invited to a late-evening reception. Anna abandons her box at the opera after she is publicly humiliated. Vronskii arrives to look for her after the performance is well under way, and returns to his hotel before the opera is over. In all of these scenes, the characters in *Anna Karenina*, much like their predecessor Eugene Onegin, treat their own lives as performances and view real theatrical events as accompaniments to the diverting spectacle of self.

The opening of *Anna Karenina* sets up the juxtaposition of life and art. Emerging from his dream and into the novel, Stiva remembers his return from the theater the evening before into a domestic situation that resembles a bad play. His wife has discovered his intrigue with their French governess by reading an incriminating letter. Stiva takes a moment to evaluate his own behavior in aesthetic, rather than moral terms: "There's something banal, a want of taste, in carrying on with one's governess." He is disturbed by his wife Dolly's "vulgar" shouting and concerned that the maids might overhear. While dining with Levin at the Angleterre, Oblonskii casts Mlle. Roland in a different light from that evoked by the memory of her "roguish black eyes . . ."[31] "A woman, a dear, gentle, affectionate creature, poor and lonely, sacrifices everything. Now when the thing is done . . . just consider, should one forsake her? Granted that one ought to part with her so as not to destroy one's family life, but oughtn't one to pity her and provide for her and make things easier?"[32] This more sentimental and flattering account of the affair proves only a divertissement, and Oblonskii is soon laughing ruefully over his predicament as a vital man with an aging wife: "What are you to do? How are you to act? It is a terrible tragedy."[33] Oblonskii is adept at gauging the dramatic mode that best fits his situation, as his ironic reference to tragedy indicates.

Operatic influences in *Anna Karenina* often emphasize how characters' and readers' expectations are formed.[34] Anna's husband, Karenin, makes a direct connection between artistic models and social circumstances, when his position as deceived husband reminds him of Offenbach's popular operetta *La Belle Hélène* (1864), a burlesque about the Trojan War that celebrates Paris's success in deceiving Helen of Troy's husband Menelaus. When Karenin returns home after the second act of an Italian opera, he stages a heated scene with Anna, seizing her letters from Vronskii and twisting her wrist. One reason for Karenin's anger seems to be his awareness that his life is theatrically derivative.

Anna Karenina invokes opera to shape the Anna-Vronskii story, which occupies the "stage" in the novel, particularly in book I, pushing other subplots to the background and forcing their characters to function as audience. Operatic elements in the Anna-Vronskii story divert the reader's attention from the less extravagant, more strictly novelistic accounts of the Levins and the Oblonskiis.[35] In this sense, the operatically pitched story of Anna and Vronsky exerts a disruptive influence on Tolstoi's novel. The story even dominates and fragments an alternative *operatic* narrative, that of the two real, unidentified and undescribed opera performances in parts II and V.

The opera-house scenes in *Anna Karenina* do not stage any actual opera performances; instead, they invite grand opera to permeate the rest of the narrative, making the distinction between opera and the novel less pronounced. The narrator signals this receptivity with Vronskii's thoughts during a discussion with Princess Betsy:

> He knew very well that he ran no risk of appearing ridiculous either in Betsy's eyes or in the eyes of Society people generally. He knew very well that in their eyes, the role of the disappointed lover of a maiden or of any single woman might be ridiculous, but the role of a man who was pursuing a married woman, and who made it the purpose of his life at all cost to draw her into adultery, was one which had in it something beautiful and dignified and could never be ridiculous.[36]

The reader knows nothing about the opera performers in this scene, only that "A famous *prima donna* was giving her second performance and all high Society was at the Opera House." Vronskii's use of the word "role" transfers the reader's expectation from the opera house to the reception at Princess Betsy's that will follow, casting Anna and Vronskii as the true performers. Anna and Vronskii enact their intimate encounter before the other reception guests much like a theatrical scene.

The generic cues linked with a character's "performance" make the notion of role more problematic. Vronskii's remark upon arriving at Princess Betsy's reception suggestively augments his earlier musings: "Where do I come from? . . . from the *Theater Bouffe*. I have been there a hundred times, and always with fresh pleasure. Excellent! I know it's a disgrace, but at the opera I go to sleep, while at the *Bouffe* I stay until the last minute enjoying it."[37] He declares to Princess Betsy, "I am afraid I am becoming ridiculous." He fears that his role will be seen by society as a laughable one, and yet, as a spectator, he prefers the piquant entertainment of the theater bouffe to the demands of tragic opera. The nineteenth-century opera bouffe, an outgrowth of the 1860s fashion for operetta, was known for parodic reenactments of lyric or epic mythological themes, and showcased fetchingly dressed female performers.[38]

Although it is at Vronskii's initiative that the affair with Anna begins, he implies from the beginning that he is unsuited for the role of operatically overstated hero. He may be an operetta-inspired bouffe character who finds himself trapped in a grand opera. He may be, as the Russian expression goes, "from another opera" (*iz drugoi opery*). Perhaps the tragic conclusion of the Anna-Vronskii line proceeds from the miscasting of Vronskii as Anna's true love. If so, the Anna-Vronskii story might be said to chart a collision between operatic genres; grand opera asserts the primacy of passion, whereas the French opera bouffe brings events to a pleasant conclusion, after entertaining its audience with a critique of contemporary mores. But perhaps it is also unjust to dismiss Vronskii as a character out of light musical theater. Although Vronskii's affair with Anna places him on unfamiliar generic and emotional ground, he struggles to the very end to meet the demands of his part, with a distinct awareness of his limitations.

Vronskii's professed affinity for opera bouffe highlights the novel's own uncertainty about this character's generic genealogy, particularly in the opening chapters. During dinner with Levin at the English Club, Oblonskii invokes Vronskii as the quintessential hero of a light stage work: "Awfully rich, handsome, with influential connections . . . a first-rate fellow."[39] The reader's first view of Vronskii comes at the Shcherbatskii home with Levin's admiring perspective on what he perceives as his rival's "simple frank smile"[40] and sincere manner. A few pages later, the old Prince describes Vronskii as a "little Petersburg fop."[41] And before the fateful Moscow ball, Anna praises Kitty's choice of Vronskii, characterizing him as "full of chivalry" and "a hero."[42] Vronskii seems the most generically inchoate of Tolstoi's characters at this point, and the quality appears self-cultivated.

During the first opera-house scene, Vronskii regales Princess Betsy with the adventures of two officers from his regiment, telling the story as a kind of variation on Gogol's story "Nevsky Prospect" (1835). The mysterious veiled woman the officers spy in a passing sledge turns out to be the pregnant wife of an apoplectic titular councillor. Betsy remarks upon Vronskii's skill in relating the story, declaring "You tell it with so much feeling that I think you yourself must have been one of the two."[43] Her assessment refers to Vronskii's appreciative emphasis of the collision between two equally conventional tales of youthful high spirits, one Romantic and the other comically realist. Although Vronskii relishes the farcelike silliness of the episode, he takes its possible consequences to his comrades seriously, according to the Russian officer's code of honor. Betsy pretends to be horrified that Vronskii leaves the celebrated Nilsson's performance at the opera theater to meet his commander at the French Theater, although, as the narrator observes, "she could not have distinguished Nilsson's voice from that of a chorus girl."[44] Vronskii lightly dismisses her objections. For him, opera is not the sacred pinnacle of the dramatic hierarchy, but one among many legitimate social modes. Vronskii will be made to pay for this early unwillingness to commit to a generic stance.

It is not until Part III that the reader learns of Vronskii's blunder in refusing a post, causing him to be passed over for a promotion: "Having then perforce to assume the role of an independent character, he played it very adroitly and cleverly."[45] His affair with Anna began just as this role had grown tedious, providing Vronskii with a much-needed opportunity to re-conceive his social self. Vronskii's suicide attempt in Part IV comes from his belief that he and Karenin have exchanged roles in Anna's sickroom, and that he has become ridiculous, always his greatest fear. In Italy, Vronskii adopts a new role "as an enlightened connoisseur and art patron, and . . . a modest artist himself, who had renounced the world, his connections and ambitions, for the sake of the woman he loved."[46] Here, Vronskii comes closest of all to looking ridiculous, tossing his cloak picturesquely over one shoulder and brushing his hair over his bald spot.[47]

The reader's final view of Vronskii at the railway station fails to resolve his generic identity. Levin's brother Koznyshev wants to see Vronskii as a hero who offers his life to the cause of Serbian national liberation. During the brief encounter between the two men, however, Vronskii's toothache prevents him from "speaking with the expression he desired."[48] Deprived of the possibility of explaining himself, Vronskii cannot prevent his story from appearing to end in an utterly conventional manner. Enlisting in the Serbian cause to meet almost certain death casts him anachronistically as a world-weary Romantic hero.[49] Perhaps the most poignant aspect of Vronskii as a literary character is his own pain at his inability to transcend the conventional roles he plays. His awareness of this shortcoming and his commitment to keeping faith with the codes of each role are his most compelling qualities.

Vronskii's remarks about the theater bouffe illustrate the point that Tolstoi makes repeatedly in *Anna Karenina*: that seemingly unaffected behavior can be extremely conventional. Kitty feels natural at the ball in part I because she has spent a great deal of trouble on her gown, hair, and adornments. She pines and droops after her loss of Vronskii in a manner scripted by the conventions of maidenly behavior. Kitty's departure from Moscow to take the waters at a European spa seems equally predictable, and she is dismayed to encounter a kind of generic twin in another similarly pale, lovesick Russian girl with mama in tow at the watering place. Similarly, Levin fantasizes about marrying a peasant girl and living a simple, peaceful life on the land. Trying to escape normative life narratives leads Levin to hit upon an equally conventional alternative right out of eighteenth-century sentimental fiction.

If *Anna Karenina* proposes Vronskii's initial affinity with opera bouffe, the novel suggests Anna as the diva in a grand opera.[50] Tolstoi does identify the two sopranos who perform in the opera-house scenes as Christine Nilsson and Adelina Patti, both of whom actually appeared in St. Petersburg during the 1872–73 winter season, while Tolstoi was writing *Anna Karenina*. But he does so simply to establish in the novel a diva-shaped space that fits his heroine. At Princess Betsy's reception, for example, the guests talk of Nilsson's performance. One gentleman observes that her poses in *Othello* and *Faust* recall illustrations of scenes from Shakespeare and Goethe in the paintings of Wilhelm von Kaulbach, thereby suggesting Nilsson's skill at making art, not from life, but *from art*. The remark about Kaulbach is itself highly conventional, since Princess Miagkaia declares that "This very same sentence about Kaulbach has been repeated to me by three different people to-day, as if by arrangement."[51] A few paragraphs later, Betsy's husband approaches Princess Miagkaia, and for lack of a better gambit, asks, "How did you like Nilsson, Princess?" Princess Miagkaia again rejects the opera diva's performance as a subject for discussion, and the general conversation turns to Anna, whom the guests alternately judge and defend. The repeated offer of Nilsson as a subject of interest links the diva with Anna in the minds of Betsy's guests *and* Tolstoi's readers. The subsequent description of Anna's entrance emphasizes her skill at self-presentation and further develops this affinity.

During the second opera-house scene in part V, Anna rebelliously attends the theater and becomes the focus of social disapprobation. This scene explicitly juxtaposes Anna's persona with that of the opera diva. As Vronskii's mother remarks, "She [Anna] is causing a sensation. No one is paying attention to Patti because of her."[52] When Vronskii arrives at the theater, he finds Anna when he notices where most members of the audience are directing their attention. The narrative only briefly evokes Patti, the real opera diva, just as it fleetingly refers to Nilsson in the first opera-house scene: "On the stage the singer, in a glitter of bare shoulders and diamonds, was bowing low and smiling and she picked up with the help of the tenor—who held her hand—bouquets that had been clumsily flung across the footlights . . . and the whole audience in the stalls and in the boxes stirred, leaned forward, shouted and applauded."[53]

The description of the diva, like that in the first opera-house scene, represents an outline onto which no identifiable female face has been drawn, a demarcated position on the stage and a relationship to the public. Anna appropriates this faceless persona, eclipsing the presumed supremacy of the opera diva, and becoming herself the primary spectacle. In fact, the reader's very first glimpse of Anna in one of the novel's opening chapters links her with the opera diva. As Stiva and Vronskii wait together at the railway station, Vronskii asks, "Well, are we to give a supper for the *diva* next Sunday?"[54] On the pretext of inquiring about this supper, Vronskii stops in at the Oblonskii home that evening, catching sight of Anna on the staircase. The opera diva is the decoy. Anna represents the true object of desire for both Vronskii and the reader.

The second opera-house scene brings the vocabulary of opera to bear on the audience rather than on the performers, and heightens the "operatization" of Anna's confrontation with high society. The ironic tone of the short conversation between Anna and Vronskii illustrates the interplay of operatic and novelistic discourses:

> "I think you got here late and missed the finest *aria*," said Anna to him, with a mocking glance as it seemed to him.
>
> "I am a poor judge," he replied, looking severely at her.
>
> "Like Prince Yashvin, who considers that Patti sings too loud," she returned with a smile.[55]

Anna's phrase "the finest *aria*" refers to the scene that ensued when Madame Kartasova in the next box publicly insulted her. Vronskii's reply "I am a poor judge" comments on the strain his loyalty to Anna has caused him. Anna's response, "Patti sings too loud," acknowledges that Vronskii finds her behavior too brazen. It is hard to love a diva. More than once, Tolstoi's novel proffers the choice of a "ballet girl" as a less troublesome alternative to the diva-like Anna. Both Vronskii's brother and Stiva Oblonskii maintain such mistresses.

After the affair with Vronskii has begun, Princess Betsy makes a trenchant observation about Anna's character, which roughly parallels Vronskii's remark about his fondness for opera bouffe: "You see a thing may be looked at tragically and turned to a torment, or looked at quite simply, and even gaily. Perhaps you are inclined to take things too tragically."[56]

Anna does indeed pitch her story toward the upper part of the generic hierarchy, into the heady air of tragedy and grand opera. Her suicidal despair is marked by her distorted perceptions of other people and her decreasing contact with anything outside of her own interior experience. She invents hurtful scenes between herself and Vronskii and writes cruel speeches for him in her imagination, "and she did not forgive him for them any more than if he had really said them."[57] Is Anna's death operatic? Certainly, she takes her life with the desire to make a grand gesture that will produce a lasting effect.[58] Anna's suicide writes her out of the gradual, novelistic deterioration of love and beauty that she fears above all else. And yet, it seems incongruous that one of the most dramatic suicides in world literature occurs when the heroine jumps awkwardly under a slow-moving freight train at a country station. Anna's death merges operatic denouement with novelistic nuance.[59]

In fact, Tolstoi intended from the outset to include a reference to a specific opera at the opening of his novel. The variants for the opening chapter of *Anna Karenina* summarize the novel's evolution from society tale to psychological and moral drama in the particular ways that opera augments the action. The original opening to Tolstoi's novel bears the intriguing title "Molodets-Baba," which may be roughly translated as an inelegant appraisal on the order of "My, what a gal!" This working title evokes operetta and variety theater, and, much like the relationship between Vronskii and the theater bouffe, calls into question Tolstoi's original generic intentions regarding the work. The working title fits the early conception of Anna, who was planned as overweight, vulgar, and coquettish.

A Pushkin prose fragment from a planned society tale gave Tolstoi the idea for a novel about contemporary Russian aristocrats: "The guests drove to the dacha of***. The room filled with ladies and gentlemen, who had come at the same time from the theater, where there had been *a new, Italian opera* [emphasis mine]."[60] The guests discuss the scandalous behavior of Zinaida, a young woman who spends most of the evening alone on the balcony with a man. The Pushkin fragment contains all of the essential elements for Tolstoi's dialogue between opera and novel: a society reception following an unidentified, real opera performance itself becomes the primary spectacle, emphasizing the theatrical conventions that shape characterization and plot. The first variant to *Anna Karenina* opens with a sentence that strongly recalls the Pushkin fragment: "*After the opera* [emphasis mine], the guests drove to the home of the young Princess Vrasskaia."

As the guests mill about in the earliest opening fragment of *Anna Karenina*, the host inquires of a beautiful woman in a black velvet dress, "How did you like Traviata, Countess?" As we know, Tolstoi eventually changed this question to "How did you like Nilsson, Princess?" The early reference to Verdi's *La Traviata* is intriguing, made as it is to a ghostly double of Anna, who herself appears at a ball in black in the final version of the novel. In making the diva, and not the opera, the subject of discussion, Tolstoi links the literary and operatic heroines. As noted, the reception guests also make this connection, and the conversation turns from Nilsson to Anna.

Although the final version of *Anna Karenina* does not refer explicitly to *La Traviata*, Verdi's opera remains a suggestive subtext to Tolstoi's novel. Anna herself suggests this relationship while suffering from puerperal fever. She compels Karenin and Vronsky to enact a scene of forgiveness before her, and, perhaps recalling the deathbed scene in the final act of *La Traviata*, points to the wallpaper and cries out, "How badly those flowers are drawn, not a bit like violets."[61] In truth, Anna's story is both like and unlike Violetta's.

La Traviata is the only one of Verdi's operas with a contemporary setting.[62] Verdi's choice to treat a nonhistorical subject prefigures Tolstoi's decision to write about contemporary social mores instead of about Russians in a "historical" context, as he did in *War and Peace*. Verdi's opera, like *Anna Karenina*, explores the consequences of flouting social convention; *La Traviata* tells the story of a demi-mondaine and her lover, a young man whose social prospects may be ruined by their relationship. *La Traviata* does not trace the actual consequences of violating society's strictures, as does *Anna Karenina*, since Violetta gives up her lover Alfredo at his father's request. In Tolstoi's novel, Anna and Vronskii do become isolated from the sphere to which they rightfully belong; Anna even comes to resemble a sort of Violetta as she presides over a provisional collection of social misfits. *La Traviata* preserves the sanctity of the bourgeois family and does not jeopardize the marital prospects of Alfredo's sister. *Anna Karenina* similarly allows the narrative of family life gradually to overwhelm the narrative of passion. The Levin-Kitty story line triumphs over the Anna-Vronskii line and outlives it in part VIII.

Tolstoi initially thought of invoking the story of *La Traviata* at the beginning of his novel, but ended up "rewriting" the Traviata story by engaging with Verdi's themes in a manner more consonant with literary realism. Tolstoi reexamines the idyll shared by Violetta and Alfredo when they retreat from society to the country through the boredom Anna and Vronskii experience abroad and at Vronskii's country estate. Verdi presents Alfredo's urging of Violetta to give herself to him as the outpouring of sincere love, whereas Tolstoi equates Vronskii's pursuit of Anna more sinisterly with the pleasures of the hunt and with the destruction of his favorite mare. Anna, too, is far more self-interested than Violetta. She does not content herself with an intimate boudoir death scene, and makes few concessions to the well-being of any family. The family as an institution is under constant siege in Tolstoi's novel.

Tolstoi's use of references to opera in the final version of the opening chapter, set in Stiva Oblonskii's study, suggests that it was always his intention to link opera and novel. Tolstoi evokes the realm of opera when Stiva Oblonskii wakes up in his study and recalls his dream: "Oh yes . . . Alabin was giving the party . . . The dinner was served on glass tables—yes, and the tables sang '*Il mio tesoro*' . . . no, not exactly '*Il mio tesoro*,' but something better than that; and then there were some kind of little decanters that were really women."[63] With the double mention of "Il mio tesoro," a well-known tenor aria from Mozart's opera *Don Giovanni*, Tolstoi invites the reader to identify the reference and recall the central preoccupations of the Mozart opera: moral retribution, sexuality, and faithlessness.

Don Ottavio sings his famous aria to Zerlina, Masetto, and Elvira, begging them to console Donna Anna, and to convey his vow to avenge her suffering. Although readers familiar with *Don Giovanni* would know that the "she" of "Il mio tesoro" is Donna Anna, the aria does not actually name its female subject. The image of Stiva as seducer prefigures the character of Vronskii, and suggests a comparison between both male characters and their prototype, Don Giovanni.[64] Similarly, the various fates of the female characters in Mozart's opera—Anna, Elvira, and Zerlina—raise the question of how far a woman may go in consenting to or inviting her own seduction, a question Tolstoi's novel asks of the Russian Anna. Tolstoi evokes the aria "Il mio tesoro" within the novel's initial context of libertinism, and on the heels of the New Testament epigraph "Vengeance is mine, I will repay."[65] In this context, Tolstoi raises the question of human versus divine retribution, a matter that bears directly on Anna's suicide.[66] The Don Juan legend as treated by Mozart poses questions about morality and the meting out of divine retribution that are not applicable to the essentially social, not moral, premises by which Verdi's opera judges Violetta's wrongdoing. *Don Giovanni* as subtext poses broader questions than those that remain largely within the province of the society tale or novel of adultery.

More important, the mention of Mozart's opera effects a merging of the novelistic and the operatic. It is, after all, the objects of the material and everyday world, the tables and decanters in Stiva's dream, that sing "Il mio tesoro." Opera does not represent a higher, alternative narrative to that of the novel here. The generic plane of the novel at the opening of *Anna Karenina* instead subsumes opera and fragments its conventions, which then fade away in ellipses as Stiva remembers his predicament. It is not actually "Il mio tesoro" that Stiva hears in his dream, "not *Il mio tesoro*, but something better."

The world of the novel, including literary dreams, both encompasses and surpasses that of the opera, the former realm of the superlative. Opera transforms the novelistic realm, causing the singing decanters in Stiva's dream to turn into tiny, singing women. But the novel can easily absorb these influences. The fact that the tables as well as the decanters are made of glass makes Stiva's dream world a kind of reflecting chamber in which miniature divas proliferate. This lovely and curious dream image serves as a kind of prelude to Anna's now delayed entrance in Tolstoi's text. The opening of *Anna Karenina* enacts in miniature the reciprocal influence between opera and the novel, and the diffuse manifestations of this influence.[67]

Eduard Granelli's little-known opera *Anna Karenina* (1906) offers a postscript to the operatic elements in Tolstoi's novel. Like Tchaikovskii's *Eugene Onegin*, Granelli's *Anna Karenina* attempts an operatic realization of a major work of nineteenth-century Russian fiction. Granelli even borrows the Tchaikovskian structuring device of linked scenes, calling his *Anna Karenina* a "lyric opera." Granelli's opera received its premiere in Kiev to a sold-out theater, but failed to meet the public's expectations. Critics contended that Granelli's opera, which consists of eight separate "pictures," was poorly constructed and lacked dramatic "coherence" (*sviaznost'*).[68] Granelli's "pictures" highlight dramatic situations such as the accident at the train station, the scene in Anna's sickroom, and the suicide, instead of playing out the evolution of these situations on stage. One critic objected to the fact that Anna and Vronskii begin their affair between "pictures," since the opera lacks "the interesting scene that would explain the *process* [emphasis mine] by which Vronskii achieves his aims."[69]

Granelli's opera looks to the nineteenth-century novel for operatic inspiration, but proves unable to effect a synthesis between the two forms. Instead, Granelli violated the central principle of the novel as expressed by Tolstoi in his most famous statement about *Anna Karenina*: "I was guided by the need to bring together ideas linked among themselves, in order to achieve self-expression. But every idea expressed by itself in words loses its meaning, becomes terribly debased when it is taken alone, out of the linking in which it is found . . . to express the essence of that linking in any way directly by words is impossible, but it is possible indirectly, with words describing images, actions, situations."[70] Tolstoi claims that his novel's structural coherence resides in a complex linkage of ideas that cannot be summarized. Granelli's *Anna Karenina* attempts to give expression to the operatic affinity in the Anna-Vronskii story, but loses touch with the essential principles of accumulation and relationship according to which Tolstoi constructed his novel. Tolstoi himself mediated between the operatic and the novelistic more successfully.

TWILIGHT OF THE LITTLE GODS: OPERATIC AND LITERARY REVOLUTIONS

Alexander Amfiteatrov's novel *Twilight of the Little Gods* (1908) posits a dynamic relationship between opera and the other genres, the psychological novel in particular. This two-volume novel depicts the conflicts and artistic differences among the troupe members of a fictional turn-of-the-century opera theater. *Twilight of the Little Gods* interrogates the nature of opera at a pre-revolutionary moment when nineteenth-century operatic *and* literary practices seemed of questionable relevance to the new ideas emerging about art among modernists and neo-realists. Amfiteatrov builds his characters, nearly all of whom are opera singers, according to the conventions associated with prose fiction; that is, he develops them gradually as the story unfolds, provides their distinct social and psychological histories, and makes them available to the reader from varying narrative perspectives.[71]

Amfiteatrov challenges the traditional distinctions between generic forms. His novel makes use of a rich vernacular; his characters interact in long conversational exchanges, using expressive, colloquial Russian and vivid imagery to talk about opera. One diva gloats over a planned triumph, for example, predicting that her rival "will fly into a rage, like a cook who's overcharged at the market."[72] The novel also transcribes conversations in a dramaturgic format, with characters seemingly fed their lines from a script. These occasional minidramas contrast with the more prevalent third-person narration. Contemporary critics assumed that Amfiteatrov's use of this device was the result of laziness: "He wearies of looking after the external details of the conversation between two heroes, and he carelessly converts the form of a novel into the form of a play . . . although he well knows that he has thus destroyed the stern harmony of an artistic novel."[73] It is more likely that Amfiteatrov intended to comment on the relationship between artistic form and generic identity.

Amfiteatrov's novel asks the reader to ponder the division between opera and prose realism. Its very title reflects a preoccupation with the connection between opera and prose fiction, referring to Wagner's *Götterdämmerung* (The twilight of the gods), the final opera in the Ring cycle, with an unexpected diminutive form, "little gods" (*bozhkov*). Amfiteatrov's ironic diminutive suggests that opera is no longer the province of the gods, which is to say, it is no longer associated with the high style. Amfiteatrov's novel depicts an opera troupe making decisions about its future artistic direction, and in doing so it brings opera down to earth, into the thematic and stylistic territory of the psychological novel. The tangled personal lives of the opera troupe members lead to the implosion of the troupe itself, the breakdown of longstanding artistic alliances, and, it is implied, the end of the nineteenth-century operatic tradition's useful life. Amfiteatrov's *Twilight of the Little Gods* also evokes Leoncavallo's opera *Pagliacci* (1892), which depicts the relationships in a traveling troupe of players. The troupe leader, Canio, crosses the boundary between staged situation and reality, stabbing his wife and her lover during a performance of a commedia dell'arte play. Leoncavallo's opera opens with a prologue in which a character tells the audience that actors experience the same passions as everyone else. Amfiteatrov's novel makes the same point in a similarly *verisimo* vein.

Twilight of the Little Gods abounds in operatic situations and mimetically reproduced operatic conventions. The soprano Nasedkina's lover hides in her bedroom while a rival woos her in the adjoining room. This scene recalls comic opera predicaments whose humor relies on dramatic irony, when the audience possesses information not available to the operatic characters. Amfiteatrov creatively transforms operatic convention during a passionate monologue by the aging, Machiavellian contralto Svetlitskaia, whose vengeful outpourings recall Mozart's "Queen of the Night" aria from *Die Zauberflöte*. Svetlitskaia's monologue swoops up and down the stylistic register, offering a tribute to an operatic tradition of injuries recounted and retribution pledged in the most florid terms.[74]

Svetlitskaia's monologue does, in fact, have an addressee: the ingenue Nasedkina, a strangely silent presence throughout this twenty-page tirade, which largely concerns Nasedkina herself and how she might figure in Svetlitskaia's plans. Svetlitskaia prefigures the equation of operatic plots with the novel's general penchant for plotting and scheming in characterizing her protegee: "you are some kind of double-woman! When you're not singing, you're one kind of woman, but once you start singing, you're another! From an ordinary and, forgive me, rather vulgar merchant's daughter . . . from a raw bun, from a stuffed heifer—you yourself don't even know into what an interesting and captivating woman you are suddenly transformed."[75]

The verb "to be transformed" (*pererozhdat'sia*), literally "to be reborn," emphasizes the similarity between playing operatic parts and recreating oneself through off-stage performances. Svetlitskaia advises Nasedkina to succumb to the advances of the director Meshkanov, and not to "play the ingenue or untouchable."[76] Nasedkina wins over Meshkanov, as "with a manner effectively adopted from Svetlitskaia, she prettily brushed away bright little tears from her eyes."[77] The other troupe members see Nasedkina as talented but inexperienced, an impression the ingenue carefully cultivates. Nasedkina, the diva for a new era, resembles an operatic Becky Sharp, displaying a novelistic sense of acumen in a setting that theatricalizes her ceaseless maneuvering. Nasedkina creates an atmosphere of operatic intrigue, transforming the prosaic machinations of an ambitious merchant's daughter into a series of betrayals that culminate in a spectacular combustion of operatic and sociopolitical concerns.

During the first part of *Twilight of the Little Gods*, Nasedkina remains an enigma to the other opera troupe members, as well as to the reader, who is denied access to her thoughts. Her initial successes in such diverse roles as Isabella in Meyerbeer's *Robert le Diable*, Tamara in Rubinshtein's *Demon*, and Brünnhilde in Wagner's *Die Walküre* reveal only her ability to summon the qualities required by a given operatic part. As Svetlitskaia does in her "Queen of the Night" monologue, various characters in the novel project their own visions and desires onto the empty space that Nasedkina represents. When Nasedkina finally reveals herself to the reader, she descends from the operatic pinnacle she has achieved with her representation of the medieval nun Trenskaia in the fictional opera *The Peasant War*, and becomes a novelistic character. This shift begins at the end of the novel's first volume, as Nasedkina strolls the city streets, savoring her new celebrity: "In the mirrored windows, Nasedkina enjoyed seeing herself, well-dressed, in a velvet blouse à la Savitskaia, in the beautiful brown furs of some American animal with a tricky name, and in an expensive hat."[78] Nasedkina works hard at constructing herself according to the visual, sartorial conventions by which nineteenth-century literary heroines lived and died. But she finds herself suddenly confronted by her former lover, the brutal Aristonov, who has come to claim a piece of her success. Dismayed by this reminder of her unsavory past, Nasedkina cannot even speak, much less sing: "sounds flew out of her throat—wild, hoarse, broken, like a dog's barking."[79] This scene, in which Nasedkina finds herself unable to control her self-presentation, represents a transitional point in Amfiteatrov's text. As the second volume of *Twilight of the Little Gods* progresses, Nasedkina topples from her operatic pedestal and finds herself trapped in a loveless marriage that she herself has contrived. She ends up ordinary.

Nasedkina's operatic successes, appropriately enough, derive from a realism that she brings to her readings of canonical operatic heroines. The critics in Amfiteatrov's novel find Nasedkina's portrayal of Rubinshtein's Tamara "rather crude . . . as if she . . . had removed all idealization from Tamara's image."[80] Nasedkina's facility reproduces the general strategy of Amfiteatrov's novel: to bring opera, both as depicted subject and genre, into the domain of the novel. Nasedkina succeeds in captivating the bass Andrei Berloga, the greatest star of the opera troupe and the most ardent proponent of the new operatic realism, because she has fascinated him with this quality in her dramatic creations. But she is too good at giving life to her realist creations, and finds herself constrained and bored by these personae:

> Outside the theater—either an unceasing succession of a curious, worshipful crowd from the public and the press, each and every one of whom she had to satisfy by appearing intelligent, nice, pleasant, and charming; or, in renouncing her individ-

> uality, work on roles; or—the artificially rapturous, feignedly modest affair with Berloga: the petty bourgeois, flattering comedy of a sentimental odalisque, sadly submitting to her adored sultan.[81]

But, as Svetlitskaia points out, the public dimension of this relationship could prove extremely useful to the ingenue's career: "The union of Berloga and Nasedkina, changing from love duets on the stage to the eternal duet of conjugal life—this is exquisite, poetic, touching. . . . The love of great performing artists always charms the crowd. I remember Patti and Nicolini. I remember Stagno and Bellincioni."[82] Nasedkina's romance with Berloga belongs to the nineteenth-century culture of opera-going and its accompanying narratives of social mobility and publicly professed passions. By the early twentieth century, however, as the cited passage implies, these plots had become hackneyed. Despite his characters' radical hopes, Amfiteatrov suggests that opera and the novel are ultimately debased by their merger.

Amfiteatrov's novel seeks a blurring of operatic and novelistic generic territory, by having his characters strive toward a radical new definition of opera. He updates opera for the twentieth century by removing it from the roster of high-style genres. Amfiteatrov describes opera in terms of a historical moment: the genre is bereft of its nineteenth-century audience, and is as homeless as the hero of any novel. Opera's defeat occurs in generic terms as the loss of a distinct identity. In thematic terms, this defeat resembles the end of a class war, in which operatic ideals are rejected. The crowd that storms the opera theater at the novel's conclusion represents the new mass reader/spectator, who craves populist, nationalistic theatrics. Ironically, pre-revolutionary Russian literary critics often cited this same mass reader as typical of Amfiteatrov's own following. This climactic scene evokes the end of the Ring cycle; when Siegfried and Brünnhilde perish, Valhalla goes up in flames, and the Rhine overflows its banks. The kingdom of the gods is no more, and a new era has arrived.

Still, the violent ending to Amfiteatrov's novel animates the spirit of *The Peasant War*, the fictional revolutionary opera that promises to radicalize the nineteenth-century tradition, updating it for the twentieth century with recourse to ideals from a distant, mythological past. Wagner's treatise *The*

Artwork of the Future (1850) similarly proposed a new nineteenth-century generic ideal for the common people (*Volk*) in a synthesis of poetry, music, and dance that privileges poetic drama. Wagner believed that this new form should arise from the very spirit of the common people, and be intended for them in particular as spectators.[83] In Herbert Lindenberger's view, "The *Ring*, like many of the great novels of the time, has helped define the mid-nineteenth century for us; perhaps one might even say it has helped create a mid-nineteenth century for us."[84] But even though Amfiteatrov, like Wagner, posits opera as the generic savior of humankind, only the novel as a form can contain the disparate energies and traditions he evokes. The novel reveals itself as the true generic repository for the twentieth century, the only artistic form of infinite, elastic amplitude.

Amfiteatrov's novel ends with the triumphant Svetlitskaia performing her favorite role of Vanya in Glinka's jingoistic nineteenth-century opera *A Life For the Tsar*, while the police chief applauds enthusiastically from the first row.[85] Amfiteatrov's novel about the operatic genre offers a prophetic allegory for the upcoming Revolution in Russia. The door to change is flung open by rebellious troupe members like Svetlitskaia and Berloga, who then become victims of the reactionary forces they unleash. Opera is left to the mercies of the police, a fitting end for a genre that shored up the social values of the European bourgeoisie.

Chapter Seven

Divining Opera
Literary Tales of Operatic Heroines

In nineteenth-century Russia, the opera prima donna assumed tangible literary form as a self-willed literary heroine who participated in an ongoing polemic about family happiness and femininity. The diva played many parts in these fictional works, among them sexual temptress, sexual prey, self-determined artist, and bad mother.[1] In such narratives, contemporary ideals of femininity collide with the increasing personal mobility of pre-revolutionary literary heroines. Like the figures of female revolutionary and woman writer, the female stage performer posed a challenge to Russian authors: how to represent a character who, by definition, transcended known forms and plots? This dilemma creates the problematics of writing, representation, and genre that permeate Russian "diva tales."[2]

LITERARY SUBJECTS

Literary works about the opera diva attempt to transform her from literary object to literary subject, from recipient and described object of poetic tributes to acting subject of prose narratives. Russian diva tales reflect the late-nineteenth-century fashion for works that treated the forbidden theatrical backstage, a development coinciding with the fullest flowering of literary realism.[3] But the diva as a heroine of late Russian prose realism seems overdetermined in this theatrical context, trapped in a funhouse of literary tropes. The productive tension between nineteenth-century realist and romantic modes, which fused so powerfully in the expressive "romantic realism" of Gogol and Dostoevskii, causes the diva-heroine to perform an aesthetic and generic fall that effectively writes her out of the story. In contrast to the worshipful distance of the poetic tribute, close-focus literary realism renders the diva monstrous, or ordinary and pitiable. Realist fiction estranges the reader from the established formal relationship to the artistic deity, and, in a pre-modernist fashion, even estranges the diva from her own artistic experience. The diva's body becomes a battleground for warring romantic and realist discourses, the very stage where this battle takes place. In the end, this contested female body disappears, figuratively and narratively. The diva remains the elusive object of representation, never truly becoming its subject.

In contrast to the lyrics that nineteenth-century poets dedicated to opera divas, prose representations seek to give the opera prima donna a voice in print. But these authorially ventriloquized fictional voices prove only marginally less ephemeral than the divas' live performance selves, whose aural component survives only in secondhand tellings and descriptions. A few real, historical female singers composed literary works, memoirs, and autobiographies. But the writing diva represents something of a chimera. Her art resembles a form of anti-writing, one that does not create a legible text, but simply draws gorgeous pictures in the air. A diva writes her life story anecdotally and allegorically, through a progression of operatic works.

Fictional diva tales, too, seem written in a kind of invisible ink. The majority of the works discussed in this chapter never found a place in the Russian literary canon. These diva tales include works by maligned female authors Maria Krestovskaia and Anastasia Verbitskaia, lesser-known texts by canonical male writers Nikolai Nekrasov and Ivan Turgenev, and literary narratives by journalists, theater professionals, and musicians, including Vladimir Nemirovich-Danchenko and Alexander Amfiteatrov. Most of these diva tales belong to the category of middlebrow literature, which so often served as a cultural scapegoat in Russia. The middle represents the place where epigones borrow from the prestige of high art, while inadvertently betraying their affinities with "vulgar" popular forms.[4] The opera diva as literary heroine languishes outside of the Russian literary tradition, in contrast to her more distinguished counterparts in English, French, and American literature. The Russian diva is a literary arriviste who never really arrived.

Perhaps the Russian diva appeared too late upon the literary scene, her presence anachronistic and compromised almost from the beginning. Following the vogue for operetta in the 1860s and the end of the Imperial monopoly on theaters in the 1880s, opera in Russia was forced to compete with a growing number of popular stage genres that featured female performers. The generic terrain of operetta, with its explicit sexual connotations, offers a telling subcategory for representations of the Russian opera diva. In this vein, Offenbach's enormously popular operetta *La Belle Hélène* (1864) offers a provocative reassessment of the generic hierarchy, bringing classical, mythological figures down to the terrain of erotic farce, while transforming the opera diva into a sexual, rather than cultural or religious, icon. In act two, Helen reposes in her private apartments and allows Paris to make love to her, happily imagining herself to be dreaming. In act three, Paris abducts Helen by boat in spite of her protests and in full view of her husband Meneleus and the rest of the court, by pretending to be the high priest from the temple to Venus. In both cases, Helen submits to the sexual and the forbidden, secure in the knowledge that it isn't her fault. Audiences, too, could enjoy the show without feeling that they had overstepped the bounds of propriety. Although Venus does not appear as a character in *La Belle Hélène*, the goddess's spirit seems to endorse the entire spectacle. During a trio number that parodies a patriotic aria from Rossini's *William Tell*, Meneleus, Agamemnon, and the high priest Calchas stand on the beach at Nauplia and complain:

> Look at the Greek nation.
> It is an immense orgy,
> And Venus, Venus Astarte
> Leads the infernal circle dance . . .
> All is pleasure and exquisite delight!
> Virtue, duty, honor, ethics,
> All are carried off by the wave!

But these accusations appear merely for form's sake within the world of the operetta, which ends with the kings fuming impotently on shore as the pleasure barge departs for Troy. In *La Belle Hélène*, the diva plays the most beautiful woman in the world, made accessible in a bedroom comedy with operatic trimmings.

In addition to operetta stars, theatergoers could hear cafe singers (*shansonetki*) who danced can-can style, variety theater vocalists, and nightclub and gypsy singers. Trained female performers in late-nineteenth-century Russia faced an increasingly commercial environment, and one that favored daring, sexually explicit performance styles. This expansion of stage genres affected all but the most elite Russian actresses and singers, who still worked largely within the Imperial theater system. Female performing artists in adjacent genres and venues borrowed from the conventions of opera culture, however. The silent film star Vera Kholodnaia and the popular songstress Anastasia Vial'tseva exemplify this process of operatic diffusion in stage arts.[5] Russian literature's diva heroines express outrage over the decline in operatic prestige through generic contamination. Their authors make diva heroines enact this decline.

Russian diva tales also contended with the "Woman Question" and its attendant concerns: marriage and divorce, sexual and reproductive politics, property and inheritance rights, rank, education, and work.[6] Many fictional representations of the opera diva in Russia seem socially reactionary, emphasizing the degradations that accompany artistic success and depicting offstage life in the bleakest terms. Such literary treatments view creative powers not as a divine gift, but as a corrupting influence. Russian diva tales enact this "corruption" in formal, generic terms as well, and can often be characterized as literary hybrids.[7] These fictional works draw upon established subgenres such as society tales, provincial stories, family novels, and adultery fictions, but render them meta-theatrically. The theatrical themes in these works destabilize generic designations, causing both heroines and narratives to exhibit literary identity crises.

The heroine of Maria Krestovskaia's story "Lelia" (1889), a provincial ingenue, begs her husband for permission to play a season with a professional troupe in Kiev. Her husband, the story's narrator, reluctantly agrees to the temporary separation, and remains at home in the provinces with their young son. The husband-narrator's worst fears are realized when Lelia becomes absorbed by her stage career and neglects her family duties. "Lelia" describes its heroine's fall by generic analogue, from roles in amateur productions of

Shakespeare and Griboyedov to professional variety-stage extravaganzas. At the story's conclusion, Lelia has become a dissolute operetta star (*kaskadnaia pevitsa*), forever lost to her family.

After Lelia's transformation and fall, her husband attends a performance of Offenbach's *La Belle Hélène*, in which she plays the most popular of all roles for nineteenth-century operetta divas: "And this woman, all sparkling with diamonds, with a ginger-colored cascade of hair in which precious stones burned and played iridescently, with lips brightly smeared with red paint, with made-up eyes, whitened and rouged, was my Lelia! . . . this was a licentious creature, who kicked up her legs in front of me, to the applause of the maddened crowd."[8]

As described by the narrator, Lelia has become a parody of womanhood, a play of false effects in jarring, incompatible hues. The preceding passage describes her simply as a "creature" (*sushchestvo*), using a neuter grammatical form in Russian. At home, Krestovskaia's narrator prominently displays a photograph of his errant wife as a gymnasium student in braids, preserving his ideal image of her.[9] "Lelia," a story written by a female author from the perspective of a male narrator, conveys the husband's anxiety about the corrupting appeal of feminine artistry. Most Russian "diva tales" exhibit a similarly ambiguous pleasure in chronicling the failures of wayward heroines, often making the fictional diva the object of the narrative's punitive force.[10] Many diva tales destabilize and then attempt to reestablish order, in both social *and* generic terms.

In Mikhail Saltykov-Shchedrin's 1870s novel, *The Golovlyov Family*, the word "young lady" (*baryshnia*) protects the Golovlyov nieces from feeling the horror of their lives as provincial operetta singers. A visit to the family estate has a sobering effect on the two young women, causing one of them, Anninka, to declare that "the position of a Russian actress is not very far from the position of a prostitute."[11] The novel similarly presents Anninka's retrospective view of her stage life in the shocked accents of a young lady:

> Up until now she had lived in a dream. She had bared herself in *La Belle Hélène*, had appeared intoxicated in *La Périchole*, had sung the most shameless things in *La Grande Duchesse de Gérolstein*, and had even been sorry that on stage "la chose" and

> "l'amour" were not represented, imagining to herself how she would have seductively quivered at the waist and stylishly twirled her train. . . . She'd made every effort only so that everything would turn out "nicely," "with chic."[12]

The nieces' claim to noble blood is largely irrelevant, since Anninka and Liubinka are the technical beneficiaries of an impoverished provincial estate. In order to supplement their earnings in the theater, the girls accept favors from admirers who value their landed status. Their physical and moral descent leads to alcoholism, prostitution, illness, and poverty. When the nieces can fall no further, Liubinka swallows phosphorus, and the consumptive Anninka returns to the Golovlyov estate to die. *The Golovlyov Family* asserts in a reactionary spirit that the stage is no place for a lady.

The Russian literary diva lives and dies by realist convention, and diva tales nearly always include a backstage view. These tales deconstruct the neoclassical and Romantic conventions that defined the diva as aesthetic object. The diva no longer provides fictional window dressing, but becomes a woman with a past.

A FEW "TELLING" EXAMPLES

Nikolai Nekrasov's story "The Female Singer" (1840) represents an early Russian attempt to insert the baffling figure of the opera diva into a genre narrative.[13] He tries to establish the diva-heroine as the narrative subject, the central character whose progress structures the story.[14] But "The Female Singer" recalls stern Victorian literary works such as the novel *East Lynne*, in which the fallen heroine is made to suffer and then allowed to die.[15]

In "The Female Singer," Count Viktor Torskoi marries Angelica, a celebrated Italian diva, and takes her back to his Russian estate. Angelica makes a restless, too exotic wife, prone to smoldering jealousies and dramatic outbursts. In this way, Nekrasov's story seems to warn against the dangers of transplanting Southern European "operaticity" to Russian soil.[16] Angelica runs off to Europe with the Baron Otto P**, who has convinced her of her husband's infidelity. After the evil Baron has been killed in a duel, Angelica's husband, now blind, arrives in Rome, seeking to revenge himself on his betrayers. In penance for her mistakes, Angelica serves her unrecognizing husband as faithful nurse and sister. After Torskoi has an operation that restores his sight, Angelica reveals her true identity. She bids him farewell and enters a convent; only the echo of her former identity remains in the title of Nekrasov's story. Nekrasov's Angelica recreates herself by turns as nobleman's wife, opera diva incognita, nurse-companion, and nun. With each costume change, the story shifts into a new generic realm: from society tale to exotic Venetian revenge narrative, from Romantic mystery story to saint's life. But Angelica's identities largely mandate secondary status, service, or silence.

This uncertainty about how to cast the opera diva extends to Russian literary works from the second half of the nineteenth century. Ivan Turgenev's story "Klara Milich" (1882) interrogates the possibility of transforming the opera diva from abstract emblem to living human character. Aratov, the story's nervous, isolated hero, attends a literary-musical evening, at which he is struck by the intensity of dramatic soprano Klara Milich. The next day, Aratov receives a note from Klara, requesting a meeting on Tverskoi Boulevard. He goes to the appointed spot, but behaves so prissily that Klara leaves abruptly, without explaining why she wanted to see him. Aratov does not even see Klara's face during this interview, since she has shrouded herself "operatically" in a veil and black mantilla. Three months later, Aratov reads of her suicide in a provincial city during a performance of an Ostrovskii play.

Aratov is haunted by images of the dead Klara, and wonders why she chose to end her life. He compulsively examines her photograph through a stereoscope to create the illusion of three-dimensionality. Aratov's obsession with the stereoscope can be read as a miniature enactment of the story's central goal: to construct a character in place of the black hole left by the diva's suicide. He travels to her native city Kazan' and speaks with her sister, pretending to gather material for Klara's biography. The sister gives him Klara's photograph and her diary, in which he finds several oblique references to an unnamed lover, possibly himself, who will "decide her fate." Aratov returns to Moscow, and continues to be plagued by strange, decadent visions of Klara. His corpse is found clutching a mysterious lock of black hair. Klara Milich has inhabited and devoured her would-be storyteller.[17]

Klara Milich exists in Turgenev's story largely as reconstruction and recollection: as an interpretation of first-person romance texts, an indistinct figure shrouded in a black veil, a photograph, a diary, a note, an unwritten biography, and, finally, as the construction of Aratov's own unreliable perceptions and dream-visions.[18] Turgenev's story poses the question of the diva's real, human identity, but the narrative is unwilling to provide an answer.[19] The diva seems an empty signifier, or perhaps an overfull one, spilling over with multiple roles and stories.

Russian literature often depicts the opera diva as a composite of the roles she has mastered, and as herself a product of the theater. In Aleksei Suvorin's play *Tatiana Repina* (1886), the performing artist declares herself too passionate a being for conventional happiness: "I have lived, how I have lived! Love, and hate, and malice, and fame, and revelry. . . . Your strength seems to grow ten times greater and you feel that your heart is so enormous. . . . It seems to enlarge and to beat like ten hearts."[20] Suvorin's diva heroine, Repina, is a mature woman who yearns for personal happiness after long years on the stage and stakes her hopes on a provincial Don Juan. After he disappoints her, she envisions a death that would represent her greatest dramatic triumph: poisoning herself on stage while performing. She goes on to realize her artistic vision in the play's final act. She performs in Ostrovskii's *Vasilisa Melent'eva*, playing the *tsaritsa* who is poisoned by her enemies at court. Enacting the tsaritsa's death simultaneously with her own, Repina literally gives the performance of her life.

Impassioned renderings of the final scene by actresses like Maria Savina and Maria Ermolova produced answering shrieks from female audience members.[21] Part of the thrill of attending a performance of Suvorin's *Tatiana Repina* came from imagining that the poisoning scene was being enacted in earnest. This possibility effected a *tripled* superimposition of images for the audience by combining the personae of Repina's real-life model Evlalia Kadmina, Suvorin's character Repina, and the actress playing her.

During the final act, the dying Repina repeatedly crosses the boundary between her dressing room and the stage, where she is summoned for bows. The staging of Suvorin's play splits the set in half: one side represents the fictional stage on which Repina performs, while the other shows the backstage area of the fictional theater, including Repina's dressing room. During her last moments, Repina strains to go out to her audience one last time, and dies hungry for more applause. She chooses theater over life, the former proving a more satisfying arena for her passionate transports. Suvorin's play makes theater out of theater as the only conceivable way to represent the diva.[22]

REPRESENTING A REPERTOIRE

During the second half of the nineteenth century, Russian opera troupes developed their standard repertoire, a process that occupied cultural critics, performers, and theater administrators. The question of repertoire was made more acute by Russian opera troupes' historic sense of inferiority in relation to the directorate's well-maintained Italian opera troupe. Russian opera troupes generally staged Western operatic works in Russian translation during the first half of the nineteenth century. The inclusion of Western operatic works sung in their original languages during the second half of the century paralleled the growth of the native Russian operatic tradition. Wagner's *Lohengrin* (1850), Gounod's *Faust* (1859), Meyerbeer's *L'Africaine* (1865), Verdi's *Aida* (1871), and Bizet's *Carmen* (1875) became staples of the Russian operatic repertoire, along with Glinka's *A Life for the Tsar* (1836) and *Ruslan and Ludmila* (1842), Dargomyzhskii's *Rusalka* (1856), Rubinshtein's *Demon* (1875), Tchaikovskii's *Eugene Onegin* (1879), and Rimskii-Korsakov's *The Snow Maiden* (1882). By the 1890s, a particularly successful decade for the Mariinskii Theater Troupe in St. Petersburg, a truly eclectic mix of Russian and Western operas showcased the diverse artistic strengths of the Russian troupe.[23] Provincial troupes were quicker to offer a mixed repertoire to their audiences, but this was a matter of economic necessity rather than of progressive artistic vision.[24] Provincial cities generally made do with a single theater troupe, whose artists could render all manner of dramatic and musical works.

The consolidation of the Russian opera repertoire coincided with the rise of the theater novel in Russia, a popular subgenre that invoked specific theatrical or operatic works as a backdrop to a performer's story. In Vladimir Nemirovich-Danchenko's *Stage Wings* (1899) and Kazimir and Olga Koval'skie's *The Two-Faced God* (1916), the operatic works staged by the fictional troupe are analogous to the experiences of the opera diva heroine. These two novels use a third-person narration to represent the heroine's consciousness during the opera performances, mirroring her confusion of operatic and novelistic narratives. These entwined narratives highlight the choices of Russian versus Western operatic works, and the chosen operas' subtextual relationship to the literary plot.

Stage Wings deploys a set of exclusively Western operatic works to represent its heroine's experiences in Russia after her artistic training in Italy. The narratives of Western opera that parallel her story are a manifestation of the heroine's "diseased" consciousness; she has been infected by Western works during her stay abroad, and experiences her own life's drama as inherently operatic. *Stage Wings* mounts a series of Western operas that complement and overdetermine the heroine's story: Meyerbeer's *Les Huguenots* and *L'Africaine*, Verdi's *Aida*, and Gounod's *Faust*, with brief, but topical digressions to Verdi's *Rigoletto* and Meyerbeer's *Robert le Diable*. The intersections between the heroine Raevskaia's story and the operatic narratives she enacts are made evident in the broadest thematic terms. The despised "foreign" heroine recurs as a central figure in *Les Huguenots*, *Aida*, and *L'Africaine*, while the consequences of faithless seduction dominate *Faust*, *Rigoletto*, and *Robert le Diable*.

The opening chapter of *Stage Wings* is titled "Raoul and Valentina," an explicit reference to *Les Huguenots*, whose plot shapes the initial encounter between Raevskaia and the cynical tenor Barskii. While walking in the hills outside of Ravenna, Raevskaia hears an unseen tenor voice singing Raoul's part from below. She cannot resist singing back as Valentina, so that when Barskii appears in person, their romantic relationship with one another has already been established. It is, of course, Raevskaia rather than Barskii who is subject to these operatic reframings, since Barskii merely profits from happy circumstance. As one of Raevskaia's associates comments quietly, "A real Raoul and Valentina! . . . But isn't it sooner the Count and Gilda?"[25] The reference to *Rigoletto* speaks to Barskii's ability to play either the noble Raoul or the concupiscent Duke of Mantua. The reader, not Raevskaia, is privy to this early warning about framing everyday surroundings in operatic terms, and misperceiving "real-life" roles. The novel's opening scene, which is set in a natural

Italian amphitheater, prefigures the real opera performances that will follow in Russia, and hints at Raevskaia's determination to see herself as an operatic heroine. Raevskaia's operatic illusions prolong her romance with Barskii; when he plays noble characters, she forgives him for disappointing her off stage.

Raevskaia's first major part after her return to Russia is Verdi's Aida, an ideal role for a literary heroine who insists on seeing herself as exiled princess and victim. The tension in the operatic narrative between Aida and the Pharaoh's daughter, Amneris, repeats itself in the rivalry between Raevskaia and Barskii's former lover, the mezzo Dosuzheva. Amneris maneuvers Aida into confessing her love for Radames, while Dosuzheva's stance on stage forces Raevskaia to sing with her back to the audience. Raevskaia's trials as a well-bred young woman unprepared for the coarse theatrical milieu correspond to the Ethiopian princess Aida's humiliations at the hands of Amneris, whom she must serve as handmaiden. Like Aida shut up in the crypt, Raevskaia is imprisoned within an operatic repertoire, and can only play heroines who pine and perish.

Barskii's efforts to seduce Raevskaia coincide with the opera troupe's production of Gounod's *Faust*, in which she plays the innocent Marguerite. The decisive moment between Raevskaia and Barskii takes place in Raevskaia's dressing room after the performance, when they seem to enact the famous Jewel Song: "The light splintered on the bracelets and earrings scattered upon the table. . . . Directly in front of her glowed a diamond. She couldn't remove her gaze from it, although it was exactly the thing that was hypnotizing her so."[26] The props from Gounod's opera reflect the compelling influence that both Barskii and the role of Marguerite exert on Raevskaia. Barskii seems to understand the fascination these operatic narratives hold, and makes overstated, theatrical declarations of love to Raevskaia in the dressing room: "I want you. . . . All, all of you, body and soul."[27] Barskii's seduction scene evokes Faust and Mephistopheles, however, not Faust and Marguerite. Barskii demands payment for the support he has offered the inexperienced Raevskaia with the theater administration and local critics. But if Raevskaia was prepared to play the innocent maiden to Barskii's masterful seducer, she refuses to yield to him in a transaction that would suit both parties.

The tension between novelistic and operatic narratives overwhelms Raevskaia during a performance of Meyerbeer's *L'Africaine*, when the entire company conspires to drown her out. As in *Aida*, Raevskaia plays a noble outsider, the captive Indian princess Selika, despised by the Portuguese court. Barskii, as Vasco de Gama, the Portuguese explorer, aptly plays a creature of the system that created him. Raevskaia transforms the operatic role into an analogue for her own situation; her willingness to accept the role in spite of the ill wishes of her enemies in the troupe mirrors Selika's decision to take poison. Raevskaia herself reflects upon this similarity, likening an artist's need to perform to an addict's need for his drug. But Raevskaia's addiction extends to operatically heightening her backstage reality. At the moment of Selika's death, Raevskaia falls into a faint at the front of the stage. She has succeeded as never before in asserting her identity through her favorite operatic heroines, authoring a spectacle of the self in which the entire troupe participates.

Raevskaia's farewell performance with the opera troupe occurs after her fiancé, the entrepreneur Kashintsev, reconfigures the theatrical world for her. In this final performance of Meyerbeer's *Les Huguenots*, Raevskaia triumphs over Barskii as both operatic artist and novelistic heroine. She sings superbly, indifferent to the tenor's charms. Once more exerting the aesthetic control she maintains throughout the novel, she uses her consciousness to edit out the final moments of Meyerbeer's opera, and she embraces the dying Raoul instead of perishing with him under fire, as the opera mandates. In Meyerbeer's opera, Raoul refuses to recant his Protestant religious heresy, and dies a martyr. Valentina, on the other hand, having promised her lover that she will give up the Catholic Church for him, dies reciting a Catholic prayer. Barskii seems, by extension, the more honest character, living and dying by the rules of his backstage world. The final scene in *Stage Wings* subverts Raevskaia's own strategy of appropriating operatic plots for her own purposes by implicating the novelistic heroine in the moral ambiguity of the operatic heroine's final actions.[28] Raevskaia cannot have it both ways; if she learns how to successfully serve her own ends in the theatrical milieu, she must renounce her old religion of victimized innocence. In symbolically killing off her tormentor Barskii, Raevskaia recasts herself as the victorious heroine. But she is now unfit for the roles she has fought to play, since in playing them she would be misrepresenting herself.

Raevskaia's fiancé Kashintsev arranges for her farewell performance of *Les Huguenots* by donating huge sums for new costumes and decorations. Kashintsev finances the reception as well as the production of Raevskaia's success; he purchases flowers and wreaths to be presented to her, and offers a bribe to an influential theater critic: "Everything must be done to bring this about. And have the troupe and orchestra help—I will pay! Prepare the public too, if necessary . . . flowers, wreaths, and so forth. Do everything on the largest scale . . . send the bill to me, just see that she doesn't know."[29]

Although Raevskaia's farewell performance is a success, she cares only for her beloved Kashintsev, who sits in the first row, smiling proudly. The wreaths and flowers ultimately belong to Kashintsev for creating and staging the illusion of success, compelling Raevskaia's former enemies and rivals to participate in the performance. If Raevskaia remains blissfully unaware that Kashintsev has written her a happy ending, the reader retains the sense that she has been rewarded for obediently playing her part in a socially reactionary novel. For Nemirovich-Danchenko's heroine, operatic and social roles constitute insistent scripts that she compulsively performs.

Kazimir and Olga Koval'skie's novel *The Two-Faced God* (1916) proposes a sequence of operatic heroines according to which Liza, the ingenue soprano, is initiated into the theater. Liza equates the experiences of the operatic heroines she represents with her own life narrative, weaving these female images into one collective bildungsroman: "Liza felt how alive, close, and joined to her own experiences were Marguerite and Tat'iana, Natasha and Martha, all of those maidenly souls, who were awaiting the secrets of love and receiving the first baptism of sorrow."[30] This bit of characterization alerts the reader to the shape of Liza's own as yet untold story, and suggests that the Koval'skies' novel will narrate Liza's life against the familiar plots of nineteenth-century opera. The novel's title refers to the two-faced Roman deity Janus, and thereby evokes the uncertain nature of theatrical life, which might reward the female performer or punish her cruelly.

The Two-Faced God associates Liza with the role of the innocent heroine in

Faust early on, when a member of the theater troupe exclaims, "Yes . . . you are truly a beauty . . . a real Gretchen."[31] Liza's affinity with Faust's heroine remains a motif throughout the novel, although Liza moves on to operatic roles that complicate the notion of female innocence. Unlike *Stage Wings*, which evokes exclusively Western operatic heroines, *The Two-Faced God* uses both Russian and Western roles as representative of Liza's situation: Tatiana in *Eugene Onegin*, Natasha in *Rusalka*, Natasha in *Demon*, and Marfa in *The Tsar's Bride*, as well as Marguerite in *Faust* and Elsa in *Lohengrin*. The Russian operatic roles in *The Two-Faced God* offer a set of faintly hopeful possibilities within the decadent world of the theater. At the end of the novel, we learn that Liza will play Tatiana in a forthcoming production of *Eugene Onegin*. This is to say that she will graduate from being miserable and utterly undone to being miserable and dignified.

Liza of *The Two-Faced God* wishes to play innocent-victim heroines on stage, since these are the available starring roles. But she does not seek to re-enact these tragic narratives in her own life. The director Volkov and the seducer-tenor Milich conspire to snare her into these operatic plots, however, and they make such enactments an implicit condition for her success in the theater. In order to stop playing Gretchen-Marguerite and move on to her next operatic role, Liza must consent to the seduction Volkov plans for her. After she offends the director with her refusal, she finds herself relegated to playing the shepherdess in the eighteenth-century pastoral vignette of Tchaikovskii's *Queen of Spades* (1890). She risks being trapped forever in the tableaux framed by the play within a play. In order to reclaim the plummy operatic roles, Liza must make the requisite sacrifices to the two-faced god of the theater.

Liza's next big role, Natasha in *Rusalka*, represents a new phase in her seduction by the theater. Like Gounod's Marguerite, Dargomyzhskii's Natasha suffers abandonment by her beloved. But Natasha reveals a capacity for fighting back, and is eventually reunited with the prince. She does not die tragically, but triumphs over the narratives of victimhood. Liza permits Milich to seduce her in his luxurious room, from whose window she can see the theater that will be the scene of her future triumphs. She becomes much more conscious of the bargains she strikes. The seduction now seems merely a necessary ritual. Liza transcends her operatic roles of hapless maidens, since she expects nothing lasting from Milich and feels no surprise when he quickly tires of their affair. She rewrites the plot of Nikolai Karamzin's *Poor Liza* (1792), an eighteenth-century sentimental tale that she re-conceives to suit a more pragmatic era.

Liza discovers that she is pregnant by Milich; her baby represents the product of the dissolute theatrical world. She miscarries as the result of a fall during a performance of *Faust*, and determines to live only for art. Her misery and eventual redemption partially complement the fate of the operatic heroine Marguerite from *Faust*, who kills her illegitimate child and is granted entry to heaven by a choir of angels in response to her dying supplications. But Liza has relinquished any operatically inspired illusions about herself. In synthesizing Russian and Western operatic subtexts, in becoming a seasoned opera professional and a mature woman who has given up girlish fantasies, Liza comes close to genuine literary heroinism.

CREATING AND PROCREATING ART

In a 1923 book about women on the stage, V. L. Iureneva tried to reconcile the fundamental opposition between being a woman and being a stage artist through the metaphor of giving birth: "Actress! A stern, happy calling. . . . There is too much of your maternity for your own children. There is too much of your love for one. There are too many sufferings for you alone. . . . Your pregnancy is unceasing, childbirth is sweet, your children are fortunate—you raise them by the thousands."[32] According to Iureneva, the female performer acts as mother to the roles she creates, as well as to the viewers, whom she educates and nurtures. But most diva-heroines in Russian literature are terrible mothers. While Iureneva's female performers give birth to the world, the diva-heroines in Russian literary works give birth to themselves at their children's expense. The literary diva is often a sterile self-creation, serving an art that merely substitutes for life, a quintessential fin-de-siècle conceit.

The question of whether a diva-heroine must sacrifice her life as a woman opens Alexander Amfiteatrov's novel *Twilight of the Little Gods* (1908), with the introduction of Elena Savitskaia, a well-preserved soprano in her forties who is also directress of an opera troupe. Savitskaia, it is rumored, has undergone a mysterious Paris operation that guarantees her eternal youth, and has no children. She smiles strangely without moving her face, and speaks in a voice with "a special crystalline ring."[33] But Savitskaia has frozen herself in time artistically as well as physically. Her former lover, the earthy bass Andrei Berloga, accuses her of worshipping opera's past instead of committing herself to its future: "Your true attachment in art is the lyricism of the old classical forms. . . . You are not cold, but the tombstone statues that you love so passionately, try to warm with your flame and bring to life, *are*."[34]

Savitskaia's beloved roles include Mozart's Donna Anna, Bellini's Norma, Meyerbeer's Alicia, Glinka's Ludmila, and Rubinshtein's Tamara. This set of Romantic opera heroines eloquently contrasts with a part Savitskaia cannot play, that of Margarita Trenskaia, the elemental fourteenth-century nun-martyress in the fictional "revolutionary" opera, *The Peasant War*. Amfiteatrov posits opera as the potential means for a transformation of twentieth-century art. Savitskaia's outmoded values signal the impending destruction of nineteenth-century artistic ideals, and she herself resembles a marble statue gracing the final resting place of nineteenth-century grand opera.

The question of whether a diva could write her own story was still unresolved when Anastasia Verbitskaia's novella *The Abandoned Man* was published in the mid-1920s. The work's title obliquely establishes the opera diva, Vera Tumanskaia, as acting subject rather than acted-upon object, since the abandoned person referred to is Vera's husband, Stanskii. As does Krestovskaia's Lelia, Vera leaves her husband and child behind. She makes an explicit declaration about self-determination and identity toward the end of the novel: "I do not regret that I went on the stage. . . . I found myself. . . . I discovered this supreme happiness: I became an individual [*lichnost'*]."[35] Like the Koval'skie siblings, Verbitskaia's novella asserts that a talented woman must sacrifice herself on the altar of art. Verbitskaia's diva tale exacts a great price from its heroine, forcing her to witness the death of her daughter Mania, and sending her off on a train journey whose destination is a lonely old age.

In Part II of Verbitskaia's novella, Vera, who has taken the stage name

Lola, stands outside her husband's tiny house in the darkness, the unseen spectator of a domestic scene. As Vera observes her husband reading, she sees a little boy crawl over to him, and he bends toward the child:

> But, Lord, Lord! Whose child was this? Why was he here? And why did Andrei caress him so tenderly? "Could it really be?" flashed the vague, distant suspicion.
>
> Suddenly Lola uttered a feeble cry, starting back for a moment from the window and again pressing her face to the glass, having forgotten all caution.
>
> A woman entered the room.
>
> Lola could not make out her features—she stood now with her back to the window, but the singer instinctively realized that the woman was young, that this was her rival. And what was most important, Lola saw that the woman who had come into the room was pregnant.[36]

The diva takes on the role of the audience, as she stands invisibly behind the window and watches the drama of family life unfold. Vera-Lola pieces together that her husband Stanskii is the little boy's father, that the unknown woman is pregnant by Stanskii, and that this new family holds him under obligations of honor. The backstage region of opera is, as this scene asserts, the province of the novel and the artistic space in which the true drama of life occurs. Here, the diva is reduced to a lonely woman who peers into other people's drawing rooms.

The final confrontation between Vera and her husband, Stanskii, directly bears upon the relationship between the opera diva and the novel. This scene occurs in the diva's own drawing room, which is deliberately lit like a stage: "A dim light illuminated Lola's luxurious drawing room. It was as if the singer was afraid of light."[37] Stanskii's first reported impressions further theatricalize the long-awaited encounter between the diva and her abandoned husband: "How often he had imagined this scene in the distant years of his loneliness! With what contempt he had planned to brand Vera! How many curses he had mentally flung in her face!"[38]

Since Stanskii has rehearsed this confrontation in his mind countless times, the stagy nature of the scene is a product of the ways in which both participants frame the situation. Vera cannot submit to the familiar narratives of the family novel or to the social novel of the principled Russian intelligentsia.

But Stanskii similarly retreats from the operatic spectacle of vengeful curses that he used to sustain himself during his lonely provincial exile. When he evokes his common-law wife, Sophie, to steel himself against his reawakened passion for Vera, he also summons up the famous renunciation scene from *Eugene Onegin*, with the gender roles reversed: "And know this, Vera: whatever it might cost me, not only will I never abandon her, but I won't even secretly or accidentally betray her. . . . This is *my* moral philosophy."[39] This scene from Verbitskaia's *The Abandoned Man* belongs to the history of the relationship between opera and novel, a retrospective view of the two genres that pays tribute to shared settings and situations.

During Vera's last encounter with Stanskii, the two play out an allegory of genre, assuming the roles of opera and novel, respectively. Vera delivers her speeches in a distinctly operatic fashion. "Don't despise me! Give me your hand! You, who were able to be happy without me!"[40] The narrator underscores the aria-like delivery of these pleas with the observation "O, how much passion and sorrow there was in that phrase!" Stanskii, for his part, speaks in long phrases, with numerous participial constructions, a language that strongly recalls the treatment of moral-philosophical themes in the Russian realist novel: "The crowd, idle, surfeited, triumphant, and celebrating the performing artist, was close and understandable to you. . . . But humanity—suffering, exhausted in the struggle for the right to live, even if half-starving; humanity, perishing in the battle for its rights—O, how far and alien it is from you!"[41]

Vera and Stanskii exchange manifesto-like statements about Art and Life couched in the terms of opera and novel, but are unable to understand each other. It is only when the two acknowledge their failure to reach a genuine understanding that they succeed in creating a bit of common ground and a moment in the narrative unclaimed by language or genre: "And for a long, long time they stood, embracing, blending kisses and tears, without the strength to tear themselves away from one another, babbling disconnected phrases as then and there they buried their feelings and the past to which there was no going back now."[42]

Verbitskaia continually reminds the reader that opera, and not the novel, affords her heroine the scope for self-expression. The central struggle in *The Abandoned Man* represents, in fact, Vera's attempt to clarify what she found lacking in conjugal life, and to express this lack in terms that the novel as a genre can accommodate. But the allegedly supreme, expressive potential of the operatic genre, which Verbitskaia's novel associates with its heroine, rarely narrates the search for female spiritual and moral autonomy. The author of *The Abandoned Man* chooses the novel as the most effective vehicle for describing Vera's experience, but also as a forum for writing about stage arts in terms of new concerns: a woman's right to self-expression.

For Vera's gifted daughter Mania, growing up and becoming a woman are synonymous with becoming a performing artist, a fate her father will do anything to avert. Verbitskaia's novella suggests that the adolescent Mania may reconcile her parents' reverse-gendered ideals of self-fulfillment (Vera) and self-sacrifice (Stanskii), but leaves this potential unrealized. Instead, Mania's death ensures that no part of Vera will outlast the diva's own passing. And Verbitskaia never lets the reader forget that Vera chooses herself over her daughter: "She was not created for a commonplace lot. Of course, one could kill off these transports in oneself, reconcile oneself and embark upon the lifeless execution of one's obligations as a wife and mother, but all that would remain of her would be a corpse."[43]

The narrative affirms Vera's right to choose herself, but doubles back and carries out a terrible punishment for this privilege: the corpse in question is not Vera, but Mania, the real victim of Vera's decision to become a performing artist. Vera's maternal devotion, awakened too late, cannot save Mania from an attack of brain fever. Mania dies of an illness that evokes her father and his relentless late-night reading and writing. And Vera never succeeds in revealing herself to Mania as the girl's mother. The narrative denies the diva this act of legitimation, although it does grant her a "voice."

Verbitskaia's novella claims an Old Testament vengeance no less severe than that inflicted on Tolstoi's Anna Karenina, a literary parallel made explicit by Mania: "She [Anna Karenina] was a bad mother, a bad one. . . . And were I in Serezha's place, I would never have forgiven her!"[44] The ending of *The Abandoned Man* rewrites Verbitskaia's insistent Tolstoyan subtext, however.

Vera Tumanskaia does not throw herself under the train, and is not crushed by it; instead, she rides the Tolstoyan train into a self-imposed exile. The train offers an apt metaphor for Vera herself, who makes the following declaration about performing artists: "we do not create anything and disappear without a trace. Not books, not statues, not paintings, not songs. . . . It is true. . . . Our image lives only in the hearts of people who disappear as we do."[45] Vera, like the train, moves onward and away, passing everything, collecting nothing. Verbitskaia's novella confers on its diva-heroine the right to spin out her tale, but warns of the pain and penalties accompanying such authorship.[46]

The Abandoned Man stands apart from Verbitskaia's earlier, pre-revolutionary novels about female performers, notably *The Keys to Happiness* (1909–13) and *The Yoke of Love* (1914–20). Written at the end of her life, when she was in her sixties, *The Abandoned Man* represents the outer edge of Verbitskaia's considerable oeuvre. Verbitskaia's fortunes had changed radically by the 1920s, and the once best-selling authoress found herself out of fashion and out of favor, already resident in the post-heroinic nowhere that awaited her aging fictional diva Vera Tumanskaia. The diva in *The Abandoned Man* suggests herself as a stand-in for the female writer, who is under siege, yet still aching to write a few more volumes. But Verbitskaia's audience had left the theater. Opera as a fully articulated metaphor for self-expression came too late to the aid of Russian fictional heroines.

SINGING THE SELF

The letters, diaries, and oral retellings by literary divas in *fictional* accounts posit a heroinic subject's voice, but make the existence of such a voice highly problematic.[47] In point of fact, the real, historical nineteenth-century opera diva rarely articulated herself through the written word. The textual legacy of these female performing artists, both in Russia and the West, generally consists of the diva's scanty and perfunctory social, contractual, and logistical correspondence. Divas in this respect offer a provocative contrast to nineteenth-century actresses, who produced a significant number of full-length autobiographies. Many of the most interesting and notable Russian divas from the imperial period, including Elizaveta Lavrovskaia, Evgenia Mravina,

Maria Kuznetsova-Benois, and Medea Figner, left no written account of themselves. For that matter, neither did Western divas Adelina Patti, Christine Nilsson, Pauline Lucca, or Desirée Artôt. There exist but a handful of written works by real-life Russian divas Evlalia Kadmina, Maria Slavina, Daria Leonova, and Alexandra Smolina.[48] These examples of diva prose attempt to mark out a territory for the self, often in generic terms.[49]

Pauline Viardot, one of the most famous nineteenth-century Western opera divas, left a few written curiosities behind. Such are the bits of writing that survived from the "portrait game" that Turgenev played with the Viardot family at their country home in 1856 and at Baden-Baden in the 1860s. During the "portrait game," Turgenev would quickly execute drawings of human profiles, whose fictional lives and characteristics the rest of the party then guessed at in writing. A cultured and accomplished woman, Viardot provided the longest and liveliest written speculations of any player, apart from Turgenev himself. Two examples of her fancies illustrate her talent for composing vivid thumbnail sketches: "Good comic actor—envious of other people's success—subtle, witty, but not easy to get on with. Is forming a button collection—likes people of distinction.—Has tried, unsuccessfully, to write vaudevilles—but his literary instincts help him to build his roles well—is observant,"[50] and

> Very meek, very amiable, very obliging young man—he must play the flute—he's a great mollycoddle. When he's at a ball, ladies send him ices, chairs, their cloaks, etc.—He's much loved in his family—His friends and acquaintances make fun of him a little, but people often have recourse to his indefatigable readiness to oblige. He is always running about doing favors. Luckily he has a little money, for he would never be able to earn his living—unless perhaps as an errand-boy.[51]

Viardot's contributions to the "portrait game" make reference to the character's theatrical or literary habits, and often describe the character in a social context by invoking standard "scenes." Always on stage, even when writing a private letter or toying with the notion of writing for a public, the nineteenth-century diva seems to have preferred to remain an icon and legend, rather than become a self-authored "literary" character.

The posthumously published story fragment "Diana Embriako" by the suicidal mezzo-soprano Evlalia Kadmina (1853–81) wistfully constructs the sort of heroine that Kadmina herself could never play. Kadmina, who was dark and sultry, made her twelfth-century heroine blonde and "dangerously" blue eyed.[52] Kadmina also gave "Diana Embriako" a setting both geographically and historically remote from her own Russian context, and, as a consequence, may not have felt herself to be on firm literary ground. Her narrator in this fragment defensively invokes literary convention throughout, declaring that while her description of the heroine's eyes might not please "purist writers and stern critics," she has no doubts that Diana's twelfth-century admirers would have warmly supported her characterization. Diana "was the embodiment of a marvelous poetic dream-vision," about whom "[i]t would be superfluous to add how the heads of all the young knights and cavaliers spun when they met her going to pray at the nearby church." Kadmina's contradictory narrator insists on the right to choose her own words, while indulging in the narrative shorthand and elisions that shared literary convention makes possible ("It would be superfluous to add. . . ."). Impatiently cutting short a description of a lovers' tryst, the narrator inquires, "But why repeat everything that these lovers expressed during this first heart-to-heart talk? Who has not loved?" Kadmina constructed her "Diana Embriako" as a literal fragment, a sign of literary tradition itself. For all her astounding grace and beauty, Kadmina's Diana can do nothing but stand on the castle ramparts, "motionless, as if turned to stone," waiting for her father and lover to return with their crusading fleet. Kadmina's literary fragment makes central not Diana's trials and tribulations, but the author's own struggle to find a narrative voice. In this sense, "Diana Embriako" can be considered a diva tale of self-authorship, as well as an amateurish attempt at historical fiction.

Accounts of life and career by Maria Slavina, Daria Leonova, and Alexandra Smolina illustrate the workings of genre and self-presentation in female stage singers' autobiographies. These retrospective narratives of self, intended for public consumption, exhibit the rhetoric that Wayne Koestenbaum calls "divaspeak": "the language of put-on (faked aristocracy, faked humility)" that "utterly believes in the effectiveness of its gestures—or pretends to."[53] The brief, unpublished autobiography of Russia's first Carmen,

Maria Slavina (1858–1951), is shot through with this self-celebratory language. After summarizing her performance career and favorite roles, Slavina lingers over an account of her 25-year anniversary benefit performance on 29 January 1903 in St. Petersburg. She reserves her most expansive prose for the gifts she received from the royal family: "The Empress Maria Fedorovna invited me to her box during the intermission, congratulated me, and presented me with a beautiful brooch. Our Sovereign the Emperor Nicholas II gladdened me with the decoration of Soloist of His Majesty, and the Grand Princes Vladimir and Aleksei Aleksandrovich presented me with an enormous silver vase, all strewn with silver coins."[54] Slavina's rapturous account of her trophies, which represent signs read as carefully as the notes of an opera score, characterizes these objects as the ultimate judgment rendered on a career in which she sang "56 roles of the most diverse character."

The 1891 autobiography of the Russian contralto Daria Leonova (1829–96) more fully manifests the rhetorical gestures of "divaspeak." Leonova's memoirs tell a story of dignity maintained, confidence unshaken by betrayals and ill-treatment, and public support received in the face of the theater directorate's hostility toward her. She writes that the desire to describe her life arose from her experience "as a performing artist who happened to come into contact with a great number of people of various social positions," and "as a woman who visited many countries and has traveled around the world."[55] Her travels as a performing artist take place on a vertical axis up and down the social hierarchy, whereas her parallel voyage as a woman occurs along the horizontal plane, between diverse geographical locations. Her identity as a performing artist permits her a greater social mobility than would be possible for her solely as a woman of a particular social standing, since she was the daughter of a former serf who served as a soldier. The twin journeys of Leonova's bifurcated self, performing artist and woman, intersect only at their point of origin, maintaining the now-familiar diva dialectic of identity. Leonova structurally reproduces the intersecting characterizations of herself as performing artist and woman with her oppositions of Russia and the West, St. Petersburg and Moscow, strength and sickness, soprano and contralto, art and money.

The first sections of Leonova's memoirs recount the discovery of her musical talents, finding retrospective portents of a brilliant future in her childish fondness for performing on a makeshift stage made out of sheets and furniture. As she grandly declares, her early musical talents were "special," her passion for music "striking," and her musical ear "exceptional." She was accepted at the training school of the St. Petersburg Bolshoi Theater, and sang soprano parts until her teachers realized that she was actually a contralto with an enormous vocal range. She briefly interrupts her tale of early recognition and triumph with an embedded narrative in a different generic vein, a story of love thwarted by class-based considerations. The diva relates that she was in love with an aristocratic youth, whose parents would not hear of his marriage to the poor but respectable Leonova. In revenge for his parents' narrow-mindedness, Leonova's suitor married a girl who Leonova claims was "at the last stage of degradation";[56] he left with his new wife for the Caucasus, and died there of a fever. This tale provides the last and only reference Leonova makes to her life as a woman, although we know that in 1856 she petitioned the emperor for permission to marry.[57] Following this embedded narrative, Leonova presents herself as a solitary woman warrior who prevailed in the face of slights and betrayals by the Imperial Theater directorate. Her father's experience at soldiering offers a metaphor for the diva's own career, and this affinity is emphasized by the senior Leonov's exclamation at her salary of 600 rubles a year: "How can this be! I've completed so many campaigns, and I still do not earn as much as you do!"[58] Money itself serves as a thematic counterpoint to the progress of Leonova's career, as she notes with great precision the amounts of her salary and raises. Her repeated insistence on rigorous notions of duty and hard work reflects the peculiarly Russian view of the opera diva as public servant.

Leonova's dignified prose complements her professional photographs in costume and street dress. These images show a large, unsmiling woman, whose stern poses and modest dress are utterly unlike the simpering portraits of Western divas from the 1850s–70s. Leonova's 1850 debut as Vanya in Glinka's *A Life for the Tsar* took place with the Russian opera troupe, in the old stone circus across the square from the St. Petersburg Bolshoi Theater. Undeterred by the Russian opera troupe's secondary status, Leonova writes of

Figure 27. Daria Leonova as the princess in *Rusalka*. The determined Leonova faces the camera squarely, just as she faced detractors and unsympathetic theater administrators throughout her career.

her debut, "for me, success on the stage was beyond question. I understood my strength and from that time on, I studied art even more seriously."[59] Leonova poignantly complements her self-characterization as heroine of her own bildungsroman with the rueful admission that she was eventually compelled to give up her favorite roles in Glinka's operas, because "my plumpness somewhat hampered me from performing in them."[60]

The assertion of self continues as the overriding theme of Leonova's memoirs, which otherwise read as a kind of travel literature: a record of journeys taken and roles performed, interwoven with a litany of complaints. From 1873 to 1879, after leaving the Imperial Theaters, Leonova toured and gave concerts throughout the Russian provinces, Europe, America, and the Far East, as an ambassador of the self. She characterizes herself as a member of the world aristocracy with the proud assertion, "Wherever I appeared with my visiting card, doors opened to me everywhere."[61] Apparently satisfied, she returned to Russia, worked as a teacher, and gave concerts to benefit orphans and war widows.

Leonova's often strident account of herself as lone martyr-heroine elides the more collaborative aspects of her artistic biography, such as her longstanding association with the composer Modest Musorgskii. Leonova and Musorgskii gave concerts together throughout Russia and Ukraine in the late 1870s, and founded a private singing school in St. Petersburg in the early 1880s. In fact, Leonova is best known today through her work with Musorgskii. In writing memoirs that so persistently assert a self of particular qualities to the exclusion of all else, a conception antithetical to the very notion of an opera diva, she leaves herself open to accusations of self-centeredness.

Leonova's file in the archive of the St. Petersburg Imperial Theater directorate suggestively augments her memoirs with a record of the official correspondence between the diva and the theater administration: requests for medical leave, contracts, and negotiations over salary and pension. This alternate narrative constructs a similarly embattled yet undaunted Leonova, who persists in her requests for additional payments and benefits. A request for a medical leave in 1863 is made in the same rolling diva prose that dominates her autobiography: "During my twelve-year service, I bore strenuous labors, while striving to be useful to the Directorate and give the public pleasure, and ruined my health, especially as regards those unpleasantnesses and troubles that I endured during the last years of my service."[62]

Leonova's memoirs and personal file provide a different sort of backstage view from that in literary diva tales, which consider salary disputes and medical leaves of less interest than romantic entanglements and theater-troupe intrigues. Despite its immodest use of the modesty trope, Leonova's autobiography presents a new model of diva conduct, a professionalism and independence hinted at but never fully realized in Verbitskaia's *The Abandoned Man*.

Professionalism also serves as a central preoccupation in the reminiscences of the operetta diva Alexandra Smolina, whose artistic career lasted from the early 1880s until the 1930s. Smolina makes the language of love into a metaphoric code for theatrical life. She declares the theater her best lover, a turn of phrase that captures one of the essential diva dilemmas: "For fifty years I belonged completely to the theater, and gave it [him] all my strength and love—and it [he] let me go when I ceased to be necessary to it [him]."[63] Although the nouns "opera" and "operetta" in Russian are grammatically gendered as feminine, and these two musical genres are often personified as women, Smolina chooses to characterize her career in relation to the Russian masculine noun "theater" (*teatr*). She reserves the relationships of stepmother and mother for opera and operetta, respectively. Of the Medved'ev Opera Theater, where Smolina got her start, the diva writes, "with such a love, one loves a very sweet, tender, and affectionate stepmother." But, operetta, the site of Smolina's greatest triumphs, "for me was my own mother."[64] Smolina constructs herself entirely from her relationship with the theater; she is its child and loving wife. Her memoirs do correspondingly little to enlighten the reader about her family background or her personal life.

The reader learns only that at age sixteen, Smolina worked in a tobacco factory, as if rehearsing to play Carmen, and that soon afterward, she became a member of the Kazan Opera Chorus at a salary of fifteen rubles per month. After working her way up to playing small solo parts, Smolina joined an operetta troupe in 1885. Her illiteracy, which obliged her to learn all new parts by ear, was the primary reason for this decision. In the operetta troupes of Smolina's time, she claims, "conversations about genres, styles, and other lofty subjects were extraordinarily rare."[65] Instead, as Smolina relates, she could rely on a repertoire of gestures and intonations that were guaranteed to please her audience.

In spite of Smolina's demurrals about her knowledge of the generic hierarchy, she uses this very hierarchy to assert a place for her beloved operetta in an overall generic scheme. She warns of the generic pitfalls inherent in operetta, where "one wrong step . . . will transform operetta into a fairground show-booth," and insists that "the best of us never lost a sense of moderation on stage."[66] But if operetta languishes as a lowly member of the generic hierarchy, it also creates an appealing, upside-down world where the serious becomes funny, and vice becomes virtue: operetta "laughed at the deceived husband and encouragingly winked at his wife." Operetta becomes a stand-in for Smolina herself, who turns the social hierarchy on its ear by becoming a grande dame of the stage.[67] Smolina's dreams for herself, described in retrospect, interweave the superlatives of the world of grand opera with the terminology of the provincial operetta theater, making reference to these hierarchies while simultaneously subverting them: "And a 'star' loomed ahead in my imagination. And this star was I, Shura . . . no, Aleksandra Alekseevna Smolina—operetta prima donna, star of the first magnitude, variety-show diva. . . . This was something to make one's head spin, even an especially practical head like mine."[68]

Smolina's vision of a herself as a star marries the vocabulary of grand opera to that of popular operetta, creating such hybrid terms as "operetta prima donna" (*operetochnaia primadonna*) and "variety-show diva" (*kaskadnaia diva*). Smolina enacts semantically the blurring of both generic and social hierarchies that represents the opera diva's most striking literary feature.

Smolina's irreverent autobiography contrasts with a tearful piece about the operetta diva V. A. Liadova, written by her son many years after her death. A graduate of the St. Petersburg Theater Institute, Liadova was famous in the 1860s for her tasteful performances of the title role in Offenbach's *La Belle Hélène*. Her son, in collaboration with the editors of the journal *Evening Time*, canonizes the diva as an exemplary public citizen and a model mother. The editors characterize her positive re-conception of the operetta diva as uniquely Russian: "The Russian Elena, having placed a candle in the chapel of the Savior, spending the night before a performance in tears and prayers, kissing the icon and crossing herself backstage—is this not a rare, a touching, a truly Russian 'genre?'"[69] Liadova's public image comes to the reader framed by her son's idealizing rhetoric and the insertions of the journal's editorial board, both of which legitimize operetta by linking it with religious ritual and the sanctity of motherhood. Represented primarily by the written accounts of others and not by her own, the opera diva was cast according to writers' own literary and ideological projects.

The Russian actress proved decidedly more forthcoming in writing about herself than did the Russian opera diva, as evidenced by a steady stream of actresses' autobiographical accounts at the turn of the century and during the early Soviet period. Maria Savina, who reigned at the St. Petersburg Aleksandrinskii Theater from the mid-1870s until the years preceding the Revolution, produced a book-length memoir of her early life and career, titled *Sorrows and Wanderings*.[70] Savina clearly relished depicting her younger self, devoting separate chapters to childhood, youth, stage debut, first love, marriage, provincial theater experience, early years in St. Petersburg, and foreign travels. Savina's one-time rival at the Aleksandrinskii, the populist actress Polina Strepetova, wrote at length in her memoir, *Fleeting Days*, about the first part of her career, from the mid-1860s through the 1870s, when she performed in the provinces. The actress Alexandra Shubert wrote substantial reminiscences about her life on the stage in St. Petersburg, Moscow, and the provinces from the 1840s through the early 1880s. Maria Ermolova of Moscow's Malyi Theater represents an exception to the Russian actress's passion for writing. Ermolova was famously close-lipped, and seems to have destroyed her entire archive to preserve her privacy. A few pages from her schoolgirl diary are all that escaped the conflagration.[71] Full-length autobiographical accounts by Russian actresses from the final part of the imperial period also include those of provincial actress Maria Velizarii, private theater actress Alexandra Glama-Meshcherskaia, and Vera Michurina-Samoilova, who hailed from the famous theatrical dynasty of Samoilov. These book-length treatments convey abundant personal revelations and ruminations on women's experiences in the Russian dramatic theater.

The autobiographies of writers Anastasia Verbitskaia and Tatiana Shchepkina-Kupernik offer a suggestive accompaniment to the collection of Russian actresses' autobiographies.[72] Both Verbitskaia and Shchepkina-Kupernik came from families involved in the dramatic theater, and their writing evolved naturally out of this environment. Verbitskaia authored two volumes of self-promoting autobiography, as well as literary works devoted to female stage performers. Shchepkina-Kupernik's autobiography, *The Days of My Life*, disproportionately concerns itself with her recollections of theater life in Moscow. Writing and the dramatic theater go together; writing and the opera stage apparently do not. The lithographic and photographic representations of opera divas at their writing desks (discussed in chapter 3) turn out to be autobiographical fictions.

The Russian diva's failure to provide an adequate written account of herself also forms a contrast to the two volumes of autobiographical writings left by Russia's most famous opera performer, the bass Fedor Chaliapin.[73] Chaliapin's first volume, *Pages from My Life*, emphasizes his early life, while the second, *Mask and Soul: My Forty Years in the Theaters*, as the title suggests, provides a retrospective view of his stage career and what he himself terms a more "analytical" perspective on himself. *Mask and Soul*, the better-known volume, was translated into a number of different languages following its 1932 publication in Paris.

Chaliapin's autobiographies are vividly expressive and idiosyncratic. *Mask and Soul* exhibits a particularly sharp awareness of itself as a literary work. In contrast to the actress-autobiographers discussed here, Chaliapin composed an author's preface to *Mask and Soul* that addresses the very fact of his literary endeavor. The author describes himself looking into the mirror and transcribes a long speech he makes to his reflection about his wanderings across Russia, which begins self-mockingly with the vocative address "Most worthy and illustrious Fedor Ivanovich." He acknowledges his participation in an established genre of self-documentation, while offering the fiction that he truly serves as his own addressee: "As is proper in such circumstances, the "speaker" gave me a pleasant anniversary present—a gold fountain-pen; I was so touched by all this that I promised myself to remember and rethink the experience of those forty years and tell about it to all who care to listen, but primarily to myself and my children."[74]

Chaliapin goes on to characterize the theater as the "magic crystal" through which he saw Russia, and compares his actor's angle of vision on the curious individuals whose paths he has crossed to that of the "Grand Duke watching the performance at the Hermitage theater."[75] He blurs the distinction between spectator and performer by declaring these individuals to be "also Russians, also actors on the Russian stage, although in different roles." Compared to most of the Russian actresses who composed autobiographies, Chaliapin was more resourceful about finding ways to describe the immediacy of theatrical and operatic effects. Even so, he ends his preface with the following ingenuous claim: "If it is appropriate for an author to speak of the quality of his labor, I should like to say that first and foremost I have striven . . . for complete truthfulness. I appear [*vystupaiu*] before the reader without stage make-up [*bez grima*]."[76]

Chaliapin's autobiography differs from the full-length accounts of Savina, Strepetova, Shubert, and others precisely in the author's awareness of writing as literary art, despite his claims to the contrary. His frequent recourse to the term "mask" in fact speaks to his discomfort about the very possibility of conveying an unvarnished truth. As he himself points out, the theater provides him with a magical refracting mechanism that turns life into literature.

IN CONCLUSION

Since genre is one of the ways in which literary works establish the bounds of narrative territory, it is not surprising that Russian diva tales exceed generic classifications. Diva tales often bring themselves to a conclusion by killing off their heroines or sending them into permanent exile. Russian diva heroines try to author new stories for themselves, but end up divested of familiar narrative apparatus. These literary divas lack both a suitable story-space and an established set of generic conventions that they can observe or violate. Instead, diva heroines enact multiple roles on stage, temporarily donning aspects of these well-worn narratives, but ultimately eluding incorporation into a generically defined context. Precisely because the diva seems overdocumented, not to mention overdetermined by the well-established plots of opera *and* literature, she manages to evade these tired tropes and trajectories, boarding a train and riding away, beyond the story's borders.

The diva tale in Russian literature plays itself out as a confrontation between role and identity. To survey this literary territory is to reenact the narrative strategy so many of these works employ: to attempt to fix the opera diva within a single generic landscape, and to admit defeat. In its own way, this admission of transcendence represents a latter-day bouquet, offered as a tribute to the diva.

But in opera's case, the conclusion is a different one. Regarding opera and its travels throughout the Russian cultural landscape, particularly in nineteenth-century St. Petersburg, it can be asserted that Russians made Western opera their own. While certain stories and motifs from Western opera proved initially resistant to Russian aesthetic and cultural mores, creative adaptations and reinterpretations allowed Russians to integrate this tradition over the course of the nineteenth century. The sum total of meanings for "opera" in Russia are among the most richly synthetic of all the opera-going nations. And this operatic aspect is central to an understanding of urban culture in nineteenth-century Russia. Opera-going culture does need to be written in order to be constituted as a subject and as an object of study. But it is also true that the travels of opera in imperial Russia, as relayed in writing, trace the outlines of Russian culture itself.

Appendix
Russian Texts

Nekrasov—"Ballet"

Например, как волшебно прекрасен
Бельэтаж—настоящий цветник!
Есть в России еще миллионы,
Стоит только на ложи взглянуть,
Где уселись банкирские жены,—
Сотня тысясь рублей, что ни грудь!
В жемчуге лебединые шеи,
Бриллиант по ореху в ушах!

Pushkin—"Onegin's Journey"

А только ль там очарований?
А разыскательный лорнет?
А закулисные свиданья?
А prima donna? а балет?
А ложа, где красой блистая,
Негоцианка молодая,
Самолюбива и томна,
Толпой рабов окружена?
Она и внемлет и не внемлет
И каватине, и мольбам,
И шутке с лестью пополам . . .
А муж—в углу за нею дремлет,
В просонках фора закричит,
Зевнет—и снова захрапит.

Grigor'ev—"Chipping in for a Box at the Italian Opera"

Кто в опере, тот чувствует все блага!
Тот на виду, да и в чести большой,
А если нет, тот и смешон и скряга,
И человек решительно дурной!

Pleshcheev—"To Desdemona"

Меж тем как шум рукоплесканья
И кликов залу оглашал.
Лишь я один сидел в молчанье,
Ничем восторг не выражал.

Я не бросал тебе букеты.
Не бросил я тебе венок;
Но стих созрел в душе поэта—
Прими же: вот и мой цветок!

"Ode on the Occasion of a Fourth Subscription to the Italian Opera"

Куда текут народа шумны волны
В дни покаяния, молитвы и поста?
Все так встревожены, все нетерпенья полны;
Глаза огнем горят, безмолвствуют уста . . .
Не возмутились-ли все бедствием народным,
О коем разнеслась по всей России весть?
Не братьям-ли спешат они помочь голодным
И жертву на алтарь Отечества принесть!

Но чтож причиною борьбы такой гигантской?
Нет, не голодных здесь спасать народ спешит!
То жертва опере несется итальянской—
Четвертый на нее абонемент открыт.
Вот как искусство мы глубоко уважаем!
В годину бедствия готовы все забыть . . .
Несем последний грош, бока себе ломаем,
Лишь только-бы билет на оперы добыть.

Benediktov—"Madwoman"

«Я все еще его, безумная, люблю».
«Я все еще» . . . едва лишь три ты эти слова
Взяла и вылила их на душу мою—
Я все предугадал: душа моя готова
Уже заранее к последнему: «люблю».
Еще не сказано: «люблю», а уж стократно
Перегорел вопрос в груди моей: «Кого?».
И ты ответствуешь: «Его». Тут все понятно;
Не нужно имени—о да, его, его! . . .

Nekrasov—"About the Weather"

Вспомним—Бозио. Чванный Петрополь
Не жалел ничего для нее.
Но напрасно ты кутала в соболь
Соловьиное горло свое,
Дочь Италии! С русским морозом
Трудно ладить полуденным розам.

Перед силой его роковой
Ты поникла челом идеальным,
И лежишь ты в отчизне чужой
На кладбище пустом и печальном.
Позабыл тебя чуждый народ
В тот же день, как земле тебя сдали,
И давно там другая поет,
Где цветами тебя осыпали.
Там светло, там гудит контрабас,
Там по-прежнему громки литавры.
Да! на севере грустном у нас
Трудны деньги и дороги лавры!

Notes

The following source abbreviations appear in the notes:

RGALI	Russian State Archive of Literature and Art
RGB	Russian State Library
RGIA	Russian State Historical Archive
RNB	State National Library
SPbGMTMI	St. Petersburg State Museum of Theater and Musical Art

Chapter 1

1. Eric Buyssens proposed operatic performance as an ideal object for semiotic study, since operatic form encompasses such a number of different communicative codes. See *Les langages et le discours*, p. 56.

2. von Geldern and McReynolds, p. xiv.

3. "Middlebrow" is primarily a twentieth-century notion, which nineteenth-century specialists now attempt to apply retrospectively to their fields of study. As Joan Shelley Rubin points out, many cultural critics in mid-twentieth-century America derided the middle element as a contaminating agent that corrupted *both* elite intellectual and unpretentious worker with its vulgar, commercial interests. This view of the middlebrow represented a rejection of the earlier possibilities the cultural middle offered as a majority audience for serious art. See Rubin, introduction.

4. Gerhard, p. 4.

5. Herbert Lindenberger provides an unparalleled survey of aesthetic pronouncements on opera, drama, and music in *Opera in History*. See the chapter "Opera Among the Arts, Opera Among Institutions."

6. For a discussion of French *tragédie lyrique* and its successor, *grand opéra*, see Gerhard.

7. de Certeau, pp. xii–xiii.

8. For an excellent summary of the early history of the Russian theater, see Simon Karlinsky, *Russian Drama from its Beginnings to the Age of Pushkin.*

9. See Richard S. Wortman, "The Return of Astraea and the Demonstration of Happiness," and "Minerva Triumphant," in *Scenarios of Power: Myth and Ceremony in Russian Monarchy: From Peter the Great to the Death of Nicholas I,* vol. 1.

10. This schedule appears in S. V. Taneev's article "Iz proshlogo imperatorskikh teatrov," p. 854.

11. "Theatre d'Odessa. Norma," *Journal d'Odessa* (1/13 February 1838), no. 9.

12. "Smes'. Pis'mo ob ital'ianskoi opere v Peterburge," *Sovremennik* t. 12 (1848): 33–34.

13. Vol'f, p. 141.

14. Greenblatt, p. 7.

15. Greenleaf and Moeller-Sally, p. 1.

16. See the essays in *The Semiotics of Russian Cultural History*, eds. Alexander D. Nakhimovsky and Alice Stone Nakhimovsky, particularly Iu. M. Lotman, "The Poetics of Everyday Behavior in Eighteenth-Century Russian Culture" and "The Decembrist in Daily Life."

17. Greenblatt, p. 12.

18. See Iu. M. Lotman, *Besedy o russkoi kul'ture*, and Todd, *Fiction and Society*, p. 7. According to Todd, the cultural practices of the early nineteenth century "aestheticized the everyday life of the Westernized gentry" such that "[s]ocial gatherings became aesthetic forms, and literary patterns served as models for behavior and its interpretation."

19. E. Shepard, p. 139.

20. Ibid., p. 135.

21. Sources on social-anthropological approaches to performance include Goffman, Schechner, and Turner.

22. Susan McClary, "The Undoing of Opera: Toward a Feminist Criticism of Music," Foreword to Clément, *Opera*, p. xviii.

23. There is some evidence that only one-third of the opera subscribers for the Paris Opéra during the years following 1830 were from the nobility, for example (Gerhard, p. 28). In Russia, there would have been a majority of noble spectators in the opera theater during the entire first half of the nine-

teenth century. Opera owed its predominance in Russia partly to the fact that the symphonic concert came to rival opera much later in Russia than in Western Europe. See Ridenour, pp. 12–14.

24. D. Levin, pp. 14–15.

25. Lindenberger, *Opera: The Extravagant Art*, p. 20. Lindenberger "confronts" opera in his book with the terms "drama," "representation," "novel," and "society."

26. Iu. M. Lotman's remarks on balls in nineteenth-century Russia apply equally well to the opera in this respect: "A ball was, on the one hand, a sphere in opposition to that of professional service—a region of unforced interaction, societal leisure, a place where the boundaries of the service hierarchy were relaxed. . . . On the other hand, a ball was a region of public representation, a form of social organization, one of the few forms of collective life permitted in Russia of that time" (p. 91).

27. Taruskin, *Defining Russia Musically*, p. 225.

28. Theodor Adorno makes this point in his famous 1959 essay "Bourgeois Opera," mentioning the sudden inventions of both opera and film, their "presentation of the body of common knowledge to the masses; as well as the massiveness of the means, employed teleologically in the material of opera as in film" (pp. 31–32). For a treatment of film's impact on Russian audiences, see Yuri Tsivian, *Early Cinema*.

29. de Certeau, p. 117.

30. Dmitriev, p. 8.

31. Sviridenko, p. 4.

32. Adorno, "Bourgeois Opera," pp. 40–41.

33. Ibid., p. 39.

34. Stakhovich, p. 195.

35. de Marinis, p. 63.

Chapter 2

1. As Herbert Lindenberger points out, opera existed as an international system from the late seventeenth century onward: "During much of this time the system was dominated by the reigning Italian style of the moment, with Italian-language companies . . . resident within a triangle defined by London, St. Petersburg, and Naples." *Opera in History*, p. 131. Note that America

offers an instructive parallel to Russia in its own importation and assimilation of opera. Like Russia, eighteenth- and nineteenth-century America was a country remote from Europe that nonetheless defined its national and cultural identity in relation to what it perceived as "Europe." See Dizikes, and Preston.

2. Tsar Nicholas I imposed strict censorship on the performance of Western operas with perceived political content. Some works, such as Rossini's *William Tell*, had to be rewritten and renamed by Russian librettists before they could be staged in Russia. See Taruskin, *Defining Russia Musically*, pp. 192–94.

3. Skal'kovskii, *V teatral'nom mire*, p. 249.

4. Vol'f, p. 170.

5. Iakhontov, p. 743.

6. Bernatskii, p. 18.

7. Recent theoretical studies of opera-going have themselves adopted these nostalgic framing strategies, taking on the shapes of opera accessories and memorabilia. Catherine Clément's *Opera, or the Undoing of Women* takes the form of a revisionist opera-lover's handbook, while Wayne Koestenbaum's *The Queen's Throat: Opera, Homosexuality, and the Mystery of Desire* models itself as a personal scrapbook.

8. For a treatment of the fetish as reified, personalized, "territorialized" historical object, see Pietz, as well as Apter and Pietz.

9. Theodor Adorno declares that opera has retained a certain audience in the twentieth century by virtue of an ersatz nostalgia. Opera appeals to those who treasure "the legendary Golden Age of the bourgeoisie, to which the Iron Age alone lends a glamour it never possessed. The medium of this unreal memory is the familiarity of individual melodies, or, as in the case of Wagner, of insistent leitmotifs." See "Opera," pp. 81–82.

10. Zvantsev's letters are in RGALI, fond 763, op. 1, ed. khr. 1 (Moscow).

11. K. I. Zvantsev, "Pis'ma o G-zhe Viardo-Garsia," l. 25 (18 June 1853).

12. de Marinis, p. 158.

13. For an extended reading of the fictional spectator's role as co-producer of the operatic spectacle, see chapter 4.

14. *Odesskii vestnik* (15 January 1836), no. 5.

15. Raphael Zotov, "Teatral'naia khronika," *Severnaia pchela* (27 October 1849), no. 239.

16. Nikolaeva, p. 64.

17. See the chapter entitled "Emerald Thrones and Living Statues: Theater and Theatricality on the Estate" in Roosevelt for an illustrated survey of the private domestic theater in eighteenth- and nineteenth-century Russia.

18. For a good overview of Petersburg theaters, see Lukomskii, "Starinnye teatry Sankt-Peterburga." For information about the kinds of performances presented by the various Petersburg theatres, see Alianskii, *Uveselitel'nye zavedeniia starogo Peterburga*; Petrovskaia and Somina; Zolotnitskaia; and Vol'f. For an account of the way the Bolshoi theater divided its week among the various troupes and genres at the turn of the century, see Vigel'. For information about the Bolshoi Theater's early prices and schedules, see Bozherianov. For information on the history of the Bolshoi's various renovations, see Taranovskaia.

19. According to Marvin Carlson, the "traditional pictorial vocabulary" of classical deities and allegorical figures used for the nineteenth-century theater interior "provided a kind of cultural authentication as important as the authentication of value provided by the equally ubiquitous chandeliers, pier mirrors, draperies, gold trimmings, and marble. In these secular cathedrals pagan gods, goddesses, and allegorical figures embellished every available space, as representations of the saints had done in the great baroque churches." *Places of Performance*, p. 187.

20. For a parallel example of operatic influences in the "lexical anomalies" of surviving Paris city structures, see Gerhard, p. 17.

21. Consider the November 1833 opening of the Italian Opera House in New York, the first building in the United States exclusively designed for opera, and its closing after two disappointing seasons. The subsequent construction of the New York Academy of Music in 1854 and the Metropolitan Opera House in the early 1880s can be best understood in the context of American cultural politics. John Dizikes asserts that the primary reason behind the construction of the Met was the need to provide opera boxes for New York's growing number of moneyed families (pp. 214–17).

22. Skal'kovskii, *V teatral'nom mire*, p. 62.

23. Stakhovich, p. 20.

24. Butler, p. 12.

25. Dizikes, pp. 126–34. See also Lowell Gallagher, "Jenny Lind and the Voice of America," in Blackmer and Smith.

26. Diamond, pp. 1–2.

27. Carlson, *Performance*, p. 2. Carlson provides a wide-ranging study of the various structures for theater in the Western world from classical antiquity to the present. He is particularly concerned with the theater's relationship to its surrounding urban context and its meaning within the urban "text."

28. See Herbert Lindenberger's *Opera: The Extravagant Art*, p. 235, for a discussion of the relationship between opera-theater architecture and nineteenth-century imperial culture.

29. Grossman, p. 14.

30. Barkhin, p. 25.

31. Nikolaeva, p. 51.

32. M. M. Ivanov, "Proshloe ital'ianskogo teatra," p. 67.

33. Carlson, *Places of Performance*, pp. 137–40.

34. Danilov, "Postoiannye publichnye teatry," pp. 153–57.

35. Zotov, *Teatral'nye vospominaniia*, p. 22.

36. Shakespeare's plays include similar asides to audience members from specific areas of the theater, as representatives of particular theatergoing subcultures.

37. V. A. Losskii, *Opernye memuary* (undated) Arkhiv teatral'nogo muzeia Bakrushina, fond 53, delo 309285, list 14 (Moscow).

38. Grossman, p. 20.

39. "Novyi konets Don Zhuana," *Severnaia pchela* 8, (December 1838), no. 279.

40. Skal'kovskii, *V teatral'nom mire*, p. ix.

41. Ibid., p. x.

42. N. A. Geineke, *Iz vospominanii opernogo teatrala (1888–1917)*, Arkhiv teatral'nogo muzeia Bakrushina, fond 53, delo 7, list 15 (Moscow).

43. Skal'kovskii, *V teatral'nom mire*, p. xii.

44. Golovacheva-Panaeva, pp. 115–16.

45. *Zhizn' v svete, doma i pri dvore* (St. Petersburg, 1890), cited in von Geldern and McReynolds, p. 98.

46. N. A. Nekrasov, *Sochineniia v 3 tomakh*, vol. 2 (Moscow: GIXL, 1959).

47. Bulgarin, "Puteshestvie," pp. 176–77.

48. Ibid., p. 177.

49. Pustynnik, p. 727.

50. See *Fiziologiia Peterburga* (Moscow: Nauka, 1991), pp. 114–41.

51. Pustynnik, p. 729.

52. Ibid.

53. Pustynnik, p. 730.

54. Pustynnik, pp. 730–31.

55. Initially, operatic events were covered by various thick journals, *The St. Petersburg News* (the state daily newspaper), *Journal de St. Petersbourg* (the French-language newspaper produced by the Foreign Ministry), and Bulgarin's shrill, opinionated *Northern Bee*. Coverage of the opera and other theatrical performances grew much broader as the nineteenth century wore on. Periodicals became more specialized, and a number were devoted to musical and theatrical topics. Audiences for periodicals also became more diverse: the boulevard press produced two daily newspapers for lower-class urban Russians called *Petersburg Newspaper* and *Petersburg Leaflet*. For an account of the independent daily newspapers that appeared after the Great Reforms of the 1860s, see Louise McReynolds, *The News Under Russia's Old Regime*.

56. Zotov, *Teatral'nye vospominaniia*, pp. 3–4.

57. For additional background on the Italian opera in Russia, see the chapter entitled "Ital'ianshchina" in Taruskin, *Defining Russia Musically*.

58. For an account of the Russian press's attempts to create a star out of the young soprano Melas during the late 1820s Italian opera venture in St. Petersburg, see Vinitsky, "Signora Melas." Melas's story represents an early prototype of later opera celebrity cults in Russia, especially in the tropes mustered to describe her talent, which were already-established requisite features of the "Italian singer" in Europe. Melas was championed with particular fervor in *The Northern Bee* by its editor, Faddei Bulgarin.

59. Skal'kovskii, *V teatral'nom mire*, p. vii.

60. Pushkin, p. 226.

61. Vigel', 2: 228.

62. *Odesskii vestnik* (13 March 1843), no. 21. For a cultural history of the Italian opera in Odessa, see Katsanov.

63. Taruskin, *Defining Russia Musically*, p. 197.

64. Odoevskii, "Russkaia ili ital'ianskaia opera?" *Muzykal'no-literaturnoe nasledie*, p. 315.

65. V. V. Stasov, "Tormozy novogo russkogo iskusstva," p. 228.

66. Skal'kovskii, *V teatral'nom mire*, p. 23.

67. Ivanskaia, no. 11, p. 58.

68. Vol'f, p. 107.

69. Iakhontov, p. 743.

70. Ivanskaia, no. 12, p. 200.

71. Stakhovich, p. 20.

72. D. N. Mamin-Sibiriak, *Cherty iz zhizni Pepko. Russkoe bogatstvo*, 1894, no. 1, p. 69.

73. D. N. Mamin-Sibiriak, *Russkoe bogatstvo*, 1984, no. 3, p. 24.

74. Ibid., p. 25.

75. Pushkin's little tragedy *Mozart and Salieri* sets the precedent for these physical recontextualizations of opera culture. A blind fiddler in a tavern delights Mozart by playing themes from *Don Giovanni*.

76. Skal'kovskii, *V teatral'nom mire*, p. viii.

77. Vol'f, p. 112.

78. Iakhontov, p. 744.

79. Zotov, *Teatral'nye vospomaniia*, p. 82.

80. See also the 1833–34 vaudeville "The Imaginary Signora Melas, or Fanatico per la musica," and Nikolai Gogol's 1836 comedy "A Busy Man's Morning," as described in Vinitsky. In Gogol's comedy, the soprano Melas is invoked during a ridiculous conversation between two St. Petersburg bureaucrats.

81. This new trend in literature about the opera makes sense when we consider that "nothing more rigorously distinguishes the different classes than the disposition objectively demanded by the legitimate consumption of legitimate works, the aptitude for taking a specifically aesthetic point of view on objects already constituted aesthetically—and therefore put forward for the admiration of those who have learned to recognize the signs of the admirable" (Bourdieu, p. 40). Displaying an ironic awareness of the display of bad taste by lower-class Russian opera-goers itself became a marker of good taste.

82. Count Vladimir Sollogub, *Bukety, ili Peterburgskoe tsvetobesie* (St. Petersburg, 1845), p. 19.

83. P. I. Grigor'ev, *Skladchina na lozhu v ital'ianskie opery* (St. Petersburg, 1843), p. 14.

84. Ibid., p. 57.

85. Ibid., p. 73.

86. Ibid., p. 105.

87. Skal'kovskii, *V teatral'nom mire*, p. 52.

88. Ivanskaia, no. 12, p. 220.

89. Michel Poizat characterizes the pleasure opera provides in terms of a Barthesian jouissance in *The Angel's Cry*: "Musical pleasure is thus a strange pleasure indeed, and if in this study I come to speak of elation, ecstasy, or gratification—of jouissance—it is insofar as this jouissance is distinct from mere pleasure" (p. 4). Poizat's study was one of the first to make explicit the connection between opera and sexuality. Poizat does not limit operatic jouissance to sexual transport; he also links it to ecstatic worship of the divine and to the yearning for pure music (cry), a voice that has completely freed itself from language. For more on jouissance, see Roland Barthes, *Pleasure*.

90. "Ital'ianskaia opera. Nevesta lunatik (Somnambula)," *Sankt-peterburgskie vedomosti* (27 November 1843), no. 270.

91. Iakhontov, p. 740.

92. Skal'kovskii, *V teatral'nom mire*, p. 271.

93. Stakhovich, p. 199.

94. Kats, *Muzyka*, pp. 71–72.

95. Skal'kovskii, *V teatral'nom mire*, p. 272.

96. Ivanskaia, no. 12, p. 181.

97. David J. Levin suggests that the violence of operatic spectacles may reflect the cultural upheaval inherent in the transfer of power from aristocratic to bourgeois spheres: "The violence that underlies this transferal is often displaced onto the stage, where it forms the explicit stuff of operas, which thus feature a struggle for accession to political and social power, a struggle that is complicated by the unstable (read: potentially illegitimate) grounds of the claim to inheritance" (p. 15).

98. For a discussion of the "hooliganism" phenomenon in Russia and its appropriation of public space at the beginning of the twentieth century, see Neuberger.

99. Bertenson, pp. 276–80.

100. Alexander Amfiteatrov, *Sumerki bozhkov*, part II, Krest'ianskaia voina (1908), p. 397.

101. Bulgarin, "Filosoficheskie vzgliady za kulisy," *Russkaia Taliia*, (1825) p. 244.

102. V. G. Benediktov, *Sochineniia*, vol. 1 (St. Petersburg: M. O. Vol'f, 1902).

103. Skal'kovskii, *V teatral'nom mire*, p. xix.

104. Nikolaeva, p. 71.

105. For descriptions of nineteenth-century masquerades, see Beliaev, Danilov, Davydov, Mil'china, Nikolaeva, Taneev, and Taranovskaia. The idea of the masquerade as a staged performance that encompassed the entire theater influenced Meierkhold's 1917 production of Mikhail Lermontov's poem "Masquerade" in the Aleksandrinskii Theater. For a discussion of Meierkhol'd's conception in a broader sociocultural context, see Clark, *Petersburg*, pp. 74–99.

106. M. Iu. Lermontov, "Maskarad," *Polnoe sobranie sochinenii*, vol. 4 (Moscow: Academia, 1935), p. 259.

107. Count Vladimir Sollogub, "Bolshoi svet." In *Povesti. Vospominaniia* (Leningrad: Khudozhestvennaia literatura, 1988), pp. 67–68.

108. See Helena Goscilo, "Stage and Page" for a discussion of stage conventions used to structure Russian short stories of the 1830s, including carefully described visual gesture, explicitly theatrical self-consciousness, emphasis on costume, stage direction, dramatic props, eavesdropping, and stock characters. These conventions belong to the important role of dramatic metaphor in Russian Romantic metaphysics, which explicitly conceived of life as theater.

109. I am grateful to Caryl Emerson for articulating the cultural phenomenon of Russian "opera-space" and its provisional freedoms.

Chapter 3

1. The past two decades have seen an explosion of scholarship on the sociocultural significance of the Western opera prima donna and opera heroine, the most notorious of which are Catherine Clément's *Opera*, and Wayne Koestenbaum's *The Queen's Throat*. Other studies include Sam Abel, *Opera in the Flesh*, Leslie C. Dunn and Nancy A. Jones, eds., *Embodied Voices*, Susan J. Leonardi and Rebecca A. Pope, *The Diva's Mouth*, Susan McClary, *Feminine Endings*, and Michel Poizat, *The Angel's Cry*. Scholarly interest in this topic shows no signs of abating. The opera prima donna serves as a battle standard for many academic and theoretical causes: feminist revisions of cultural and literary history (Clément, Dunn, and Jones), challenges to the methodologi-

cal and ideological framework of traditional musicology (McClary), Lacanian psychoanalytic theory in viewing the female voice as one of the primary objects of human drives (Poizat), and queer studies (Koestenbaum, Abel, Leonardi, and Pope).

2. Mordden, pp. 18–21.

3. For a discussion of gendered national symbols, see chapter 5 in Mosse.

4. Skal'kovskii, *V teatral'nom mire*, p. 393.

5. A rare exception to the traditional separation between poetry deifying the prima donna and narratives of her movements in nineteenth-century culture is provided by George Eliot's dramatic poem "Armgart" from the 1870s, discussed in Blake, and in Leonardi. Eliot's poem, like so many prose works about the female performer, focuses on the prima donna's choice between love and art.

6. For a study of the actress in Russia during the period 1870–1910, see Schuler.

7. Kommissarzhevskaia's father, Fedor Petrovich, was a popular opera singer at the Mariinskii Theater.

8. See Catherine Schuler's account of Kommissarzhevskaia's unsuccessful 1908 tour to America. According to Schuler, Kommissarzhevskaia "not only performed in Russian, but deliberately maintained cultural markers that emphasized her connections with the Russian intelligentsia and the European avant garde" (p. 182).

9. "Smes'. Zhurnal'naia vsiakaia vsiachina. Luchiia," *Severnaia pchela* (4 December 1843), no. 271.

"But the most surprising thing of all, is that in a *new* role, Madame Viardot-Garcia did not recall *her former roles* with a single gesture or a single passage in singing . . . ! In a *new* role, everything is *new*! Unfathomable woman, creative genius!"

10. Wayne Koestenbaum amusingly juxtaposes two photographs of Patti, one as Norina in *Don Pasquale*, the other as Lucia in *Lucia di Lammermoor*. Although Patti wears different costumes, her poses in the two photographs are identical. Echoing many nineteenth-century opera critics, Koestenbaum declares that "Patti imperiously refuses to alter her gestures from role to role; and her indifference to realism thrills us." See Koestenbaum, p. 110.

11. "O zakliuchenii kontrakta s pevitsei Polinoi Viardo-Garsia, 1843–5," RGIA, fond 497, delo 9316.

12. See RGIA, "O sluzhbe aktrisy opernoi truppy Dar'i Leonovoi (1852–74)," fond 497, delo 13644.

13. "Odesskii teatr. Norma, opera Bellini," *Odesskii vestnik* (15 January 1836), no. 5.

14. A. A. Verbitskaia, *Pokinutyi* (Riga 1925/26), p. 134.

15. "Theatre d'Odessa. Reprise de la Norma," *Journal d'Odessa* (17/29 July 1836), no. 57.

16. Iu. Arnol'd, "Teatral'naia khronika," *Sanktpeterburgskie vedomosti* (25 October 1850), no. 247.

17. *Odesskii vestnik* (23 July 1853), no 83.

18. M. Sabinina, "Zapiski," *Russkii arkhiv* 2, kn. 6 (1900): 121.

19. "Ital'ianskaia opera v Peterburge," *Literaturnaia gazeta* 47 (30 November 1844).

20. Ivanskaia, no. 11, p. 71.

21. Thomas, p. 55.

22. The etymological deification of the opera diva comes full circle with Maria Callas in the twentieth century, called "La Divina" by her worshipful public.

23. Vol'f, p. 106. See also Stark, p. 26, and Ivanskaia, no. 11, p. 71.

24. V. I. Nemirovich-Danchenko, *Kulisy* (St. Petersburg, 1899), pp. 4–13.

25. For a discussion of the etymological history and contemporary meanings of the word "diva" in Russian, see I. L. Reznichenko's "Ustarelo li slovo 'diva'?" Reznichenko surveys the various definitions of "diva" in Russian references. He claims that the term has been renewed by regular, ironic usage in contemporary contexts, and concludes that the word "diva" is not antiquated, but that its official (non-ironic) definitions are.

26. Poizat, p. 180.

27. M. M. Ivanov, *Pervoe desiatiletie*, p. 25.

28. In fact, as Wayne Koestenbaum points out, "battling divas"—the fight for supremacy between two would-be prima donnas played out as public spectacle—represents a venerable tradition in opera-going culture (Koestenbaum, 113).

29. Pokhitonov, p. 154.

30. A. N. Davydov, "Vospominaniia o Patti," SPbGMTMI, rukopisnyi otdel: HBM 1195/5.

31. A. S. Pushkin, "Pikovaia dama," *Polnoe sobranie sochinenii v desiati tomakh*, vol. 6 (Moscow: Nauka, 1964), p. 328.

32. H. Sutherland Edwards, 2: 103–4.

33. For more information on the serf theaters, see Roosevelt; Senelick.

34. R. Zotov, *Teatral'nye vospominaniia*, pp. 74–88.

35. Stites, "The Domestic Muse," p. 191.

36. A few representative examples from RGIA fond 497 include delo 2534, "O sluzhbe pevitsy russkoi truppy Aleksandry Ivanovoi (1824–31)," delo 6024, "O sluzhbe pevitsy russkoi opernoi truppy Marii Stepanovoi (1833–54)," delo 12701, "O sluzhbe khoristki imperatorskoi truppy Anny Skvortsovoi (1850–66)," delo 12628, "O sluzhbe aktrisy opernoi truppy Karaliny Kolkovskoi (1850–79)," delo 14099, "O sluzhbe aktrisy russkoi opernoi truppy Ekateriny Malyshevoi (1853–81)," and delo 14561, "O sluzhbe aktrisy russkoi opernoi truppy Anis'i Bulakhovoi po teatru Lavrovoi (1854–76)."

37. See Asenkova, "Kartiny proshedshego: Zapiski russkoi artistki."

38. Taneev, "Iz proshlogo imperatorskikh teatrov," p. 865.

39. Grossman, p. 10.

40. Golovacheva-Panaeva, p. 52.

41. For a treatment of "travesty" roles in the larger context of opera and gender, see Blackmer and Smith.

42. "Russkii teatr v Sankt-Peterburge. Bol'shoi teatr," *Literaturnoe pribavlenie k russkomu invalidu* (15 October 1837), no. 42.

43. It is instructive to think about Russia's attempts to produce its own homegrown prima donnas in light of Judith Butler's, Ann Pellegrini's, and other recent treatments of gender, race, and nationality as *performative* and *citational.* The Russian prima donna becomes herself by literally "acting it out."

44. Sviridenko, pp. 47–48.

45. See Bartlett.

46. Verbitskaia, *Pokinutyi*, p. 13.

47. Skal'kovskii, *V teatral'nom mire*, p. 26.

48. H. Sutherland Edwards, 1: 230.

49. For more information about Zhemchugova's life, see Iazykov, and Elizarova.

50. Vol'f, p. 139.

51. Ivanskaia, no. 2, p. 210.

52. Vol'f, pp. 136–37.

53. Patti's life and career were characterized not only as opera but as a novel in the very conception of the extremely free biographical account by Vakano, entitled *Roman Adeliny Patti po angliiskim, ispanskim i ustnym istochnikam*, published in Russia in 1875. Vakano's biography contains long stretches of dialogue and description, as if it were a work of fiction. The claim to authenticity based on legitimate sources made explicitly by the title of the book also suggests that these sources, as well as Patti herself, were complicit in shaping her story into a novel.

54. Vigel', 1: 336.

55. Meshcherskii, p. 496.

56. For example, M. M. Ivanov's two-part series on the Italian opera in St. Petersburg, covering the period 1843–63, contains detailed information on the fees received by singers in the troupe. See "Pervoe desiatiletie postoiannogo ital'ianskogo teatra v Sankt-Peterburge v XIX veke (1843–53)" and "Proshloe ital'ianskogo teatra v Peterburge v XIX veke. Vtoroe desiatiletie (1853–63).

57. See RGIA, fond 497, delo 12701, "O sluzhbe khoristki Imperatorskoi truppy Anny Skvortsovoi (1850–66)," and delo 13644, "O sluzhbe aktrisy opernoi truppy Dar'i Leonovoi (1852–74)."

K. I. Skal'kovskii observes that female dancers received 400 to 1,200 rubles a year, but provided a historical context for this figure in pointing out that it was approximately the same salary received by male officers and clerks, and twice as much as that of governesses and teachers, the other paying female occupations of the time. Skal'kovskii also claims that this 40–1,200-ruble figure must be evaluated when considering that these dancers generally lived at home with their families, and were therefore not responsible for supporting a household (Skal'kovskii, *V teatral'nom mire*, p. 61).

58. Vigel', 1: 180–81.

59. Ivanskaia, no. 12, p. 195.

60. Vol'f, pp. 126–28.

61. See Walter Benjamin's famous essay, "The Work of Art in the Age of Mechanical Reproduction."

62. See Beth Holmgren's essay "Gendering the Icon" for a fascinating reading of similarly commodified visual representations of women writers.

According to Holmgren, the new images of the female writer were part of "a general tendency toward embodying, sexing, materializing, and even theatricalizing the person of the writer" (p. 327). See also Laura Engelstein's chapter entitled "From Avant-Garde to Boulevard: Literary Sex" in *The Keys to Happiness.*

63. For an important treatment of the relationship between the detail, the aesthetic, and the feminine, see Schor. Schor examines the detail's participation not only in the aesthetics of realism, but in a "larger semantic network, bounded on the one side by the *ornamental,* with its traditional connotations of effeminacy and decadence, and on the other, by the *everyday,* whose 'prosiness' is rooted in the domestic sphere of social life presided over by women. . . . The detail does not occupy a conceptual space beyond the laws of sexual difference: the detail is gendered and doubly gendered as feminine" (p. 4). Another source for the semiotics of self-presentation and gendered identity through the details of fashion is A. Hollander, *Sex and Suits.*

64. Grav. P. Kurenkov, *Iskra* (25 August 1861), no. 32, p. 453.

65. "Zametka," *Sanktpeterburgskie vedomosti* (22 December 1845).

66. I. S. Turgenev, *Polnoe sobranie sochinenii i pisem v dvadtsati vos'mi tomakh,* vol. 13 (Moscow: Nauka, 1967).

67. Pavlovsky, pp. 150–51.

68. Stakhovich, p. 184.

69. As Beth Holmgren points out, visual representations of the Russian writer often "posed a writer 'at work' (reading, writing, or looking pensive) and toured the grounds of his or her desktop, study, library, house, and local landscape" (p. 328).

70. P. I. Tchaikovskii, "O kontsertakh gospozhi Patti," in *Muzykal'nye fel'etony i zametki P. I. Tchaikovskogo (1868–76 gg.),* p. 257.

71. Tchaikovskii remarks about Carlotta Patti prefigure the actual operatic representation of the prima donna as a mechanical doll in Offenbach's *The Tales of Hoffmann* (1881). In the first act of this opera, the young student Hoffmann falls in love with the doll Olympia, who amazes her listeners with coloratura feats.

Chapter 4

1. The most important studies of opera and representation include Conrad's *Romantic Opera,* Kerman's *Opera as Drama,* and Lindenberger's *Opera: The*

Extravagant Art. Jean-Jacques Nattiez's *Music and Discourse* returns to the ancient problem of music and meaning, using recent theories of culture and the sign.

2. Marco de Marinis's *The Semiotics of Performance* has provided much of the theoretical basis for my discussion of the spectator's creative contribution to representations of the operatic scene. His study presents performance and reception as more than derivatives of the literary or musical text, as elusive objects of study that must be reconstituted from cultural context and synchrony.

3. Viktor Shklovskii cites precisely this passage from Tolstoi as an example of the way that art makes its audience perceive an object anew, rather than allowing them to simply "recognize" this object. See pp. 8–9.

4. Tolstoi, *War and Peace*, p. 498.

5. L. N. Tolstoi, "Letter to P. I. Bartenev, 1 November 1867," in V. G. Chertkov, ed., *Polnoe sobranie sochinenii*, vol. 61 (Moscow: Gosudarstvennoe izdatel'stvo "Khudozhestvennaia literatura," 1953), p. 180.

6. Edward Wasiolek writes of Tolstoi's "devastatingly bitter" satire of opera, "Tolstoy alienates our sympathy by what one might call an extreme realism. It is a kind of faithful and stupid realism, where the viewer refuses to go along with the illusion that art demands" (p. 108). In the passage cited, "the viewer" refers to Natasha. But it seems to me that the text encourages the reader to assume Natasha's narrative perspective as the scene progresses. The estranged perspective on the operatic spectacle that the reader might initially resist comes to feel like home.

7. Gozenpud, "Natasha Rostova na opernom spektakle," pp. 120–23. Some Tolstoi scholars differ with this reading. David Lowe, for example, sees Tolstoi's historically anachronistic literary "opera" as evidence of Tolstoi's general lack of knowledge about the kinds of operas staged in Moscow of the 1812 period. Lowe traces the operatic motifs in Tolstoi's description and contrasts these with the operatic works that Natasha might actually have seen.

8. de Marinis, p. 80.

9. Consider also Roland Barthes's essay "From Work to Text," in which the author characterizes textual play, in contrast to consumption, as that which joins reading and writing into a single signifying practice:

> *reading*, in the sense of consuming, is far from *playing* the text. 'Playing' must be understood here in all its polysemy: the text itself *plays* (like a

> door, like a machine with 'play') and the reader plays twice over, playing the Text as one plays a game, looking for a practice which re-produces it, but, in order that the practice not be reduced to a passive, inner *mimesis* . . . , also playing the Text in the musical sense of the term." (p. 162)

Here, Barthes re-conceives the reader as a practicing amateur, one for whom "playing" and "listening" are almost the same activity.

10. Klenov's reception of Pasta as Norma may have been complicated by Petersburg's perception of the aging prima donna as both *the* Norma and as merely the latest in a *series* of Normas. Bellini created the role of Norma for Pasta herself, who gave the role its first performance in 1831. Owing to Petersburg's remoteness from the European opera capitals, however, *Norma* reached Russian audiences only in 1836, and Pasta arrived five years after that. The role of Norma, like Pasta herself, was at once old and new for its Russian audience.

11. N. V. Kukol'nik, "Tri opery," in *Sochineniia Nestora Kukol'nika*, vol. 3 (St. Petersburg, 1852), p. 101.

12. Kukol'nik, pp. 130–31. Klenov is here in accord with the reviewer, who, in evaluating Pasta's 1841 performances, chastises the Russian public for being critical of her failing powers. Like Klenov, this reviewer cites Pasta's ability to transcend the mutual incomprehensibility between words and music: "we demand from the first female singer that she be without fail a good actress, and besides, be young and beautiful . . . Madame Pasta has realized the idea of poets and composers of genius: she has transfused drama (that is, life) into sounds, and given to sounds the meaning of thought and feeling." From "Bol'shoi teatr. Ital'ianskaia opera. Gospozha Pasta v roliakh Normy, Semiramidy i Anny Bolen," *Severnaia pchela* (14 May 1841), no. 104.

13. Kukol'nik, pp. 125–26.

14. Ibid., pp. 132–33.

15. A. A. Grigor'ev, "Robert-D'iavol (iz zapisok diletanta)." *Vospominaniia* (Moscow, 1988), p. 177.

16. Ibid., p. 178.

17. Some literary scholars consider Grigor'ev's "Robert le Diable" an autobiographical work, in part because it is included in a volume of his memoirs. Grigor'ev's long poem "Encounter" (1846) also includes references to a performance of Meyerbeer's *Robert le Diable*.

18. Meyerbeer's opera was extremely popular in Russia during the 1830s and 1840s. As Raphael Zotov declared, "Who among the lovers of music does not

know the entire score of this lofty creation by heart! . . . Who has not delighted in these divine sounds, which shake every fiber of the most coarsened heart, which enflame the coldest imagination!" *Severnaia pchela* (10 February 1848), no. 32.

19. Grigor'ev, p. 183.

20. A poem by Petr Ershov entitled "Music" (1840) also describes the spectator's experience of the overture from Meyerbeer's *Robert le Diable*. Ershov's version invokes a "magical temple" in which the lyrical self is borne aloft into the realm of the imagination upon waves of music. As in Grigor'ev's case, Ershov's poem posits an identity between the fallen spirit of Bertram and the listening consciousness of the narrator. See *Biblioteka dlia chteniia*, vol. 40, 1840, ch. 1 (Russkaia Slovesnost'), pp. 7–9.

21. Russian translations of Hoffmann's "Don Juan" appeared in March 1833 in the literary supplement to the newspaper *The Odessa Herald*, and then in 1838 in *The Moscow Observer* (vol. 16). More important, a translation of Hoffmann's sketch appeared in 1840 in volume 2 of the new journal *Pantheon*, which was close in conception to the journal *Repertoire and Pantheon*, in which Apollon Grigor'ev 's "Lucia" and "Robert le Diable" appeared six years later. Pushkin's 1830 drama *The Stone Guest* may also have been inspired to some degree by the original version of Hoffmann's "Don Juan."

For information about the publication and translation of Hoffmann's works in Russia, see Ingham.

22. For a summary of the ways in which Hoffmann's rereading of Mozart departs from traditional interpretations of *Don Giovanni*, see R. Murray Schafer, *E. T. A. Hoffmann and Music*, pp. 59–62. For a discussion of the problematics of interpretation posed by Hoffmann's text itself, see David E. Wellbery, "E. T. A. Hoffmann and Romantic Hermeneutics," pp. 455–73.

Note that V. F. Odoevskii concurred with Hoffmann's reinterpretation of Donna Anna's role, which makes central her love for Don Juan, declaring that "From the time of Hoffmann, few singers understood the role of Donna Anna in this sense, for they looked for it in the text and not in the music." See Odoevskii, p. 244.

23. "Don Juan, or A Fabulous Adventure that Befell a Music Enthusiast on his Travels," in *Tales of Hoffmann*, (New York: Heritage Press, 1943), p. 106.

24. Ibid., p. 108.

25. Ibid., p. 110.

26. Ibid., p. 108. As Herbert Lindenberger points out, the diva has interpreted Donna Anna as the narrator-composer wished. Her death can thus "be attributed to her having misinterpreted several lines of her part as a prophecy of the opera character's death." Lindenberger here refers to Donna Anna's request to Don Ottavio that they postpone their marriage for a year, and to the narrator's conviction that she will not survive that year and the prospect of marrying someone other than Don Juan. See *Opera: The Extravagant Art*, p. 181. James M. McGlathery similarly sees the soprano's death as confirming her clairvoyant understanding of the narrator's radical interpretation of Mozart's opera. See p. 21.

27. For a discussion of Hoffmann's story as a dramatization of the author's attempt to convey his creative and interpretive relationship with Mozart-the-creator to the reader, see Greenleaf, pp. 314, 324–35.

28. For a description of Bauer's work in films, see McReynolds, "The Silent Movie Melodrama," and "Home."

29. Grigor'ev, p. 186.

30. One of the most interesting aspects of Bauer's *Daydreams* is that, although the resemblance between Elena and Tina is a central premise for the film, the two women are in fact played by two different actresses. Bauer's use of two actresses emphasizes the idea that Nedelin's desires exaggerate the affinities between Elena and Tina. Verkhovtseva, the actress playing Elena, appears in the deathbed scene, in two visitations, and in the memory-vision of Nedelin and Elena walking in the park. Chernobaeva, the actress playing Tina, appears in all the other scenes.

31. For a brief account of Alchevskaia's efforts as a proponent of popular education and literacy, see J. Brooks, pp. 323–24.

32. In 1912, in commemoration of Alchevskaia's fifty years of service as a pedagogue, a volume of her writings appeared in print. In a brief preface, the editors note that these samples of her writing represent a tiny fraction of her voluminous output in diaries, letters, and notes, and were selected to give the reader a sense of her widely ranging interests and activities. The editors refer to the ambiguous nature of these "private" documents, declaring that they were written "either for herself, or for a close circle of friends or colleagues." In fact, Alchevskaia's writings (not unlike Dostoevskii's *Diary of a Writer*) encompass a broad spectrum of written genres: descriptions of her remembered meetings with Dostoevskii, Tolstoi, and Turgenev, "rural sketches" in a moralistic, naturalistic vein, sentimental reminiscences about school-holiday

celebrations, and dramatic impressions of wounded men she encountered at the time of the Russo-Turkish War. See Alchevskaia: *Peredumannoe i perezhitoe.* This volume does not include the 1892 account of the Mariinskii performance of *Eugene Onegin*, although it does describe several days spent in Moscow during the same trip.

33. "Otryvok iz dnevnika Kh. D. Alchevskoi (Oktiabr' 1892)," SPbGMTMI, rukopisnyi otdel: KP 3202/2, ORU–7. Since the Theater Museum holds only a handwritten transcription of Alchevskaia's diary entry, future citations will not include page references.

34. Alchevskaia, *Peredumannoe i perezhitoe*, p. 261.

35. Alchevskaia herself had served as something of a Russian cultural ambassador, when she spent three months at the Paris World's Fair in 1889, as described in a speech delivered to a conference of teachers (ibid., pp. 285–406).

36. As many critics have noted, Pushkin's novel does not actually provide specific details about Tatiana's appearance. The Tatiana cult is based on readers' assumptions about how she looked, especially in comparison with the "moon-faced" Olga.

37. Note that Alchevskaia's reportage here only roughly approximates Tchaikovskii's own stage directions for the opening act of *Eugene Onegin.* This strategy prefigures Alchevskaia's habit of (mis)quoting by memory, and illustrates her insistence on describing her personal response to the opera, even as she posits this response as a cultural norm.

38. For a discussion of the range of cultural referents a reader of Pushkin's own sophistication could derive from the novel *Eugene Onegin*, see Todd, "Eugene Onegin: 'Life's Novel,'" in *Fiction and Society.*

39. Iu. M. Lotman, *Roman v stikhakh Pushkina 'Evgenii Onegin'* (Tartu, 1975), pp. 92–108.

40. For an original, alternative reading of the novel's final encounter between Onegin and Tatiana, as well as a discussion of Tatiana as a central, received image in the Russian literary tradition, see Caryl Emerson's "Tatiana," pp. 6–20. Emerson sees Tchaikovskii's opera as a "crucial stage in the maturation of the cult" regarding Tatiana.

41. Hoisington, *Russian Views*, p. 6.

42. In fact, Alchevskaia's mode of cultural enshrinement and pedagogy continues to structure contemporary Russian perspectives on Pushkin's novel.

See, for example, the presentation of *Eugene Onegin* in cultural context for literature teachers in Kozhevnikov.

43. Asaf'ev, *Izbrannye trudy* 2: 89–90.

44. Gozenpud, "Pushkin i russkaia opernaia klassika," p. 6. This point is made unintentionally ironic by the fact that Turgenev himself did not condone the changes Tchaikovskii made in Pushkin's text. But Tchaikovskii does update Pushkin's Tatiana more or less according to the model of the Turgenevian heroine in Russian literature, at least if this model is compared to the "infernal" Dostoevskian heroine. See I. S. Turgenev, "Letter to L. N. Tolstoi, 15 November 1878," *Polnoe sobranie sochinenii i pisem*, t. 12, kn. 1 (1876–78) (Moscow: Izdatel'stvo akademii nauk SSSR, 1966), pp. 383–84.

45. Nabokov, 2: 333, 530.

46. Kerman, *Opera as Drama*, pp. 59–63.

47. Carl Dahlhaus finds that with the "dissolution of periodic structure" in music, this quintessentially Romantic nineteenth-century art form responded in a limited way to the realist tendencies of the times. See pp. 120–21.

48. In an unfinished article from 1944, for example, A. Al'shvang traces the narrative development of Dostoevskii's novel *Crime and Punishment* in terms of symphonic structure, pointing out that both Dostoevskii's novel and Tchaikovskii's First Symphony appeared in 1866. See A. Al'shvang, pp. 73–97.

49. As Caryl Emerson notes, "setting prose to music was not just an aesthetic task; it was a whole world view, a means by which art could pay tribute to real experience." See *Boris Godunov*, pp. 163–70.

50. Schmidgall, p. 237.

51. Zhekulin, p. 285.

52. Taruskin, *Defining Russia Musically*, pp. 54, 245–46. Taruskin makes the older women's concluding maxim, adapted from Chateaubriand, serve as a kind of epigraph to *Eugene Onegin* itself: "Habit is given to us from above as substitute for happiness."

53. Tynianov, pp. 68–75.

54. Taruskin, *Opera and Drama*, p. x. This citation is from V. N. Pogozhev, "Vospominaniia o P. I. Tchaikovskom," in I. Glebov, ed., *P. I. Tchaikovskii: vospominaniia i pis'ma* (Petrograd: Gosudarstvennaia akademicheskaia filarmoniia, 1924), p. 78.

55. Strakhov, p. 373.

56. Jakobson, p. 44. Jakobson is citing a pronouncement by Dostoevskii that can be found in the *Polnoe sobranie sochinenii*, vol. 13, p. 540.

57. Taruskin, *Defining Russia Musically*, p. 54.

58. M. I. Tchaikovskii, vol. 2.

59. M. Ivanov, "Muzykal'nye nabroski," *Novoe vremia* (11 February 1880), no. 1421.

60. "Fel'eton. Muzykal'naia letopis'," *Russkaia pravda* (14 [26] December 1878), no. 75.

61. S. Kruglikov, "'Eugene Onegin,' opera P. I. Tchaikovskogo," *Artist*, kn. 2 (October 1889).

62. Ibid.

63. En-En. "'Evgenii Onegin,' opera P. I. Tchaikovskogo," Pis'mo k redaktoru, *Sankt-Peterburgskie novosti* (6 ([18] April 1879), no. 93.

64. "Fel'eton. Muzykal'naia letopis'," *Russkaia pravda* (14 [26] December 1878), no. 75.

65. The strict distinction between recitatives and arias is most characteristic of eighteenth-century opera seria. Nineteenth-century opera made huge strides in giving recitative-like passages greater expressive scope. Tchaikovskii can rightly be considered to have contributed to this advance.

66. S. Kruglikov, "'Evgenii Onegin,' opera P. I. Tchaikovskogo," *Artist*, kn. 2 (October 1889).

67. See Belinskii's famous article on Pushkin's *Eugene Onegin* as an "encyclopedia of Russian life," published in the journal *Notes of the Fatherland* in 1844.

68. See Hoisington, *Russian Views*, for English-language translations of these twentieth-century accounts of the novel.

69. "Moskovskii fel'eton," *Novoe vremia* (16 December 1878), no. 1007. Note that Catherine Clément places special emphasis on the jam in the opening scene of *Evgenii Onegin*: "This is certainly the only opera that starts with preserves. This jam. . . . How could anyone imagine it is the key to *Eugene Onegin*?" By the end of the opera, "The curtain falls on youthful loves; the girl is gone. The time to make preserves has come" (pp. 79–82). Clément finds a new sort of poetry in the domestic scene of making preserves, using this detail as the key to a fresh reading of the opera.

70. "Moskovskie nabroski," *Russkaia pravda* 55 (26 July 1879).

71. "Fel'eton. Muzykal'naia letopis'," *Russkaia pravda* 75 (14 [26] December 1878).

72. Taruskin, *Defining Russia Musically*, p. 244.

73. Asaf'ev, "'Evgenii Onegin,'" p. 37.

74. Ibid., pp. 38–39.

75. Ibid., p. 8.

76. In contrast, Richard Taruskin characterizes the Russian art song as a mix of Western and Russian musical "morphemes" that matched Tchaikovskii's own mixed, Europeanized musical sensibility. See *Defining Russia Musically*, p. 52.

Chapter 5

1. Linda Hutcheon and Michael Hutcheon summarize the Western cultural associations for tuberculosis, romantic creativity, love, and erotic appeal in *Opera: Desire, Disease, Death*.

2. Roland Barthes terms the love between Marguerite and Armand "the archetype of petit-bourgeois sentimentality" (*Mythologies*, p. 104). For an elaboration of bourgeois mores and practices, see Perrot.

3. For a summary of the difference in status accorded the Italian opera troupe and the Russian opera troupe during the 1850s in Petersburg, see Ridenour. For an acount of the performances of *La Traviata* connected with the tsar's coronation, see M. M. Ivanov, "Proshloe ital'ianskogo teatra."

4. Rostislav, "Muzykal'nye besedy. Novaia opera Verdi 'La Traviata,'" *Severnaia pchela* (13 November 1856), no. 252. Note that Catherine Clément makes Verdi's use of waltzes central to her reading of *La Traviata*: "Waltzes. Slow waltzes, loving or sad—even the cadence is stifling; brilliant, breathless waltzes, propelled by hidden legs rushing across waxed floors. Trival, vulgar, rotten waltzes. . . . Who whirls like this in a three-beat rhythm, in a heart passing from one to the other, in alternating current, from arm to arm? The *Traviata*'s way of the cross is not made up of sorrowful stations on a straight, uphill road. She spins from waltz to waltz, scarcely settling, like a tired bird, long enough to catch her unhealthy breath. . . . She waltzes her sorrow and her days; she embodies the dancer in the secret schemes of the seated bourgeoisie, who adorn her, dress her, undress her, and prostitute her." See pp. 60–61.

5. Rappaport, "Bol'shoi teatr. 'Traviata,' opera Verdi," *Muzykal'nyi i teatral'nyi vestnik* (28 October 1856), no. 43.

6. A. N. Serov, "'La Traviata,' opera Verdi," *Muzykal'nyi i teatral'nyi vestnik* (11 November 1856), no. 45.

7. A. de H., "'La Traviata,' debut de Mlle. J. Altieri," *Journal d'Odessa* (5/17 August 1860), no. 90.

8. This outburst was treated indulgently by the reviewer, who admitted "It is true that the furniture is gilded and of an utterly splendid red color." Theatre d'Odessa, *Journal d'Odessa* (8/20 August 1860), no. 91.

9. M. R. (Rappaport), "Teatral'naia letopis'," *Syn otechestva* (28 April 1868), no. 17. Government censors felt similarly about Dumas's play *La Dame aux camélias* (1849), on which the opera was based. The play was banned from the Russian stage until the 1867–68 season, more than ten years after the Russian premiere of Verdi's *La Traviata*. For a notice of the play's first performance in Russia, see Vol'f, p. 158.

10. (Cui), "Muzykal'nye zametki," *Sanktpeterburgskie vedomosti* (4 May 1868), no. 120.

11. H. Sutherland Edwards, p. 119.

12. The elusive quality in constructions of Marguerite's identity as a woman across the various generic incarnations that depict her is the subject of Roland A. Champagne, "My Cup Runneth Over: The Semiotic States of the Courtesan Myth in the Metamorphoses of Marguerite Gautier."

13. Joseph Kerman, "Opera, Novel, Drama," p. 48.

14. Verdi scholar Julian Budden writes of *La Traviata*: "Marguerite Gauthier . . . as Violetta Valery . . . is nobler still—a kept woman, a *demi-mondaine*, but not necessarily promiscuous. . . . Violetta, idealized as she is, becomes in Verdi's hands intensely human and yet heroic as well; and no one need feel the loss of the novel's realistic detail. . . . Dumas's play remains a faded period drama needing the talents of a great actress to restore it to life; *La Traviata* is an undying masterpiece." See Budden, *The Operas of Verdi*, p. 121.

15. G. A. Larosh, "Muzykal'naia khronika," *Moskovskie vedomosti* (29 October 1869), no. 235.

16. "Peterburgskaia letopis'. Novaia drama vnushennaia 'Traviatoi,'" *Sanktpeterburgskie vedomosti* (25 November 1856), no. 259.

17. A. N. Serov, "'La Traviata,' opera Verdi," *Muzykal'nyi i teatral'nyi vestnik* (11 November 1856), no. 45.

18. M. P. (Rappaport), "Teatral'naia letopis'," *Syn otechestva* (28 April 1868), no. 17.

19. "Muzykal'naia khronika," *Moskovskie vedomosti* (17 October 1875), no. 264.

20. M. Rappaport, "Teatral'naia letopis'," *Teatral'nyi i muzykal'nyi vestnik* (5 October 1858), no. 39.

21. "Peterburskaia letopis', Bosio v 'Traviate,'" *Sanktpeterburgskie vedomosti* (18 November 1856), no. 254.

22. Jules Leconte, "Parizhskie pis'ma," *Sanktpeterburgskie vedomosti* (18 March 1855), no. 61.

23. "Teatry," *Teatral'nyi i muzykal'nyi vestnik* (24 November 1857), no. 46.

24. Note, however, that Petersburg may have been initially unreceptive to Bosio because she was married to a Greek merchant. As M. M. Ivanov relates, "our theater-lovers, who considered Bosio for some reason a 'Hungarian' or a 'housemaid' (they heard the unpronounceable name of her husband), at first were indifferent to her." See "Proshloe ital'ianskogo teatra," p. 73.

25. H. Sutherland Edwards, 2: 42.

26. Ibid., 2: 39–41.

27. Neznakomets, "No. 8 ital'ianskogo abonementa. Traviata," *Antrakt* (28 April 1868), no. 16.

28. *Muzykal'nyi svet* (July 1859), no. 7.

29. I. S. Turgenev, "Letter to I. A. Goncharov, 7 April 1859," in *Polnoe sobranie sochinenii v 30 tomakh*, vol. 4 (Moscow: Izdatel'vsto akademii nauk SSSR, 1987), p. 37.

30. "Peterburgskaia letopis'—Bolezn' i konchina pevitsy Bosio. Neskol'ko slov o nei," *Sanktpeterburgskie vedomosti* (5 April 1859), no. 75.

31. "Dnevnik Grafa Petra Aleksandrovicha Valueva (1847–1860)," *Russkaia starina* (August 1891): 274–75.

32. Entry for 1 April, 1859. Reprinted in B. Modzalevskii, *Biriuch petrogradskikh gosudarstvennykh teatrov* (December 1918), no. 5, p. 31.

33. Note that members of the Petersburg Italian opera troupe actually did sing Mozart's Requiem at Bosio's funeral, an event that could well have been the original inspiration for Voevodskii's story.

34. M. M. Ivanov, "Proshloe ital'ianskogo teatra," p. 73.

35. Golovacheva-Panaeva, p. 120.

36. Golovacheva-Panaeva's story of Bosio's elderly admirer resonates with a paragraph in the theater chronicle of the otherwise decorous Vol'f, who, upon reporting Bosio's death, includes a description of an aged prince who was passionately devoted to the prima donna: "The loss of the beloved woman finally

clouded the old man's reason, and he, just like a Nebuchadnezzar, imagined himself transformed into an animal, crawled on all fours, and wanted to eat only from a trough; he did not long outlive the object of his last love." (Vol'f, p. 112).

37. A. N. Serov, "Ocherki o muzyke v pis'makh," letter to M. P. Anastas'eva, 7/19 April 1859. *Russkaia starina* 20 (1877): 534.

38. "Melochi. Dva poklonnika talanta Bozio," *Razvlechenie* (25 April 1859), no. 16, p. 188.

39. "Pis'mo I. Kokoreva k M. P. Pogodinu," RGB, rukopisnyi otdel, fond 231, karton 15, ed. khr. 106, l. 11.

40. "Konchina Andzhioliny Bozio," *Teatral'nyi i muzykal'nyi vestnik* (5 April 1859), no. 14.

41. Kats, *Osip Mandelshtam*, p. 10.

42. Bernatskii, pp. 22–23.

43. Bosio's monument was inscribed with the following verses:

Elle avait tout ce qu'on envie;
Elle reçut tout en naissant,
Tout, excepté la longue vie,
Elle est morte en la commençant!
La mort, jalouse de sa gloire,
Brisant un avenir si beau,
N'ensevelit pas sa mémoire
Sous le marbre de ce tombeau.
Elle n'est plus, sa gloire reste;
Dieu le veut, respectons ses loix;
Dans les anges du choeur céleste
Il manquait, sans doute, une voix!

44. See Kobak, pp. 560–62.

45. *Russkii khudozhestvennyi listok* (1 May 1859), no 13.

46. G. Verdi, *La Traviata*, English National Opera Guide (John Calder: London, 1981), p. 69.

47. "Teatral'noe obozrenie," *Severnaia pchela* (2 March 1861), no. 50.

48. "Muzykal'nye zametki," *Sanktpeterburgskie vedomosti* (4 May 1868), no. 120.

49. M. P. (Rappaport), "Teatral'naia i muzykal'naia letopis'," *Novoe vremia* (16 November 1870), no. 315.

50. "Vnutrennie novosti," *Golos* (7 December 1876), no. 338.

51. S. Ivanskaia, "Byloe nashei ital'ianskoi opery (okonchanie)," *Kolos'ia* (December 1889), no. 12, p. 197.

52. "Moskovskaia zhizn'," *Golos* (30 April 1868), no. 119.

53. For a treatment of the "fallen woman" in the mid-Victorian literary tradition, see Anderson. For two good summary accounts of the Russian tradition, see Siegel and Matich. For reflections on the relationship between plot and female protagonist in Russian literature, see Hoisington, ed., *A Plot.*

54. Anderson, p. 10.

55. Siegel, p. 99. Siegel is particularly good on this aspect of the Russian literary tradition. He surveys texts by Gogol', Nekraskov, Chernyshevskii, Krestovskii, Garshin, Tolstoi, Chekhov, and Gorkii.

56. Matich, p. 337.

57. In *La Traviata*, Alfredo wounds the Baron during their duel, and is obliged to go abroad for a time. Leskov's story repeats the motif of the hero defending the heroine's honor, which has been called into question.

58. Here Olga seems to be reprising the role of Emma Bovary, who has a similar experience at a performance of *Lucia di Lammermoor.*

59. M. V. Krestovskaia, *Artistka*, p. 229.

60. See Catherine Clément for remarks about this "distressing chapter" as a rite of passage in the life of a young male bourgeois (p. 64).

61. See A. Skabichevskii, "M. V. Krestovskaia," *Novoe slovo* (September 1896), no. 12.

62. As Jane Costlow observes, the city of Venice itself provides "an uncomfortable aesthetic identification of beauty, death and youth" that parallels the associations between Violetta and Insarov. See p. 96.

63. Lindenberger, *Opera: The Extravagant Art*, p. 178.

64. Irene Masing-Delic sees Turgenev's novel in terms of a different operatic subtext: "Insarov, a hero whose vision of the world is dramatically altered through love, shows a profound affinity to the hero of Wagner's opera *Tristan and Isolde.*" See "Metaphysics of Liberation."

65. Costlow does not read the ending of Turgenev's novel as heroic or affirmative, claiming that Turgenev qualified the heroic project in terms of the lyric by "bringing his final hero, Elena, to a consciousness of solitude and indeterminacy." According to Costlow, "The sole trace preserved is literary,

the sole memory is the artist's" (p. 102). I am arguing for a redefinition of heroic, as well as for a merging of oppositions like heroic/lyric, public/private, and male/female in the novel.

66. For a study of the ways in which Chernyshevskii's novel blends life and art, see Paperno, *Chernyshevsky*.

67. N. G. Chernyshevskii, *Chto delat'?* (Moscow-Leningrad: Akademiia, 1937), p. 208.

68. Bosio did occasionally perform Russian romances, to the public's great delight—a tradition continued by Adelina Patti.

69. For a discussion of the parallels between Dostoevskii and Dumas in this scene, see Rayfield, pp. 76–80. See also J. Frank, pp. 322 and 339.

70. F. M. Dostoevskii, *Polnoe sobranie sochinenii v 30 tomakh*, vol. 8 (Leningrad: Nauka, 1973), p. 11.

71. See the chapter entitled "The Saintly Whore" in Dalton for a discussion of the ambiguities in Nastasia's image.

72. L. N. Tolstoi, *Voskresenie. Polnoe sobranie sochinenii v 90 tomakh*, vol. 32 (Moscow-Leningrad: Gosudarstvennoe izdatel'stvo "Khudozhestvennoi literatury," 1933), p. 301.

73. For a perceptive reading of Bauer's cinematic innovations and their contribution to the telling of this story on film, see McReynolds, "The Silent Movie Melodrama."

74. K. G. Paustovski, "Muzyka Verdi," *Sobranie sochinenii v 6 tomakh*, vol. 4. (Moscow, 1959), p. 506.

75. I am grateful to Caryl Emerson for pointing out this unexpected affinity.

76. Paustovskii, p. 509. Note that Verdi's opera was originally performed in costumes of the seventeenth-century Venetian court, a performance tradition that continued into the twentieth century.

77. Inber's account of her libretto appears in her article "Shkaf s portretami (vospominaniia)" in *Teatr* 11 (1963), no. 11, 97–104.

Chapter 6

1. See Lindenberger, *Opera in History*, pp. 107–33, for an analytical overview of such pronouncements, from Count Algarotti and Schelling through Hegel, Wagner, and Nietzsche.

2. Kerman, *Opera as Drama*, p. 10.

3. Clément, p. 22.

4. Caryl Emerson provides support for this affinity in pointing out that music—and by extension, musical drama and opera—"must happen in real time, and it is accretive: like prosaic values and prosaic habits, music accumulates in its effects and wholeness. It also must be *performed* in an ongoing present, not merely completed by the artist and then gazed at by the spectator" ("Prosaics in *Anna Karenina*," p. 165). On the other hand, Emerson finds literature to diverge from the immediacy of music, in that literary works remain with their readers in tangible, material form. Literary narrative is moreover not always up to the challenge of fully conveying events after the fact. In this sense, literature seems less "prosaic" than music.

5. Mikhail Bakhtin, p. 39.

6. Litvak, p. 61. Litvak claims that theatricality in the nineteenth-century novel simultaneously enables and subverts "various coercive cultural mechanisms," and that the self in this literature is "not just a text but a contingent cluster of theatrical roles" (pp. xi–xii).

Nina Auerbach similarly unmasks a hidden theatricality in the ostensibly anti-theatrical culture of nineteenth-century British private life. See *Private Theatricals*.

7. Fisher and Fisher, p. 109.

8. Diment, p. 3.

9. Ivan Goncharov, *Oblomov*, trans. David Magarshack (New York: Penguin Books, 1983), p. 453.

10. Beth Holmgren argues differently in her essay "Questions of Heroism." Holmgren extends the radical nineteenth-century critic Dobroliubov's valorization of Olga, suggesting that Olga is heroinic because she is not satisfied by the conventional resolutions to a woman's plot: a loving husband, a good marriage, and motherhood. According to Holmgren, Olga points toward unrealized possibilities for heroinic spiritual development.

11. Irene Masing-Delic discusses the Pygmalion myth in connection with Goncharov's novel in her essay "Creating the Living Work of Art." Masing-Delic characterizes Olga as Pygmalion in relation to Oblomov's Galatea, but as a "realist intelligentsia" Galatea in relation to her husband Stolz.

12. Goncharov, p. 361.

13. See Dobroliubov's famous essay on *oblomovshchina*, "What is Oblomovitis?"

14. For a treatment of the structure of space in *Oblomov* as an artistic whole, see Löve.

15. Goncharov, pp. 194–95.

16. Ibid., p. 179.

17. See Goldstein for an insightful reading of a scene between Oblomov and Agafya Matveevna that emphasizes the transformative properties of the kitchen environment.

18. Goncharov, p. 178.

19. Ibid., p. 311.

20. Ibid., pp. 428–29.

21. See Monika Greenleaf's discussion of Charskii's luxuriously appointed room and elaborate costume in *Pushkin and Romantic Fashion: Fragment, Elegy, Orient, Irony*. The affinity with Gogol's hero was also inspired by a link Greenleaf made between Pushkin and Pliushkin during a 1996 talk at Harvard.

22. Goncharov, p. 15.

23. Ibid., p. 249.

24. Ibid., p. 482.

25. For a treatment of framing techniques and *ecphrasis* in *Anna Karenina*, see Mandelker. See also D. Herman.

26. Gary Saul Morson discusses Anna's story in terms of her narrative narcissism, emphasizing the novelistic fatalism and foreshadowings that Anna uses to structure her own story. This fatalism leads to a lack of responsibility on Anna's part concerning her own life plot, which she mistakenly perceives as art. For Morson, one of the greatest differences between Anna and Tolstoi's other characters is her sense of the structured nature of time, expressed in generic terms as romantic novel or melodrama.

27. L. N. Tolstoi, "Chto takoe iskusstvo?" In V. G. Chertkov, ed., *Polnoe sobranie sochinenii*, vol. 30, (Moscow: Gosudarstvennoe izdatel'stvo "Khudozhestvennaia literatura," 1951), pp. 129–30.

28. Gozenpud, "Natasha Rostova," p. 113. For accounts of Tolstoi's musical tastes and experiences, see Gusev and Gol'denveizer, and Paliukh and Prokhorova.

29. See Mandelker, particularly part 1.

30. Morson, "Anna Karenina's Omens," pp. 150–51.

31. Translated excerpts are all taken from the Norton Critical Edition, ed. George Gibian (New York: Norton, 1970). This passage appears on p. 3.

32. Ibid., pp. 37–38.

33. Ibid., p. 38.

34. Gina Kovarsky argues that Tolstoi provides the reader with a moral education in *Anna Karenina* by drawing him or her into a relationship with the novel's characters at key moments. The reader is seduced into mimetically reproducing characters' flawed moral responses (smiling indulgently, feeling contempt, being attracted, intoxicated, etc.), and is then made conscious of this susceptibility. The reader is urged to relinquish this morally faulty (but understandable) response in favor of an ethical sense of compassion.

35. Many critics view the contrasting story lines of Anna and Vronskii versus Kitty and Levin in terms of genre and narrative. See Armstrong, Eikhenbaum, Evans, and Wasiolek, among others. Judith Armstrong makes the interesting observation that the language used to describe and discuss Levin is largely "untroped," whereas Anna's story "is thickly scattered with metaphors, similes, and symbols." Armstrong, p. 85.

36. Tolstoi, *Anna Karenina*, p. 117.

37. Ibid., p. 124.

38. Vronskii attended the Theater Bouffe on Alexander Square, which featured visiting French operetta artists. Bouffe continued to be popular up until the Russian Revolution. St. Petersburg had a French bouffe in the 1880s at the Restaurant Cascade, a summer bouffe on the Fontanka Canal, and a winter bouffe on the Admiralty embankment during the pre-revolutionary years of the twentieth century. See Alianskii, *Uveselitel'nye zavedeniia starogo Peterburga.*

39. Tolstoi, *Anna Karenina*, p. 36.

40. Ibid., p. 47.

41. Ibid., p. 51.

42. Ibid., p. 67.

43. Ibid., p. 118.

44. Ibid., p. 117.

45. Ibid., p. 279.

46. Ibid., p. 423.

47. Caryl Emerson offers a different reading of Vronsky, declaring that he

becomes "increasingly pragmatic in his relations with her, aware of himself, and responsible. He develops prosaically" ("Prosaics in *Anna Karenina*," p. 171). "Prosaics" refers to Gary Saul Morson's work on an anti-systemic way of reading a particular kind of text. "Prosaics" is counterpoised to the rule-based Aristotelian notion of "Poetics," which values lyric and epic poetry above other literary forms. Prosaics is oriented toward process, "a way of thinking about human events that focuses on the ordinary, messy, quotidian facts of daily life" and "offers a reason to take novels with renewed seriousness" ("Prosaics: An Approach," p. 516).

48. Tolstoi, *Anna Karenina*, p. 706.

49. This sort of ending had been treated ambiguously by Pushkin in his much earlier work "The Shot" (1830). Pushkin's anti-hero Silvio dies in a suicidal mission to liberate Greece from Turkey in 1821.

50. I offer this interpretation as a complement to the work by Armstrong, Mandelker, and others on the prevalence of static portrait and sculptural images used to characterize Anna. Armstrong does describe Anna as a *hero* because of her quasi-divine attributes: "Obviously, Anna is invested with this quality of 'extra.' Not only does she outshine every other woman in the novel, she is also more vital, more noticeable, more commanding of attention than any of the males, including Levin and Vronsky" (Armstrong, p. 120).

51. Tolstoi, *Anna Karenina*, p. 121.

52. Ibid., p. 498.

53. Ibid., part v, ch. 33, pp. 495–96.

54. Ibid., p. 54.

55. Ibid., p. 499.

56. Ibid., p. 272.

57. Ibid., p. 679.

58. See the chapter entitled "The Execution of Anna Karenina: Heroines Framed and Hung," in Mandelker for a provocative survey of the deaths chosen by nineteenth-century literary heroines, and these deaths' various symbolic and historical meanings.

59. Gary Saul Morson sees the novel's ending differently, declaring, "One might say that Anna Karenina dies from a lack of prosaics, from her attempt to base her life with Vronsky entirely on passion and the excitement of desire" ("Prosaics: An Approach," p. 524).

60. A. S. Pushkin, *Polnoe sobranie sochinenii v 10 tomakh*, vol. 6 (Moscow: Nauka, 1964), p. 560. For a discussion of Tolstoi's fascination with Pushkin's prose during the 1870s, see Eikhenbaum, pp. 147–56. Eikhenbaum claims that a remark made about Zinaida by a guest in the Pushkin fragment could have served as the epigraph to *Anna Karenina*: "There is much good in her, and much less bad than people think. But her passions will destroy her."

61. Tolstoi, *Anna Karenina*, p. 376. I am grateful to Gina Kovarsky for sharing this observation with me.

62. The contemporary setting of Verdi's *La Traviata* was considered shocking when the opera received its premiere in 1853. As a result, it was often performed in the costume of Louis XIV's France, and only gradually came to be set in the nineteenth century. Adelina Patti played Violetta in a contemporary ballgown, a choice that seemed daring to Russian opera audiences of the 1870s.

63. Tolstoi, *Anna Karenina*, p. 1.

64. For an exploration of eighteenth-century libertinism and its connection with Tolstoi's novel, see Goscilo, "Tolstoy."

65. Romans 12:19.

66. Ian Saylor treats the reference to Mozart's *Don Giovanni* as specifically intended to illuminate the meaning of the epigraph to *Anna Karenina*. He points out that Anna actually attends a performance of Mozart's opera in an earlier draft of the novel, but leaves the theater upset, presumably by the opera's treatment of unrepentant sensuality. Saylor also links the glass tables with the arrival of the commendatore, who has been invited to dine by the Don.

67. James Rice traces the evolution of this literary dream from earlier variants of *Anna Karenina*. For Rice, "something better" indicates Stiva's wish to indulge in adultery without moral consequences, as well as his awareness of possible punishment. The little glass decanter-women in Stiva's dream are fragile, and, moreover, they sing of vengeance.

68. "Literatura i iskusstvo," *Kievlianin* (15 November 1906), no. 316.

69. Ibid.

70. L. N. Tolstoi, "Letter to N. N. Strakhov, 23 and 26 April 1876," in V. G. Chertkov, ed., *Polnoe sobranie sochinenii*, vol. 62 (Moscow: Gosudarstvennoe izdatel'stvo "Khudozhestvennaia literatura," 1953), p. 269.

71. Amfiteatrov's own early professional life mingled operatic and prosaic

concerns; during the period 1886–87 he lived in Milan and received training as an operatic baritone, while writing articles as a foreign correspondent for a Russian newspaper. Amfiteatrov played two seasons on provincial opera stages in Tiflis and Kazan. Toward the end of the 1880s, he decided to devote himself entirely to journalism and literary work, although he often returned to his beloved operatic themes.

72. Citations are from A. Amfiteatrov, *Sumerki bozhkov*, part 1, Serebrianaia feia (1908). This quotation appears on page 140.

73. A. A. Izmailov, "Vcherashnii den' v belletristicheskom zerkale. Roman Amfiteatrova 'Sumerki bozhkov,'" *Novoe slovo* (1909), no. 5.

74. Catherine Clément reflects upon the Queen of the Night precisely in terms of the music/language dialectic in opera: "The Queen of the Night is the only one who expresses herself in a part that is technically unbearable, untenable tessitura. It is an intransmissable language . . . she sings purely affective language far beyond the words stringing out the signified" (73). Svetlitskaia's monologue aims to emulate this affective musical aria with written words.

75. Amfiteatrov, *Sumerki bozhkov*, p. 151.

76. Ibid., p. 152.

77. Ibid., p. 172.

78. Ibid., p. 248.

79. Ibid., p. 259.

80. Ibid., p. 223.

81. Ibid., part II, Krest'ianskaia voina, p. 353.

82. Ibid.

83. Wagner's operatic cycle *The Ring of the Nibelungs* (completed in 1876), of which *Twilight of the Gods* is the final part, represents the culmination of these ideas. The *Ring* libretto itself is noteworthy from a literary standpoint, in that it "seeks a new linguistic mode to recapture the spirit of a lost national past," using philological studies as sources (Lindenberger, *Opera in History*, p. 135). Although Wagner's treatise singled out drama as the expressive form of supreme potential, the *Ring* bears a much stronger resemblance to the epic, a narrative of great temporal scope whose "national and communal functions" were largely assumed by the historical novel during the nineteenth century. But Wagner sought to transform epic by rendering it dramatic, primarily

through musical structures derived from the Beethoven symphonies (Lindenberger, *Opera in History*, pp. 134–59).

84. Ibid., p. 158.

85. For an extended treatment of the novel as deliquent genre, and of hegemony and discipline in the nineteenth-century English novel, see D. A. Miller.

Chapter 7

1. Consider the spectrum of literary and social roles accorded the opera prima donna in Offenbach's opera *The Tales of Hoffmann*, which transforms its diva heroine Stella into three different female characters through the narration of its male protagonist, while Stella herself is performing *Don Giovanni* in a nearby theater: the mechanical doll Olympia, the singing courtesan Giulietta, and the ingenue soprano Antonia. Each of the three disappoint Hoffmann, who becomes so drunk during the course of his narration that he misses his opportunity for a meeting with Stella.

2. The mythology of the female stage performer as a composite woman could occasionally take a lighter tone. The Koval'skie siblings' story "The Unsuccessful Woman" (1912) rewrites Chekhov's "The Darling" (1899) within a theatrical context. The "unsuccessful" woman adopts the theatrical orientation of each successive lover, transforming herself by turns into a graceful decadent, a daring realist, and a comedienne. At the story's conclusion, the heroine is alone, bereft of either artistic or personal identity. See the journal *Studiia (Zhurnal iskusstva i stseny)* 36–37 (23 June 1912).

3. This chapter limits itself to literary works that specifically concern the opera theater. There are numerous Russian literary works that feature nonoperatic female stage artists, particularly actresses and dancers, including Ostrovskii's plays *Talents and Admirers* (1882) and *Guilty Without Fault* (1884), Chekhov's play *The Seagull* (1896), and Verbitskaia's novel *The Keys to Happiness* (1909–13). The figure of the actress also makes frequent appearances in Western literary works from the nineteenth and early twentieth centuries.

4. Another example of opera's association with retrogressive, middlebrow art is Mikhail Kuzmin's notorious novel *Wings* (1906), the first extended treatment of homosexual themes in Russian fictional literature. The young protagonist Vanya Smurov undergoes a process of transformation and liberation, bracketed by two trips to the opera, where he attends performances of *Carmen* and *Tristan and Isolde*. These operas of heterosexual passion and transcendent

love provide no more than a scenic backdrop to Vanya's story, which constitutes a radical reworking of these operatic themes. The female stage performer in Kuzmin's two opera-house scenes is not even mentioned.

5. See "Vera Kholodnaia" and Louise McReynolds, " 'The Incomparable' Anastasiia Vial'tseva" for information about these two artists.

6. For background on the "Woman Question" in Russia, see Engel, Natalia Pushkareva, and Stites, *The Women's Liberation Movement*.

7. For purposes of comparison, it is worth mentioning some of the most notable of the Western literary works from the same period that fictionalize the opera prima donna. This tradition begins with Madame de Staël's novel *Corinne* (1807), and continues with George Sand's *Consuelo* (1842), George Eliot's poem "Armgart" (1870) and her novel *Daniel Deronda* (1876), George du Maurier's *Trilby* (1895), Gaston Leroux's *The Phantom of the Opera* (1911), and Willa Cather's *The Song of the Lark* (1915). Most of these works are discussed in Leonardi and Pope. See also my article "Novelistic Figuration."

8. M. V. Krestovskaia, "Lelia," *Ugolki teatral'nogo mirka* (St. Petersburg, 1889), pp. 374–75.

9. Krestovskaia's reviewers did not find the story's presentation of the heroine's decline at all ambiguous. One critic, for example, hailed the author's "masterful description of that social environment in which the purest souls are made dirty," declaring that "the very process of this contamination, drop by drop, step by step, constitutes the story of Lelia." See V. Kliushnikov, "Sovremennye belletristy. M. V. Krestovskaia," *Moskovskie vedomosti* (6 June 1889), no. 154. At this point in her career, Krestovskaia was hailed as a fresh new talent, a poet of Truth and Beauty. But her novel *Artistka* (1891), which portrays the aspirations of its actress heroine to live for her art, was poorly received.

10. In this sense, Russian diva tales correspond to Catherine Clément's view of opera as staging the defeat of transgressive elements: "The triumphant ones are the fathers, the kings, the uncles, the lovers. . . . Defeated are paganism with its many gods, the rebellious, desirable existence of the sorceress" (p. 22).

11. M. E. Saltykov-Shchedrin, *Gospoda Golovlevy. Sobranie sochinenii v 20 tomakh*, vol. 13 (Moscow: Khudozhestvennaia literatura, 1972), p. 156.

12. Ibid.

13. Consider this story as an attempt by its author to insert himself into the Russian literary tradition. Nekrasov wrote "The Female Singer" while struggling to complete his university studies in St. Petersburg. His florid, improb-

able story bears no resemblance to the civic poetry on contemporary Russian social themes for which he later became famous. Nekrasov's "The Female Singer" appeared in print during the same year as did his first collection of romantic poems (1840), which received unfavorable reviews.

14. By "narrative subject" I mean the subject actant or the narrative's fundamental role, as defined by A. J. Greimas. This term also corresponds to Lotman's notion of the "archipersona." The narrative subject strives to attain the narrative object, and the narrative trajectory typically establishes this subject as such. In Russian diva tales, the narrative object is often the achievement of narrative subjecthood. See Greimas and Courtes.

15. The Academy edition of Nekrasov declares that this story "has all the signs of a thing written exclusively under the influence of extreme circumstances and for money." Soviet cultural authorities found this story incompatible with the author's canonical image. See N. A. Nekrasov, "Pevitsa," in *Polnoe sobranie sochinenii i pisem*, vol. 7 (Leningrad, 1983), p. 547.

16. Nekrasov's story bears some resemblance to "La Prima Donna" (1831), an early story by George Sand written in collaboration with her friend Jules Sandeau. In Sand's story, an atmosphere of mystery surrounds the Verona Theater, where the soprano Gina will perform after several years' absence from the opera. Gina married a duke, but pined for her beloved theater until her doctor recommended that she return to the stage. Overcome by emotion and passion during the performance, Gina dies. Sand's story exhibits confusion about inserting its opera diva heroine into a literary narrative. "La Prima Donna" solves this problem through embedded narration, having Gina's lover Valterna relate most of her story. Gina appears as the construction of Valterna's own fevered operatic consciousness. See *Revue de Paris* 25 (1831).

17. Russian and Western critics have read Turgenev's "Klara Milich" as the product of the author's long relationship with the opera singer Pauline Viardot. There exists an entire body of critical and anecdotal literature about this relationship, of which I. M. Grevs's colorful *Istoriia odnoi liubvi* is but one example.

18. For a treatment of the real-life model for Turgenev's heroine, the mezzo Evlalia Kadmina, who staged her own death, see my article "Her Final Debut." See also Iagolim, *Kometa divnoi krasoty*.

19. Contemporary reviewers of Turgenev's story saw Klara Milich as a unified literary character, not the antithesis of one, as I do. A reviewer from the journal *Golos* described the heroine's character as a series of absolutes: "What a

purely Russian type—Klara Milich! This is a woman, pure and beautiful morally but with a capricious and demanding nature, who does not know the compromises of life, and who, once she gives herself to something, gives herself completely and forever!" See A. Vvedenskii, "Literaturnaia letopis'. Novaia povest' Turgeneva, 'Klara Milich,'" *Golos* (6 [18] January 1883), no. 6.

20. A. S. Suvorin, *Tatiana Repina* (St. Petersburg, 1899), p. 37.

21. The journal *Teatr i zhizn'* attests to this phenomenon, noting that "during Repina's death scene, five ladies became hysterical, the crying and sobbing throughout the hall interfered with our hearing the end of the last scene." See *Teatr i zhizn'* (19 January 1889) no. 249.

22. Suvorin's *Tatiana Repina* offers a kind of retelling of Eugène Scribe's popular play *Adrienne Lecouvreur* (1849), in which the actress and a princess vie for the love of Polish Count Maurice de Saxe. The princess steals a bouquet given by Adrienne to Maurice, fills it with deadly poison powder, and sends it back to the actress. When Adrienne kisses the bouquet sadly, thinking that Maurice is rejecting her, she receives a fatal dose and dies. *Adrienne Lecouvreur* abounds in references to specific neoclassical tragedies, quoted by the heroine to characterize her own plight. Scribe's play acts out a battle between disparate genres: neoclassical tragedy and meta-theatrical woman's novel. Suvorin's *Tatiana Repina* gives its title character greater control over theatrical effects in the shape of the heroine's story. It is not the more "literary" character who kills the actress, but the female performer who literally lives out her roles.

23. For information about Russian opera troupe repertoire at the turn of the century, see Bogoliubov, Pokhitonov, Stark, and Sviridenko.

24. For information about the operatic tradition in the Russian provinces, see Shteinpress.

25. V. I. Nemirovich-Danchenko, *Kulisy* (St. Petersburg, 1899), p. 17.

26. Ibid., p. 77.

27. Ibid., p. 79.

28. Actually, it is arguable whether Raevskaia or the theater administration is responsible for the changed ending of Meyerbeer's *The Huguenots*. The final three scenes of the opera depict a street battle between the Protestants and the Catholics, in which the lovers die. Since the opera is extremely long, nineteenth-century opera troupes sometimes abridged the concluding sections. But the ending described in *Stage Wings* suits Raevskaia's purposes admirably, in either event.

29. Nemirovich-Danchenko, p. 108.

30. K. A. Koval'skie and O. N Koval'skie, *Dvulikii bog* (Petrograd, 1916), p. 62.

31. Ibid., p. 71.

32. Iureneva, p. 65.

33. A. Amfiteatrov, *Sumerki bozhkov*, part 1, Serebrianaia feia (St. Petersburg, 1908), p. 10.

34. Ibid., pp. 54–55.

35. A. A. Verbitskaia, *Pokinutyi* (Riga, 1925/26), p. 161.

36. Ibid., p. 119.

37. Ibid., p. 149.

38. Ibid.

39. Ibid., p. 153.

40. Ibid., p. 154.

41. Ibid., p. 160.

42. Ibid., p. 163.

43. Ibid., p. 74.

44. Ibid., p. 102.

45. Ibid., p. 159.

46. Verbitskaia's heroines provoked an angry critical response from reviewers concerned about the perpetuation of the Russian literary canon. Mania, the heroine of her novel *The Keys to Happiness*, in particular seemed a threat to the continued survival of the traditional Russian literary heroine:

> If Verbitskaia conquers Tolstoi and Turgenev, this means that . . . Mania El'tsova . . . conquers Turgenev's maidens and Tolstoi's women! We are not speaking about our reveries, our dreams, about our ideals! But you—real, earthly Turgenevian maidens, you, the pure and genuine, where are you? Natasha, Kitty, all of you, whose pure images look out at us from the prophetic pages of Tolstoi's works—is it possible that forever, is it possible that for all time, you have disappeared from our life? Is it possible that Mania El'tsova, the lewd, brazen and deceitful kept woman of Shteinbakh, has replaced all of you in our astonishing, our unfortunate country?

See I. Vasilevskii, "Geroinia nashego vremei (Romany A. Verbitskoi i sovremennyi chitatel')," *Novoe slovo* (1913), no. 4. For similarly outraged commentary on Verbitskaia's female characters, see also V. Kranikhfel'd, "O novykh liudiakh A. Verbitskoi. Literaturnye otkliki," *Sovremennyi mir* (August 1910).

47. For a wide-ranging treatment of women's autobiography in pre-revolutionary Russia, see the introduction to Clyman and Vowles. Note that this volume includes the memoirs from the early life of Liubov Pavlovna Nikulina-Kositskaia, a woman from a serf family who became a provincial actress during the second half of the nineteenth century.

48. In the Western tradition, opera divas began to produce their autobiographies and memoirs in significant numbers only during the first decades of the twentieth century. Western diva-authors from the first half of the century include Frances Alda, Emma Calve, Geraldine Farrar, Kirsten Flagstad, Olive Fremstad, Mary Garden, Lotte Lehmann, and Luisa Tetrazzini.

49. Beth Holmgren's "Gendering the Icon: Marketing Women Writers in Fin-de-Siècle Russia" is no less suggestive in considering the female opera singer as author than in examining commodified representations of the opera diva. See particularly Holmgren's juxtaposition of the personal-authorial narratives projected by the photographs and autobiographies of writers like Verbitskaia and Charskaia.

50. Mainwaring, p. 28.

51. Ibid., p. 100.

52. Kadmina's story fragment was published three years after her death, and appeared in an anthology called *Pomoshch' brat'iam: Literaturnyi sbornik v pol'zu postradavshikh ot navodneniia* (Kiev, 1884). The editors of the volume took it upon themselves to edit out unnecessary details and description from the fragment, but acknowledged making these changes in an accompanying footnote.

53. Koestenbaum, *The Queen's Throat*, pp. 131–32.

54. *Biograficheskie dannye M.A. Slavinoi*, RNB, rukopisnyi otdel. fond 1110, opis' 1, delo 272.

55. D. M. Leonova, "Vospominaniia artistki imperatorskikh teatrov D.M. Leonovoi," *Istoricheskii vestnik* (1891), t. 43, no. 1, p. 120.

56. Ibid., p. 135.

57. "O sluzhbe aktrisy opernoi truppy Dar'i Leonovoi," Pis'mo August 1856. RGIA, fond 497, delo 13644. Note that the standard contract between a female singer and the theater directorate stipulated that she could not marry without official permission.

58. Leonova, "Vospominaniia," p. 137.

59. Ibid., p. 136.

60. D. M. Leonova, "Vospominaniia artistki imperatorskikh teatrov D.M. Leonovoi," *Istoricheskii vestnik*, (1891), t. 44, no. 4, p. 345.

61. D. M. Leonova, "Vospominaniia artistki imperatorskikh teatrov D. M. Leonovoi." *Istoricheskii vestnik* (1891), t. 43, no. 3 , p. 635.

62. "O sluzhbe aktrisy opernoi truppy Dar'i Leonovoi," Pis'mo 20 April 1863, RGIA, fond 497, delo 13644.

63. A. A. Smolina, "Vospominaniia," *Russkii provintsial'nyi teatr* (Leningrad-Moscow: Vserossiiskoe teatral'noe obshchestvo, 1937), p. 209.

64. Ibid., p. 227.

65. Ibid., p. 217.

66. Ibid., p. 218.

67. Sources on the operetta theater in Russia include "Operetta na stsene Aleksandrinskogo teatre. Vospominaniia teatral'nogo starozhila," in *Ezhegodnik imperatorskikh teatrov*, 1910, vyp. 3, and P. Gnedich's "Operetta 60-kh godov," *Teatr i iskusstvo* (1913), no. 52.

68. Smolina, p. 231.

69. L. Ivanov, "Istoriia Prekrasnoi Eleny (V. A. Liadova): Vospominaniia o moei materi," *Vechernee vremia* (31 January [13 February] 1913), no. 367.

70. For an account of Savina's artistic career and legacy. as well as those of Strepetova, Fedotova, Ermolova, Iavorskaia, and Kommissarzhevskaia, see Schuler.

71. M. N. Ermolova, "Dnevnik i pis'ma," *Malyi teatr*, vol. 1 *(1824–1917)*, (Moscow: Vserossiiskoe teatral'noe obshchestvo, 1978).

72. See A. A. Verbitskaia, *Moemu chitateliu. Avtobiograficheskie ocherki s portretom avtora i semeinymi portretami (Detstvo, Gody ucheniia)*, bk. 1 (Moscow, 1908); *Moi vospominaniia (Iunost'. Grezy)*, bk. 2 (Moscow, 1911). See also T. L. Shchepkina-Kupernik, *Dni moei zhizni: teatr, literatura, obshchestvennaia zhizn'* (Moscow: Federatsiia, 1928). Shchepkina-Kupernik published a biography of Ermolova, as well as unpublished recollections about the Silver Age actress Lidia Iavorskaia.

73. F. I. Chaliapin, *Stranitsy iz moei zhizni: Povesti*, and *Maska i dusha: Moi sorok let na teatrakh* (Moscow: Knizhnaia palata, 1990).

74. F. I. Chaliapin, *Maska i dusha*, p. 224.

75. Ibid.

76. Ibid., p. 225.

Bibliography

Abbate, Carolyn. *Unsung Voices: Opera and Musical Narrative in the Nineteenth Century*. Princeton, N.J.: Princeton University Press, 1991.

Abel, Sam. *Opera in the Flesh: Sexuality in Operatic Performance*. Boulder, Colo.: Westview Press, 1996.

Adorno, Theodor W. "Opera." In E. B. Ashton, trans., *Introduction to the Sociology of Music*. New York: Seabury, 1976.

———. "Bourgeois Opera." In David J. Levin, ed. and trans., *Opera Through Other Eyes*. Stanford, Calif.: Stanford University Press, 1994.

Alchevskaia, Kh. D. *Peredumannoe i perezhitoe: Dnevniki, pis'ma, vospominaniia*. Moscow: Tip. I. D. Sytina, 1912.

Alekseeva, E. "Evgeniia Mravina." *Sovetskaia muzyka* (1964), no. 4.

Alianskii Iu. *Veseliashchiisia Peterburg: (Po materialam sobraniia G. A. Ivanova)*. T. 1–4. St. Petersburg: Peterburgskii klub miniaturistov, 1992–96.

———. *Uveselitel'nye zavedeniia starogo Peterburga*. St. Petersburg: AOZT "PF," 1996.

Al'shvang, A. "Russkaia simfoniia i nekotorye analogii s russkim romanom." *Izbrannye sochineniia v 2-x tomakh*. Vol. 1. Moscow: Muzyka, 1964.

Al'tshuller, A. Ia., ed. *Ocherki istorii russkoi teatral'noi kritiki*. Leningrad: Iskusstvo, 1976.

Amfiteatrov, Alexander. *Sumerki bozhkov* (Twilight of the little gods). St. Petersburg, 1908.

Anderson, Amanda. *Tainted Souls and Painted Faces: The Rhetoric of Fallenness in Victorian Culture*. Ithaca, N.Y.: Cornell University Press, 1993.

Appelbaum, David. *Voice*. Albany: State University of New York Press, 1990.

Apter, Emily, and William Pietz, eds. *Fetishism as Cultural Discourse*. Ithaca, N.Y.: Cornell University Press, 1993.

Arapov, P. *Letopis' russkogo teatra*. St. Petersburg: Tip. N. Tiblena, 1861.

Armstrong, Judith. *The Unsaid Anna Karenina*. Basingstoke, England: Macmillan, 1988.

Aronson, M., and S. Reiser, eds. *Literaturnye kruzhki i salony*. Leningrad: Priboi, 1929.

Asaf'ev, B. *"Evgenii Onegin". Liricheskie stseny P. I. Chaikovskogo. Opyt intonatsionnogo analiza stilia i muzykal'noi dramaturgii*. Moscow: Muzgiz, 1944.

———. *Izbrannye trudy*. 5 vols. Moscow: Izdatel'stvo Akademii Nauk SSSR, 1953–57.

———. *Ob opere: izbrannye stat'i*. Leningrad: Muzyka, 1976.

Asenkova, A. "Kartiny proshedshego: Zapiski russkoi artistki." *Teatral'nyi i muzykal'nyi vestnik* 36–37, 39, 42, 44, 46, 49–51 (1857).

Ashbrook, William. *Donizetti and his Operas*. Cambridge: Cambridge University Press, 1982.

Attali, Jacques. *Noise: The Political Economy of Music*. Trans. Brian Massumi. Minneapolis: University of Minnesota Press, 1985.

Auerbach, Nina. "Alluring Vacancies in the Victorian Character." *The Kenyon Review* 8, no. 3 (summer 1986).

———. *Private Theatricals: The Lives of the Victorians*. Cambridge: Harvard University Press, 1990.

———. *Woman and the Demon: The Life of a Victorian Myth*. Cambridge: Harvard University Press, 1982.

Austin, J. L. *How to Do Things with Words*. 2nd ed. Cambridge: Harvard University Press, 1975.

———. *Philosophical Papers*. Ed. J. O. Urmson and G. L. Warnock. Oxford: Oxford University Press, 1979.

Baker, Jennifer. "Dargomyzhsky, Realism, and *The Stone Guest*." *Music Review* 37, no. 3 (August 1976).

Bakhtin, M. M. *The Dialogic Imagination*. Ed. Michael Holquist. Austin: University of Texas Press, 1981.

Barish, Jonas. *The Antitheatrical Prejudice*. Berkeley: University of California Press, 1981.

Barkhin, G. B. *Arkhitektura teatra*. Moscow: Izdatel'stvo Akademii Arkhitektury SSSR, 1947.

Barthes, Roland. "From Work to Text." In *Textual Strategies: Perspectives in Post-Structuralist Criticism*. Ithaca, N.Y.: Cornell University Press, 1986.

———. *Image—Music—Text.* Trans. Stephen Heath. New York: Hill and Wang , 1977.

———. *Mythologies.* Trans. Annette Lavers. New York: Hill and Wang, 1972.

———. *The Pleasure of the Text.* Trans. Richard Miller. New York: Hill and Wang, 1975.

Bartlett, Rosamund. *Wagner and Russia.* Cambridge: Cambridge University Press, 1995.

Bauer, Evgenii. "Sumerki zhenskoi dushi" (Twilight of a woman's soul). 35mm, 1913.

———. "Grezy" (Daydreams). 35mm, 1915.

Bayley, John. *Tolstoy and the Novel.* Chicago: University of Chicago Press, 1988.

Beizer, Janet. *Ventriloquized Bodies: Narratives of Hysteria in Nineteenth-Century France.* Ithaca, N.Y.: Cornell University Press, 1994.

Beliaev, I. S. "K istorii razvlechenii moskvichei v polovine XVIII stoletiia. Maskarad i opera Lokatelli." In *Staraia Moscow.* Vyp. 2. Moscow, 1914.

Belkina, M. A. "Svetskaia povest' 30-kh godov i 'Kniaginia Ligovskaia' Lermontova." In N. L. Brodskii, ed., *Zhizn' i tvorchestvo M. Iu. Lermontova.* Moscow: Gosudarstvennoe izdatel'stvo "Khudozhestvennaia literatura," 1941.

Belza, I. *Pushkin i Mitskevich v istorii muzykal'noi kul'tury.* Moscow: Muzyka, 1988.

Benjamin, Walter. "The Work of Art in the Age of Mechanical Reproduction." In *Illuminations.* New York: Schocken Books, 1968.

Benson, Ruth Crego. *Women in Tolstoy: The Ideal and the Erotic.* Urbana: University of Illinois Press, 1973.

Berger, P. L., and T. Luckmann. *The Social Construction of Reality.* Garden City, N.Y.: Anchor, 1967.

Berkov, V. *Gogol' o muzyke.* Moscow: Gosudarstvennoe muzykal'noe izdatel'stvo, 1952.

Berlioz, H. *Les Soirées de l'orchestre.* Paris: Calmann-Levy, 1895.

Bernandt, G. *Slovar' oper vpervye postavlennykh ili izdannykh v dorevoliutsionnoi Rossii i v SSSR, 1736–1959.* Moscow: Sovetskii kompozitor, 1962.

Bernatskii, V. A. "Iz zolotogo veka ital'ianskoi opery v Peterburge." *Russkaia starina* (1916), no. 168.

Bernheimer, Charles. *Figures of Ill Repute: Representing Prostitution in Nineteenth-Century France.* Durham, N.C.: Duke University Press, 1997.

Bertenson, V. B. *Za 30 let (listki iz vospominanii).* St. Petersburg: Tip. A. S. Suvorina "Novoe vremia," 1914.

Blackmer, Corinne E., and Patricia Juliana Smith, eds. *En Travesti: Women, Gender Subversion, Opera.* New York: Columbia University Press, 1995.

Blake, Kathleen. "*Armgart*—George Eliot on the Woman Artist." *Victorian Poetry* 18, no. 1 (spring 1980).

Boborykin, P. *Moi vospominaniia.* Ed. E. Vilenskaia and L. Roitberg. Moscow: Khudozhestvennaia literatura, 1965.

Bogoliubov, N. *Polveka na opernoi stsene. Teatral'nye memuary.* Moscow, 1957.

Bourdieu, Pierre. *Distinction: A Social Critique of the Judgement of Taste*, Trans. Richard Nice. Cambridge: Harvard University Press, 1984.

Bozherianov, I. N. *Stoletie SPb imperatorskogo Bol'shogo teatra.* St. Petersburg, 1883.

Bozherianov, I. N., and N. N. Karpov. *Illiustrirovannaia istoriia russkogo teatra XIX veka.* St. Petersburg, 1903.

Brett, Philip, Elizabeth Wood, and Gary C. Thomas, eds. *Queering the Pitch: The New Gay and Lesbian Musicology.* New York: Routledge, 1994.

Brissett, Dennis, and Charles Edgley, eds. *Life as Theater: A Dramaturgical Sourcebook.* New York: Aldine de Gruyter, 1990.

Brooks, Jeffrey. *When Russia Learned to Read: Literacy and Popular Culture, 1861–1917.* Princeton, N.J.: Princeton University Press, 1985.

Brooks, Peter. *The Melodramatic Imagination: Balzac, Henry James, Melodrama, and the Mode of Excess.* New Haven, Conn.: Yale University Press, 1976.

Brown, Calvin S. *Music and Literature: A Comparison of the Arts.* Hanover: University Press of New England, 1987.

Brownstein, Rachel M. *Becoming a Heroine: Reading About Women in Novels.* New York: Viking, 1982.

———. *Tragic Muse: Rachel of the Comédie-Française.* New York: Alfred A. Knopf, 1993.

Buckler, Julie. "Her Final Debut: The Kadmina Legend in Russian Literature." In Andrew Baruch Wachtel, ed., *Intersections and Transpositions: Russian Music, Literature, and Society.* Evanston, Ill.: Northwestern University Press, 1998.

———. "Novelistic Figuration, Narrative Metaphor: Western and Russian

Models of the Prima Donna." *Comparative Literature* 50, no. 2 (spring 1998).

Budden, Julian. *The Operas of Verdi*. Vol 1. *From "Oberto" to "Rigoletto."* Oxford: Oxford University Press, 1973.

———. *The Operas of Verdi*. Vol 2. *From "Il Trovatore" to "La Forza del destino."* Oxford: Oxford University Press, 1979.

Bulgarin, F. "Filosoficheskie vzgliady za kulisy," *Russkaia talia*, 1825.

———. "Panoramicheskii vzgliad na sovremennoe sostoianie teatrov v Sanktpeterburge. Kharakteristicheskie ocherki teatral'noi publiki, dramaticheskikh artistov i pisatelei." *Repertuar russkogo teatra*. T. 1, kn. 3 (1840).

———. "Puteshestvie iz raika v lozhu pervogo iarusa" (Journey from the paradis to a box in the first ring). *Russkaia taliia*, 1825.

Burns, Elizabeth. *Theatricality: A Study of Convention in the Theatre and in Social Life*. London: Longman, 1972.

Bushnell, Howard. *Maria Malibran*. University Park: The Pennsylvania State University Press, 1979.

Butler, Judith. *Bodies That Matter: On the Discursive Limits of Sex*. New York: Routledge, 1993.

Buyssens, Eric. *Les langages et le discours*. Brussels: Office de publicité, 1943.

Byerly, Alison. *Realism, Representation, and the Arts in Nineteenth-Century Literature*. Cambridge: Cambridge University Press, 1997.

Carlson, Marvin. *Performance: A Critical Introduction*. London: Routledge, 1996.

———. *Places of Performance: The Semiotics of Theatre Architecture*. Ithaca, N.Y.: Cornell University Press, 1989.

Chaliapin, F. I. *Maska i dusha: moi sorok let na teatrakh*. Moscow: Knizhnaia palata, 1990.

———. *Stranitsy iz moei zhizni: Povesti*. Moscow: Knizhnaia palata, 1990.

Champagne, Roland. "My Cup Runneth Over: The Semiotic Stakes of the Courtesan Myth in the Metamorphoses of Marguerite Gautier." *American Journal of Semiotics* 8, no. 4 (1991).

Chatman, Seymour. *Coming to Terms: The Rhetoric of Narrative in Fiction and Film*. Ithaca, N.Y.: Cornell University Press, 1990.

Chernyshevskii, N. G. *Chto delat'?* (What is to be done?). Moscow-Leningrad: Akademiia, 1937. Originally published in 1863.

Cheshikhin, V. *Istoriia russkoi opery*. Moscow: P. Iurgenson, 1905.

Chodorow, Nancy. *The Reproduction of Mothering: Psychoanalysis and the Sociology of Gender*. Berkeley: University of California Press, 1978.

Chorley, Henry F. *Thirty Years' Musical Recollections*. New York: Vienna House, 1972.

Christiansen, Rupert. *Prima Donna: A History*. New York: Viking, 1984.

Clark, Katerina. *Petersburg: Crucible of Cultural Revolution*. Cambridge: Harvard University Press, 1995.

Clayton, Ellen Creathorne. *Queens of Song*. Reprint from 1865, Freeport: Books for Libraries Press, 1972.

Clément, Catherine. *Opera, or the Undoing of Women*. Trans. Betsy Wing; foreword by Susan McClary. Minneapolis: University of Minnesota Press, 1988. Originally published as *L'opéra ou la défaite des femmes*. Paris: Éditions Grasset & Fasquelle, 1979.

Clowes, Edith W., Samuel D. Kassow, and James L. West, eds. *Between Tsar and People: Educated Society and the Quest for Public Identity in Late Imperial Russia*. Princeton, N.J.: Princeton University Press, 1991.

Clyman, Toby W., and Judith Vowles, eds. *Russia Through Women's Eyes: Autobiographies from Tsarist Russia*. New Haven, Conn.: Yale University Press, 1996.

Cone, Edward T. *The Composer's Voice*. Berkeley: University of California Press, 1974.

Conrad, Peter. *Romantic Opera and Literary Form*. Berkeley: University of California Press, 1977.

———. *A Song of Love and Death: The Meaning of Opera*. New York: Poseidon, 1987.

Costlow, Jane T. *Worlds Within Worlds: The Novels of Ivan Turgenev*. Princeton, N.J.: Princeton University Press, 1990.

Cui, C. *Izbrannye stat'i*. Leningrad: Gosudarstvennoe muzykal'noe izdatel'stvo, 1952.

———. *La musique en Russie*. Paris: Sandoz, 1880.

Dahlhaus, Carl. *Realism in Nineteenth-Century Music*. Trans. Mary Whittall. Cambridge: Cambridge University Press, 1995.

Dalton, Elizabeth. *Unconscious Structure in* The Idiot*: A Study in Literature and Psychoanalysis*. Princeton, N.J.: Princeton University Press, 1979.

Danilov, S. S. *Gogol' i teatr*. Leningrad: Khudozhestvennaia literatura, 1936.

———. "Po teatram starogo Peterburga." *Iskusstvo i zhizn'* 7, 8, 10, (1939); 3, 8 (1940).

———. "Postoiannye publichnye teatry v Peterburge v XIX veke." In

O teatre: Vremennik Otdela Istorii i Teorii Teatra Gosudarstvennogo Instituta Istorii Iskusstv. Leningrad, 1929.

———. *Russkii teatr v khudozhestvennoi literature*. Moscow: Iskusstvo, 1939.

Davidovich, M. G. "Zhenskii portret u russkikh romantikov pervoi poloviny XIX veka." In A. I. Beletskii, ed., *Russkii romantizm*. Leningrad: Akademiia, 1927.

Davydov, N. V. *Iz proshlogo*. Moscow: I. D. Sytina, 1914.

de Certeau, Michel. *The Practice of Everyday Life*. Trans. Steven Rendall. Berkeley: University of California Press, 1984.

de Jonge, Alex. *Dostoevsky and the Age of Intensity*. London: Secker & Warburg, 1975.

de Lauretis, Teresa. *Alice Doesn't: Feminism, Semiotics, Cinema*. Bloomington: Indiana University Press, 1984.

Dellamora, Richard, and Daniel Fischlin, eds. *The Work of Opera: Genre, Nationhood, and Sexual Difference*. New York: Columbia University Press, 1997.

de Marinis, Marco. *The Semiotics of Performance*. Trans. Áine O'Healy. Bloomington: Indiana University Press, 1993.

Diamond, Elin, ed. *Performance and Cultural Politics*. New York: Routledge, 1996.

Diment, Galya, ed. *Goncharov's Oblomov: A Critical Companion*. Evanston, Ill.: Northwestern University Press, 1998.

Dizikes, John. *Opera in America: A Cultural History*. New Haven, Conn.: Yale University Press, 1994.

Dmitriev, N. *Opernaia stsena Moskovskogo imperatorskogo teatra*. Moscow, 1897.

Dobroliubov, N. A. "What is Oblomovitis?" In Ralph E. Matlaw, ed. *Belinsky, Chernyshevsky, and Dobrolyubov: Selected Criticism*. Bloomington: Indiana Universty Press, 1976.

Doerner, Klaus. *Madmen and the Bourgeoisie: A Social History of Insanity and Psychiatry*. Trans. Joachim Neugroschel and Jean Steinberg. Oxford: Basil Blackwell, 1981.

Donington, Robert. *Opera and Its Symbols: The Unity of Words, Music, and Staging*. New Haven, Conn.: Yale University Press, 1990.

Dostoevskii, F. M. *Idiot*. In vol. 8 of *Polnoe sobranie sochinenii v 30 tomakh*. Leningrad: Nauka, 1973. Originally published in 1868.

Drizen, N. V. *Stopiatidesiatiletie imperatorskikh St. Petersburgskikh teatrov*. St. Petersburg, 1906.

Druskin, M. "Dostoevskii glazami muzykanta." In *Ocherki, stat'i, zametki.* Leningrad: Sovetskii kompozitor, 1987.

———. " 'Evgenii Onegin' Chaikovskogo." In *Istoriia i sovremennost'. Stat'i o muzyke.* Leningrad: Sovetskii Kompozitor, 1960.

———. "Studencheskaia pesnia v Rossii 40-kh–60-kh godov." In *Ocherki po istorii i teorii muzyki.* Ed. A. I. Mashirov. Leningrad: Gosudarstvennoe nauchno-issled. institut teatra i muzyki, 1939.

———. *Voprosy muzykal'noi dramaturgii opery.* Leningrad: Gosudarstvennoe muzykal'noe izdatel'stvo, 1952.

Dunn, Leslie C., and Nancy A. Jones, eds. *Embodied Voices: Representing Female Vocality in Western Culture.* Cambridge: Cambridge University Press, 1994.

Duvignaud, Jean. *Le Sociologie du Théâtre.* Paris: Presses Universitaires de France, 1963.

Edgcumbe, Richard. *Musical Reminiscences of an Old Amateur for Fifty Years, from 1773 to 1823.* London: W. Clarke, 1824.

Edwards, Anne. *La Divina.* New York: William Morrow, 1994.

Edwards, H. Sutherland. *The Prima Donna: Her History and Surroundings from the Seventeenth to the Nineteenth Century.* 2 vols. London: Remington, 1888.

Eiges, I. *Muzyka v zhizni i tvorchestve Pushkina.* Moscow: Muzgiz, 1937.

Eikhenbaum, Boris. *Lev Tolstoi: Semidesiatye gody.* Leningrad: Khudozhestvennaia literatura, 1974.

Elizarova, N. A. *Krepostnaia aktrisa P. I. Kovaleva-Zhemchugova.* Moscow: 1969.

Emerson, Caryl. *Boris Godunov: Transpositions of a Russian Theme.* Bloomington: Indiana University Press, 1986.

———. "Musorgsky's Libretti on Historical Themes: From *The Two Boris*es to *Khovanshchina.*" In Arthur Groos and Roger Parker, eds., *Reading Opera.* Princeton, N.J.: Princeton University Press, 1988.

———. "Prosaics in *Anna Karenina*: Pro and Con." *Tolstoy Studies Journal* 8 (1995–96).

———. "Tatiana." *A Plot of Her Own: The Female Protagonist in Russian Literature.* Ed. Sona Stephan Hoisington. Evanston, Ill.: Northwestern University Press, 1995.

Engel, Barbara Alpern. *Mothers and Daughters: Women of the Intelligentsia in Nineteenth-Century Russia.* Cambridge: Cambridge University Press, 1985.

Engelstein, Laura. *The Keys to Happiness: Sex and the Search for Modernity in Fin-de-Siècle Russia*. Ithaca, N.Y.: Cornell University Press, 1992.

Evans, Mary. *Reflecting on Anna Karenina*. London: Routledge, 1989.

Evzerikhina, V. A. " 'Kniazhna Meri' M. Iu. Lermontova i 'svetskaia povest'" 1830-kh godov." *Uchenye zapiski*. T. 219. *Voprosy istorii literatury* (1961).

Fanger, Donald. *Dostoevsky and Romantic Realism: A Study of Dostoevsky in Relation to Balzac, Dickens, and Gogol*. Cambridge: Harvard University Press, 1965.

Fedotova, G. N. "Vospominaniia iunosti i pis'ma." In *Malyi teatr*, 1824–1917. Vol. 1. Moscow: Vserossiiskoe teatral'noe obshchestvo, 1978.

Felman, Shoshana. *The Literary Speech Act: Don Juan with J. L. Austin, or Seduction in Two Languages*. Trans. Catherine Porter. Ithaca, N.Y.: Cornell University Press, 1983.

Ferman, V. F. *Opernyi teatr (stat'i i issledovaniia)*. Moscow: Gosudarstvennoe muzykal'noe izdatel'stvo, 1961.

Feuer, Kathryn B. *Tolstoy and the Genesis of War and Peace*. Ithaca, N.Y.: Cornell University Press, 1996.

Findeizen, N. *Russkaia khudozhestvennaia pesnia (romans)*. Moscow: Iurgenson, 1905.

Fisher, Lynn, and Wesley Fisher. "Bellini's 'Casta diva' and Goncharov's *Oblomov*." *Mnemozina: Studia litteraria russica in honorem Vsevolod Setchkarev*. Munich: Fink Verlag, 1974.

Fitzlyon, April. *Maria Malibran: Diva of the Romantic Age*. London: Souvenir, 1987.

———. *The Price of Genius, a Life of Pauline Viardot*. London: John Calder, Ltd., 1964.

Flynn, Elizabeth A., and Patrocinio P. Schweickart, eds. *Gender and Reading: Essays on Readers, Texts, and Contexts*. Baltimore, Md.: Johns Hopkins University Press, 1986.

Foucault, Michel. *Madness and Civilization: A History of Insanity in the Age of Reason*. Trans. Richard Howard. New York: Vintage, 1988.

Frank, Joseph. *Dostoevsky: The Miraculous Years (1865–1871)*. Princeton, N.J.: Princeton University Press, 1995.

Frank, Stephen P., and Mark D. Steinberg, eds. *Cultures in Flux: Lower-Class Values, Practices and Resistance in Late Imperial Russia*. Princeton, N.J.: Princeton University Press, 1994.

Gallagher, Catherine, and Thomas Laqueur, eds. *The Making of the Modern*

Body: Sexuality and Society in the Nineteenth Century. Berkeley: University of California Press, 1987.

Garber, Marjorie. *Vested Interests: Cross-Dressing and Cultural Anxiety*. New York: HarperCollins, 1993.

Gates, Barbara T. *Victorian Suicide: Mad Crimes and Sad Histories*. Princeton, N.J.: Princeton University Press, 1988.

Gerhard, Anselm. *The Urbanization of Opera: Music Theater in Paris in the Nineteenth Century*. Trans. Mary Whittall. Chicago: University of Chicago Press, 1998.

Gerngross, V. "Teatral'nye zdaniia v St. Petersburge v XVIII stoletii." *Starye gody* (February and March 1910).

Gilbert, Sandra M., and Susan Gubar. *The Madwoman in the Attic: The Woman Writer and the Nineteenth-Century Literary Imagination*. New Haven, Conn.: Yale University Press, 1984.

Ginzburg, L. Ia. *O psikhologicheskoi proze*. Leningrad: Khudozhestvennaia literatura, 1971.

Glama-Meshcherskaia, A. Ia. *Vospominaniia*. Leningrad: Iskusstvo, 1937.

Glumov, A. *Muzyka v russkom dramaticheskom teatre*. Moscow: Muzgiz, 1955.

———. *Muzykal'nyi mir Pushkina*. Moscow-Leningrad: Gosudarstvennoe muzykal'noe izdatel'stvo, 1950.

Gnedich, P. P. "Operetka 60-kh godov. Iz vospominanii P. P. Gnedicha." *Teatr i iskusstvo* (1913), no. 52.

Goffman, Erving. *The Presentation of Self in Everyday Life*. Garden City, N.Y.: Doubleday, 1959.

Goldstein, Darra. "Domestic Porkbarreling in Nineteenth-Century Russia, or Who Holds the Keys to the Larder?" In Helena Goscilo and Beth Holmgren, eds., *Russia Women Culture*. Bloomington: Indiana University Press, 1996.

Golovacheva-Panaeva, A. Ia. *Vospominaniia. Russkie pisateli i artisty 1824–1870*. St. Petersburg, 1890.

Goncharov, I. A. *Oblomov*. Translated David Magarshack. New York: Penguin Books, 1983. Originally published in 1859.

Goscilo, Helena. "Stage and Page: Drama's Incursion into Russian Fiction of the 1830s." *Studia Filologiczne* 18, no. 7 (1985).

———. "Tolstoy, Laclos, and the Libertine." *The Modern Language Review* 81, no. 2 (April 1986).

Goscilo, Helena and Beth Holmgren, eds. *Russia Women Culture*. Bloomington: Indiana University Press, 1996.

Gozenpud, A. A. *Dom Engel'gardta: Iz istorii kontsertnoi zhizni Peterburga pervoi poloviny XIX veka*. St. Petersburg: Sovetskii kompozitor, 1992.

———. "Gogol' v muzyke." In *Izbrannye stat'i*. Leningrad: Sovetskii kompozitor, 1971.

———. "Natasha Rostova na opernom spektakle." In *Izbrannye stat'i*. Leningrad: Sovetskii kompozitor, 1971.

———. "Pushkin i russkaia opernaia klassika." In *Izbrannye stat'i*. Leningrad: Sovetskii kompozitor, 1971.

———. *Russkii opernyi teatr mezhdu dvukh revoliutsii (1905–17)*. Leningrad: Muzyka, 1975.

———. *Russkii opernyi teatr na rubezhe XIX–XX vekov i Shaliapin (1890–1904)*. Leningrad: Muzyka, 1974.

———. *Russkii opernyi teatr XIX veka*. 3 vols. Leningrad: Muzyka, 1969.

Graves, Robert. *The White Goddess: A Historical Grammar of Poetic Myth*. New York: Farrar, Straus and Giroux, 1966.

Greenblatt, Stephen. *Shakespearean Negotiations: The Circulation of Social Energy in Renaissance England*. Oxford: Oxford University Press, 1988.

Greenleaf, Monika. *Pushkin and Romantic Fashion: Fragment, Elegy, Orient, Irony*. Stanford, Calif.: Stanford University Press, 1994.

Greenleaf, Monika, and Stephen Moeller-Sally, eds. *Russian Subjects: Empire, Nation, and the Culture of the Golden Age*. Evanston, Ill.: Northwestern University Press, 1998.

Greimas, A. J., and Joseph Courtes. *Semiotics and Language: An Analytical Dictionary*. Trans. Larry Crist, et al. Bloomington: Indiana University Press, 1982.

Grevs, I. M. *Istoriia odnoi liubvi*. Moscow: Sovremennye problemy, 1928.

Grigor'ev, Apollon. "Robert le Diable." In *Vospominaniia*. Moscow, 1988. Originally published in 1859.

Grigor'ev, P. I. "Skladchina na lozhu v ital'ianskie opery" (Chipping in for a box at the Italian opera). St. Petersburg, 1843.

Grigoreva, A. *E. K. Mravina*. Moscow: Sovetskii kompozitor, 1970.

Groos, Arthur, and Roger Parker, eds. *Reading Opera*. Princeton, N.J.: Princeton University Press, 1988.

Grossman, Leonid. *Pushkin v teatral'nykh kreslakh*. Leningrad: Brokgaus-Ephron, 1926.

Guillory, John. *Cultural Capital: The Problem of Literary Canon Formation*. Chicago: University of Chicago Press, 1993.

Gusev, N. N., and A. Gol'denveizer. *Lev Tolstoi i muzyka (Vospominaniia).* Moscow: Gosudarstvennoe muzykal'noe izdatel'stvo, 1953.

Hauser, Arnold. *The Social History of Art.* Vol. 9. New York: Vintage, 1985.

Heilbrun, Carolyn, and Margaret R. Higonnet, eds. *The Representation of Women in Fiction.* Baltimore, Md.: Johns Hopkins University Press, 1981.

Heldt, Barbara. *Terrible Perfection: Women and Russian Literature.* Bloomington: Indiana University Press, 1987.

Herman David. "Stricken by Infection: Art and Adultery in *Anna Karenina* and *Kreutzer Sonata.*" *Slavic Review* 56, no. 1 (spring 1997).

Herman, Luc. *Concepts of Realism.* Columbia, S.C.: Camden House, 1996.

Hobsbawm, Eric. *The Age of Empire (1875–1914).* New York: Vintage, 1987.

Hodge, Thomas Peter. "Mutatis Mutandis: Poetry of the Musical Romance in Early Nineteenth-Century Russia." Ph.D. diss., Stanford University, 1992.

Hoffmann, E. T. A. "Don Juan, or A Fabulous Adventure that Befell a Music Enthusiast on his Travels." In *Tales of Hoffmann.* New York: Heritage Press, 1943. Originally published in 1812.

Hoisington, Sona Stephan, ed. *A Plot of Her Own: The Female Protagonist in Russian Literature.* Evanston, Ill.: Northwestern University Press, 1995.

———. *Russian Views of Pushkin's Eugene Onegin.* Bloomington: Indiana University Press, 1988.

Hollander, Anne. *Sex and Suits.* New York: Alfred A. Knopf, 1994.

Hollander, John. *The Untuning of the Sky.* New York: W. W. Norton, 1970.

Holmgren, Beth. "Gendering the Icon: Marketing Women Writers in Fin-de-Siècle Russia." In Helena Goscilo and Beth Holmgren, eds., *Russia Women Culture.* Bloomington: Indiana University Press, 1996.

———. "Questions of Heroism in Goncharov's *Oblomov.*" In Galya Diment, ed., *Goncharov's Oblomov: A Critical Companion.* Evanston, Ill.: Northwestern University Press, 1998.

Holub, Robert C. *Reception Theory: A Critical Introduction.* London: Methuen, 1984.

Hughes, Spike. *Great Opera Houses.* London: Weidenfeld and Nicolson, 1956.

Hutcheon, Linda, and Michael Hutcheon. *Opera: Desire, Disease, Death.* Lincoln: University of Nebraska Press, 1996.

Iagolim, B. S. "E. A. Lavrovskaia: k 30-letiiu so dnia smerti." *Sovetskaia muzyka* (1949), no. 3.

———. *Kometa divnoi krasoty. Zhizn' i tvorchestvo Evlalii Kadminoi.* Moscow: Iskusstvo, 1970.

Iakhontov, A. N. "Peterburgskaia ital'ianskaia opera v 1840-kh godakh." *Russkaia Starina.* (December 1886).

Iakovlev, V. *Chaikovskii na moskovskoi stsene: Pervye postanovki v gody ego zhizni.* Moscow: Iskusstvo, 1940.

———. *D. M. Leonova.* Moscow, 1950.

———. "Moskovskaia opernaia stsena v sorokovykh godakh." In *Vremennik russkogo teatral'nogo obshchestva.* Moscow, 1924.

———. *Pushkin i muzyka.* Moscow: Gosudarstvennoe muzykal'noe izdatel'stvo, 1957.

Iarustovskii, B. *Dramaturgiia russkoi opernoi klassiki.* Moscow, 1952.

Iazykov, D. *Grafinia Praskov'ia Ivanovna Sheremeteva: Biograficheskii ocherk.* Moscow, 1903.

Iezuitova, R. V. "Svetskaia povest'." In B. S. Meilakh, ed., *Russkaia povest' XIX veka.* Leningrad, 1973.

Ignatov, I. N. *Teatr i zritel'.* Part I. Moscow: 1916.

Inber, Vera. "Shkaf s portretami (vospominaniia)." *Teatr* (1963), no. 11.

Ingham, Norman W. *E. T. A. Hoffmann's Reception in Russia.* Wurzburg: Jal-Verlag, 1974.

Iser, Wolfgang. "The Reading Process: A Phenomenological Approach." In *The Implied Reader: Patterns of Communication in Prose Fiction from Bunyan to Beckett.* Baltimore, Md.: Johns Hopkins University Press, 1975.

Issacharoff, Michael. *Discourse As Performance.* Stanford, Calif.: Stanford University Press, 1989.

Issacharoff, Michael, and Robin F. Jones, eds. *Performing Texts.* Philadelphia: University of Pennsylvania Press, 1988.

Issartel, Christiane. *Les Dames aux Camélias, de l'histoire à la légende.* Paris: Chene Hachette, 1981.

Iureneva, V. L. *Zhenshchiny teatra.* Petrograd: Mysl', 1923.

Ivanov, L. "Istoriia Prekrasnoi Eleny (V. A. Liadova): Vospominaniia o moei materi." *Vechernee vremia* 31, (January 1913), no. 367.

Ivanov, M. M. "Pervoe desiatiletie postoiannogo ital'ianskogo teatra v Peterburge v XIX veke (1843–53 gg.)." In *Ezhegodnik imperatorskikh teatrov.* St. Petersburg, 1893–94.

———. "Proshloe ital'ianskogo teatra v Peterburge v XIX veke. Vtoroe desiatiletie (1853–63 gg.)." In *Ezhegodnik imperatorskikh teatrov. Prilozhenie k knige vtoroi*, 1894–95.

Ivanskaia, S. "Byloe nashei ital'ianskoi opery (iz vospominanii ital'ianomana 1862–1885 gg.)." *Kolos'ia* 11 and 12 (November 1889).

Jakobson, Roman. "On Realism in Art." In Ladislav Matejka and Krystyna Pomorska, eds., *Readings in Russian Poetics: Formalist and Structuralist Views*. Ann Arbor: Michigan Slavic Publications, 1978.

John, Nicholas, ed. *Violetta and Her Sisters: The Lady of the Camellias, Responses to the Myth*. London: Faber and Faber, 1994.

Karlinsky, Simon. *Russian Drama from its Beginnings to the Age of Pushkin*. Berkeley: University of California Press, 1985.

Karnovich, E. P. "Teatral'nye zrelishcha v Rossii." *Nov'*. T. 29, no. 18 (1889).

Kashin, N. P. *Teatr N. B. Iusupova*. Moscow: Gos. akademiia khudozh. Nauk, 1927.

Kashkin, N. (Dmitriev, N.). *Opernaia stsena Moskovskogo imperatorskogo teatra*. Moscow, 1897.

Kats, B. A. *Muzyka v zerkale poezii*. Vyp. 1. Leningrad: Sovetskii kompozitor, 1985.

———. *Osip Mandelstam: "Polon muzyki, muzy i muki . . ."* Leningrad: Sovetskii kompozitor, 1991.

Katsanov, Ia. S. "Iz istorii muzykal'noi kul'tury Odessy (1794–1855)." In B. S. Shteinpress, ed., *Iz muzykal'nogo proshlogo*. Vol. 1. Moscow: Gosudarstvennoe muzykal'noe izdatel'stvo, 1960.

Kelly, Catriona. *Petrushka: The Russian Carnival Puppet Theatre*. Cambridge: Cambridge University Press, 1990.

Kerman, Joseph. *Contemplating Music: Challenges to Musicology*. Cambridge: Harvard University Press, 1985.

———. *Opera as Drama*. Berkeley: University of California Press, 1988.

———. "Opera, Novel, Drama: The Case of *La Traviata*." *Yearbook of Comparative and General Literature* 27 (1978).

Kirsanova, R. M. *Stsenicheskii kostium i teatral'naia publika v Rossii XIX veka*. Moscow: Artist. Rezhisser. Teatr, 1997.

Klein, Herman. *The Reign of Patti*. New York: Century, 1920.

Knapp, Bettina Liebowitz. *Music, Archetype, and the Writer: a Jungian View*. University Park: The Pennsylvania State University Press, 1988.

Kobak, A. V. "Unichtozhennye kladbishcha." *Istoricheskie kladbishcha Peterburga*. St. Petersburg: Izdatel'stvo Chernysheva, 1993.

Koestenbaum, Wayne. *The Queen's Throat: Opera, Homosexuality, and the Mystery of Desire*. New York: Poseidon, 1993.

———. "Wilde's Divas and the Pathos of the Gay Page." *Southwest Review* 77, no. 1 (winter 1992).

Kolosova E. M., and V. Filippov, eds. *Ostrovskii i russkie kompozitory*. Moscow: Iskusstvo, 1937.

Koval'skie, K. A. and O. N. Koval'skie. *Dvulikii bog* (The two-faced god). Petrograd, 1916.

Kovarsky, Gina. "Mimesis and Moral Education in *Anna Karenina*." *Tolstoy Studies Journal* 8 (1995–96).

Kozhevnikov, V. A. "*Vsia zhizn', vsia dusha, vsia liubov'* . . . ": *Perechityvaia 'Evgeniia Onegina (Kniga dlia uchitelia)'*. Moscow: Prosveshchenie, 1993.

Kramer, Lawrence. *Music As Cultural Practice, 1800–1900*. Berkeley: University of California Press, 1990.

Kremlev, Iu. *Russkaia mysl' v muzyke. Ocherki istorii russkoi muzykal'noi kritiki i estetiki v XIX veke*. 3 vols. Leningrad: Gosudarstvennoe muzykal'noe izdatel'stvo, 1954–58.

Krestovskaia, M. V. "Lelia" *Ugolki teatral'nogo mirka*. St. Petersburg, 1889.

———. *Artistka*. St. Petersburg, 1896. Originally published in 1891.

Kriukov, A. *Turgenev i muzyka*. Leningrad, 1963.

Kukol'nik, N. V. "Tri opery" (Three operas). In *Sochineniia Nestora Kukol'nika*. Vol 3. St. Petersburg, 1852. Originally published in 1841.

Kulikov, N. I. "Peterburgskoe teatral'noe uchilishche v vospominaniiakh Nikolaia Ivanovicha Kulikova." *Russkaia starina*. T. 52 (December 1886).

Lambert, Gavin. *Nazimova: A Biography*. New York: Alfred A. Knopf, 1997.

Larosh, (H.). *Izbrannye stat'i*. Leningrad: Muzyka, 1976.

———. *Sobranie muzykal'no-kriticheskikh statei*. Moscow, 1913.

Lauw, Louisa. *Fourteen Years with Adelina Patti*. Trans. Jeremiah Loder. New York: Norman L. Munro, 1884.

Law, Joe K. "The Prima Donnas of *Vanity Fair*." *College Language Association Journal* 31, no. 1 (September 1987).

Lebedev, D. *Ispolnitel'skie traditsii russkikh opernykh pevtsov*. Moscow-Leningrad: Muzyka, 1964.

———. *Mastera russkoi opernoi\stseny*. Leningrad: Muzyka, 1973.

Leonardi, Susan J. "To Have a Voice: The Politics of the Diva." *Perspectives on Contemporary Literature* 13 (1987).

Leonardi, Susan J., and Rebecca A. Pope. *The Diva's Mouth: Body, Voice, Prima Donna Politics*. New Brunswick, N.J.: Rutgers University Press, 1996.

Leonova, D. M. "Vospominaniia artistki imperatorskikh teatrov D. M. Leonovoi." *Istoricheskii vestnik* (1891), no. 43, 1–3; no. 44, 4.

Leppert, Richard, and Susan McClary, eds. *Music and Society: The Politics of Composition, Performance and Reception*. Cambridge: Cambridge University Press, 1987.

Levin, David J., ed. *Opera Through Other Eyes*. Stanford, Calif.: Stanford University Press, 1994.

Levin, Harry. *The Gates of Horn: A Study of Five French Realists*. New York: Oxford University Press, 1963.

Levin, Iu. I. "Zerkalo kak potentsial'nyi semioticheskii ob'ekt." In *Uchenye zapiski Tartuskogo gosudarstvennogo universiteta. Trudy po znakovym sistemam XXII*. Tartu, 1988.

Levine, George, ed. *Realism and Representation: Essays on the Problem of Realism in Relation to Science, Literature, and Culture*. Madison: University of Wisconsin Press, 1993.

Lewis, D. K. *Convention*. Cambridge: Harvard University Press, 1969.

Lindenberger, Herbert. *Opera: The Extravagant Art*. Ithaca, N.Y.: Cornell University Press, 1984.

———. *Opera in History: From Monteverdi to Cage*. Stanford, Calif.: Stanford University Press, 1998.

Litvak, Joseph. *Caught in the Act: Theatricality in the Nineteenth-Century English Novel*. Berkeley: University of California Press, 1992.

Livanova, T. *Motsart i russkaia muzykal'naia kul'tura*. Moscow: Gosudarstvennoe muzykal'noe izdatel'stvo, 1956.

———. *Muzykal'naia bibliografiia russkoi periodicheskoi pechati XIX veka 1801–1880*. 8 vols. Moscow: Gosudarstvennoe muzykal'noe izdatel'stvo, 1960–79.

———. *Opernaia kritika v Rossii*. 6 vols. Moscow: Muzyka, 1966–73.

———. *Russkaia muzykal'naia kul'tura XVIII veka v ee sviazakh s literaturoi, teatrom i bytom*. 2 vols. Moscow: Gosudarstvennoe muzykal'noe izdatel'stvo, 1952–53.

Lotman, Iu. M. *Besedy o russkoi kul'ture: byt i traditsii russkogo dvorianstva (XVIII—nachalo XIX veka)*. St. Petersburg: Iskusstvo, 1994.

———. *Roman v stikhakh Pushkina 'Evgenii Onegin'*. Tartu: TGU, 1975.

———. *Struktura khudozhestvennogo teksta*. Providence, R.I.: Brown University Press, 1971.

———. "Stsena i zhivopis' kak kodiruiushchie ustroistva kul'turnogo povedeniia cheloveka nachala XIX stoletiia." *Stat'i po tipologii kul'tury*. Tartu: TGU, 1973.

———. "Teatr i teatral'nost' v stroe kul'tury nachala XIX veka." *Stat'i po tipologii kul'tury*. Tartu: TGU, 1973.

Löve, Katharina Hansen. *The Evolution of Space in Russian Literature: A Spatial Reading of Nineteenth and Twentieth Century Narrative Literature*. Amsterdam: Rodopi, 1994.

Lovell, Terry. *Consuming Fiction*. London: Verso, 1987.

Lowe, David. "The Sources for the Opera in *War and Peace*." In *James Daniel Armstrong: In Memorium*. Columbus, Oh.: Slavica Publishers, Inc., 1994.

Lukacs, Georg. *Studies in European Realism*. New York: Grosset & Dunlap, 1964.

Lukomskii, G. K. *Starinnye teatry*. St. Petersburg, 1913.

———. "Starinnye teatry St. Petersburga." *Stolitsa i usad'ba* (1914), no. 7.

———. *Staryi Peterburg. Progulki po starinnym kvartalam*. Petrograd: Svobodnoe iskusstvo, 1917.

McClary, Susan. *Feminine Endings: Music, Gender, and Sexuality*. Minneapolis: University of Minnesota Press, 1991.

McGlathery, James M. *Interpretations of the Tales*. Part II of *Mysticism and Sexuality: E. T. A. Hoffmann*. Berne: Peter Lang, 1985.

McReynolds, Louise. "Home Was Never Where the Heart Was: Domestic Dystopias in Russia's Silent Movie Melodramas." Manuscript.

———. " 'The Incomparable' Anastasiia Vial'tseva and the Culture of Personality." In Helena Goscilo and Beth Holmgren, eds., *Russia Women Culture*. Bloomington: Indiana University Press, 1996.

———. *The News Under Russia's Old Regime: The Development of a Mass-Circulation Press*. Princeton, N.J.: Princeton University Press, 1991.

———, ed. *Russian Studies in History*. Special Issue on "Russian Nightlife, Fin-de-Siècle" 31, no. 3 (winter 1992–93).

———. "The Silent Movie Melodrama: Evgenii Bauer Fashions the Hero(in)ic Self." In Stephanie Sandler and Laura Engelstein, eds., *Self and Story in Russian History*. Ithaca, N.Y.: Cornell University Press, forthcoming.

Mainwaring, Marion, ed. *The Portrait Game: Drawings by Ivan Turgenev*,

Text by Ivan Turgenev, Pauline Viardot and Others. London: Chatto and Windus, 1973.

Mamin-Sibiriak, D. N. *Cherty iz zhizni Pepko* (Features from the life of Pepko). *Russkoe bogatstvo*, 1894, nos. 1–3.

Mandelker, Amy. *Framing Anna Karenina: Tolstoy, the Woman Question, and the Victorian Novel*. Columbus: Ohio State University Press, 1993.

Martens, Frederick H. *The Art of the Prima Donna and Concert Singer*. New York: D. Appleton, 1923.

Martorella, Rosanne. *The Sociology of Opera*. New York: Praeger, 1982.

Masing-Delic, Irene. "Creating the Living Work of Art: The Symbolist Pygmalion and His Antecedents." In Irina Paperno and Joan Delaney Grossman, eds., *Creating Life: The Aesthetic Utopia of Russian Modernism*. Stanford, Calif.: Stanford University Press, 1994.

———. "The Metaphysics of Liberation: Insarov as Tristan." *Die Welt der Slaven* 32, no. 1 (1987).

Matich, Olga. "A Typology of Fallen Women in Nineteenth-Century Russian Literature." In *American Contributions to the Ninth International Congress of Slavists*. Vol 2. Kiev, published by Columbus, Ohio: Slavica, 1983.

Medvedev, P. M. *Avtobiografiia*. Kazan', 1886.

Meierkhol'd, Vs. E. *Pikovaia dama (sbornik statei i materialov k postanovke opery)*. Leningrad, 1935.

(Merlin). *Madame Malibran par la Comtesse Merlin*. 2 vols. Bruxelles, 1838.

Meshcherskii, A. V. "Iz moei stariny. Zapiski." *Russkii arkhiv*. T. 1 (1901).

Michurina-Samoilova, V. A. *Pol veka na stsene Aleksandrinskogo teatra*. Leningrad: Gosudarstvennyi akademicheskii teatr dramy, 1935.

Mikhnevich, V. O. *Peterburg ves' na ladoni*. St. Petersburg: K. N. Plotnikov, 1874.

Mil'china, V. A. "Maskarad v russkoi kul'ture XVIII—nachala XIX v." *Kul'turologicheskie aspekty teorii i istorii russkoi literatury*. Moscow: Izdatel'stvo moskovskogo universita, 1978.

Miller, D. A. *The Novel and the Police*. Berkeley: University of California Press, 1988.

Miller, Nancy. *The Heroine's Text: Readings in the French and English Novel*. New York: Columbia University Press, 1986.

M-me A. Patti v anekdotakh i kharakteristikakh. Sobranie anekdotov i interesnykh faktov iz zhizni znamenitoi. St. Petersburg, 1891.

Moers, Ellen. *Literary Women*. New York: Doubleday, 1976.

Moon, Michael, and Eve Kosofsky Sedgwick, "Divinity: A Dossier/A Performance Piece/A Little-Understood Emotion." In Eve Kosofsky Sedgwick, ed., *Tendencies*. Durham, N.C.: Duke University Press, 1993.

Mordden, Ethan. *Demented: The World of the Opera Diva*. New York: Franklin Watts, 1984.

Morson, Gary Saul. "Anna Karenina's Omens." In Elizabeth Cheresh Allen and Gary Saul Morson, eds., *Freedom and Responsibility in Russian Literature: Essays in Honor of Robert Louis Jackson*. Evanston, Ill.: Northwestern University Press, 1995.

———. "The Potentials and Hazards of Prosaics." *Tolstoy Studies Journal* 2 (1989).

———. "Prosaics and *Anna Karenina*." *Tolstoy Studies Journal* 1 (1988).

———. "Prosaics: An Approach to the Humanities." *The American Scholar* (fall 1988).

Mosse, George L. *Nationalism and Sexuality: Respectability and Abnormal Sexuality in Modern Europe*. New York: Howard Fertig, 1985.

Musorgskii, M. *Pis'ma i dokumenty*. Moscow, 1932.

———. *Pis'ma k A. A. Golenishchevu-Kutuzovu*. Moscow, 1939.

Nabokov, Vladimir. *Eugene Onegin: A Novel in Verse*. Vol. 2. Princeton, N.J.: Princeton University Press, 1990.

Nakhimovsky, Alexander. D., and Alice Stone Nakhimovsky, eds. *The Semiotics of Russian Cultural History*. Ithaca, N.Y.: Cornell University Press, 1985.

Naletova, I. N. *Problemy dramaturgii russkoi liriko-psikhologicheskoi opery XIX veka (arkhitektonika, formoobrazuiushchie protsessy)*. Moscow, 1976.

Napravnik, E. F. *Avtobiograficheskie, tvorcheskie materialy, dokumenty, pis'ma*. Leningrad: Muzgiz, 1959.

Napravnik, V. *Eduard Frantsovich Napravnik i ego sovremenniki*. Leningrad: Muzyka, 1991.

Natarova, A. P. "Iz vospominanii artistki." *Istoricheskii vestnik*. T. 94, nos. 10–12 (1903).

Nattiez, Jean-Jacques. *Music and Discourse: Toward a Semiology of Music*. Trans. Carolyn Abbate. Princeton, N.J.: Princeton University Press, 1990.

Nekrasov, N. A. "Pevitsa" (The female singer). In vol. 7 of *Polnoe sobranie sochinenii i pisem*. Leningrad, 1983. Originally published in 1840.

Nemirovich-Danchenko, V. I. *Kulisy* (Stage wings). St. Petersburg, 1899.

Neuberger, Joan. *Hooliganism: Crime, Culture, and Power in St. Petersburg, 1900–1914*. Los Angeles: University of California Press, 1993.

Nikolaeva, T. I. *Teatral'naia ploshchad'*. Leningrad: Lenizdat, 1984.

Nil'skii, A. A. *Zakulisnaia khronika 1856–94*. St. Petersburg, 1897.

Noske, Frits. *The Signifier and the Signified: Studies in the Operas of Mozart and Verdi*. The Hague: Nijhoff, 1977.

Odoevskii, V. F. *Muzykal'no-literaturnoe nasledie*, Ed. G. B. Bernandt. Moscow: Gosudarstvennoe muzykal'noe izdatel'stvo, 1956.

Oglovets, A. *Materialy i dokumenty po istorii russkoi realisticheskoi muzykal'noi estetiki*. Moscow: Gosudarstvennoe muzykal'noe izdatel'stvo, 1954–56.

"Operetta na stsene Aleksandrinskogo teatra. Vospominaniia teatral'nogo starozhila." *Ezhegodnik imperatorskogo teatrov*. Vyp. 3 (1910).

Orlova, E. *Romansy Tchaikovskogo*. Moscow: Muzgiz, 1948.

Osborne, Charles. *Verdi: A Life in the Theatre*. New York: Alfred A. Knopf, 1987.

Otradin, M. V. *Proza I. A. Goncharova v literaturnom kontekste*. St. Petersburg: Izdatel'stvo S-Peterburgskogo universiteta, 1994.

Ozarovskii, Iu. E. "Khram Talii i Mel'pomeny (teatr aleksandrovskoi epokhi)." *Starye gody*, July–September 1908.

Paliukh, Z. G., and A. V. Prokhorova. *Lev Tolstoi i muzyka*. Moscow: Sovetskii kompozitor, 1977.

Paperno, Irina. *Chernyshevsky and the Age of Realism: A Study in the Semiotics of Behavior*. Stanford, Calif.: Stanford University Press, 1988.

———. *Suicide as a Cultural Institution in Dostoevsky's Russia*. Ithaca, N.Y.: Cornell University Press, 1997.

Paperno Irina, and Joan Delaney Grossman, eds. *Creating Life: The Aesthetic Utopia of Russian Modernism*. Stanford, Calif.: Stanford University Press, 1994.

Parker, Patricia. *Literary Fat Ladies: Rhetoric, Gender, Property*. London: Methuen, 1987.

Paustovskii, K. G. "Muzyka Verdi" (Verdi's music). In *Sobranie sochinenii v 6 tomakh*. Vol. 4. Moscow, 1959. Originally published in 1935.

Pavlova, N. G. *Muzyka i literatura (1917–72) Bibliograficheskii ukazatel* . Ed. A. D. Rklitskaia. Moscow: Gos. bibl. SSSR, 1975.

Pavlovsky, I. *Souvenirs sur Tourgueneff*. Paris: A. Savine, 1887.

Pellegrini, Ann. *Performance Anxieties: Staging Psychoanalysis, Staging Race*. New York: Routledge, 1997.

Perrot, Michelle. *A History of Private Life: From the Fires of Revolution to the Great War*. Trans. Arthur Goldhammer. Cambridge: The Belknap Press of Harvard Press, 1990.

Petrova, A. (Vorob'eva). "Vospominaniia." *Russkaia starina* 27 (1880).

Petrovskaia, I. F. *Teatr i zritel' provintsial'noi Rossii*. Leningrad: Iskusstvo, 1979.

Petrovskaia, I. F., and V. V. Somina. *Teatral'nyi Peterburg*. St. Petersburg: Rossiskii Institut Iskusstv, 1994.

Pietz, William. "The Problem of the Fetish." *Res* 9 (spring 1985), 13 (spring 1987), and 16 (fall 1988).

Pleasants, Henry. *The Great Singers: From Jenny Lind and Caruso to Callas and Pavarotti*. New York: Simon and Schuster, 1981.

Poizat, Michel. *The Angel's Cry: Beyond the Pleasure Principle in Opera*. Trans. Arthur Denner. Ithaca, N.Y.: Cornell University Press, 1992. Originally published as *L'Opéra, ou Le Cri de l'ange: Essai sur la jouissance de l'amateur d'opéra*. Paris: Éditions A. M. Metailie, 1986.

Pokhitonov, D. I. *Iz proshlogo russkoi opery*. Leningrad: Vserossiiskoe teatral'-noe obshchestvo, 1949.

Preston, Katherine K. *Opera on the Road: Travelling Opera Troupes in the United States, 1825–60*. Champaign: Illinois University Press, 1994.

Pushkareva, Natalia. *Women in Russian History: From the Tenth to the Twentieth Century*. Trans. and ed. Eve Levin. New York: M. E. Sharpe, 1997.

Pushkin, A. S. *Eugene Onegin*. Trans. James E. Falen. Oxford: Oxford University Press, 1995. Originally published in 1833.

Pustynnik, P. "Teatral'naia publika: Iz rasskazov turista po teatram." *Literaturnaia gazeta* (13 November 1847), no. 46.

Pyliaev, M. I. *Staryi Peterburg*. Leningrad: Titul, 1990.

———. *Zabytoe proshloe okrestnostei Peterburga*. 1889. Reprint, St. Petersburg, Lenizdat, 1994.

Rasponi, Lanfranco. *The Last Prima Donnas*. New York: Alfred A. Knopf, 1990.

Rayfield, Donald. "Dumas and Dostoevskii—Deflowering the Camellia." In Arnold McMillin, ed., *From Pushkin to Palisandriia: Essays on the Russian Novel in Honour of Richard Freeborn*. London: Macmillan, 1990.

Raynor, Henry. *A Social History of Music: From the Middle Ages to Beethoven*. New York: Shocken Books, 1972.

Reinelt, Janelle G., and Joseph R. Roach, eds. *Critical Theory and Performance.* Ann Arbor: University of Michigan Press, 1992.

Reznichenko, I. L. "Ustarelo li slovo 'diva'?" *Russkaia rech'* (May–June 1983).

Rice, James. "Some Observations on Stiva's Dream." *Tolstoy Studies Journal* 8 (1995–96).

Ricoeur, Paul. *The Rule of Metaphor: Multi-disciplinary Studies of the Creation of Meaning in Language.* Trans. Robert Czerny, with Kathleen McLaughlin and John Costello. Toronto: University of Toronto Press, 1977.

Ridenour, Robert C. *Nationalism, Modernism, and Personal Rivalry in Nineteenth-Century Russian Music.* Ann Arbor, Mich.: UMI Research Press, 1981.

Rischin, Ruth. "*Allegro Tumultuosissimamente*: Beethoven in Tolstoy's Fiction." In Hugh McLean, ed., *In the Shade of the Giant: Essays on Tolstoy.* Berkeley: University of California Press, 1989.

Rivière, Joan. "Womanliness as a Masquerade." *International Journal of Psychoanalysis* 10 (1929).

Robinson, Paul. *Opera and Ideas: From Mozart to Strauss.* Ithaca, N.Y.: Cornell University Press, 1985.

———. "Reading Libretti and Misreading Opera." In Arthur Groos and Roger Parker, ed., *Reading Opera.* Princeton, N.J.: Princeton University Press, 1988.

Roosevelt, Priscilla. *Life on the Russian Country Estate: A Social and Cultural History.* New Haven, Conn.: Yale University Press, 1995.

Rosand, Ellen. *Opera in Seventeenth-Century Venice: The Creation of a Genre.* Berkeley: University of California Press, 1991.

Rossikhina, V. *Opernyi teatr S. Mamontova.* Moscow: Muzyka, 1985.

Rozanov, A. *Polina Viardo-Garsia.* 3rd. ed. Leningrad: Muzyka, 1982.

Rubin, Joan Shelley. *The Making of Middlebrow Culture.* Chapel Hill: University of North Carolina Press, 1992.

Said, Edward W. *Musical Elaborations.* New York: Columbia University Press, 1991.

Saltykov-Shchedrin, M. E. *Gospoda Golovlovy* (The Golovlyov family). In vol. 13 of *Sobranie Sochinenii v 20 tomakh.* Moscow: Khudozhestvennaia literatura, 1972. Originally published in 1875–80.

Savina, M. G. *Goresti i skitaniia. Zapiski, 1854–77.* Moscow: Iskusstvo, 1961.

Saylor, Ian. "*Anna Karenina* and *Don Giovanni*: The Vengeance Motif in Oblonsky's Dream." *Tolstoy Studies Journal* 8 (1995–96).

Schafer, R. Murray. *E. T. A. Hoffmann and Music*. Toronto: University of Toronto Press, 1975.

Schechner, Richard. *Between Theater and Anthropology*. Philadelphia: University of Pennsylvania Press, 1985.

Schechner, Richard, and Mady Schuman, eds. *Ritual, Play, and Performance: Readings in The Social Sciences/Theatre*. New York: Seabury, 1976.

Scher, Steven Paul. "Literature and Music." In Jean-Pierre Barricelli and Joseph Gibaldi, ed., *Interrelations of Literature*. New York: Modern Language Association, 1982.

Schmidgall, Gary. *Literature as Opera*. Oxford: Oxford University Press, 1977.

Schor, Naomi. *Reading in Detail: Aesthetics and the Feminine*. New York: Routledge, 1987.

Schuler, Catherine A. *Women in Russian Theatre: The Actress in the Silver Age*. New York: Routledge, 1996.

Segal, Naomi. *The Adulteress's Child: Authorship and Desire in the Nineteenth-Century Novel*. Cambridge, Mass.: Polity, 1992.

Senelick, Laurence. "The Erotic Bondage of Serf Theatre." *Russian Review* 50 (1991).

Serapin, S. *Pushkin i muzyka*. Sofiia, n.d.

Serov, A. N. *Kriticheskie stat'i*. 4 vols. St. Petersburg, 1892–95.

———. *Izbrannye stat'i*. Vol. 1. Moscow: Muzgiz, 1950.

———. *Izbrannye stat'i*. Vol. 2. Leningrad: Gosudarstvennoe muzykal'noe izdatel'stvo, 1957.

Shepard, Elizabeth C. "The Society Tale and the Innovative Argument in Russian Prose Fiction of the 1830s." *Russian Literature* 10 (1981).

Shepard, John. *Music as Social Text*. Cambridge, Mass.: Polity, 1991.

Shklovskii, Viktor. "Art as Device." In Benjamin Sher, trans., *Theory of Prose*. Elmwood Park, Ill.: Dalkey Archive Press, 1990.

Shol'p, A. E. "I. S. Turgenev i 'Evgenii Onegin' Tchaikovskogo." In *I.S. Turgenev (1818–1883–1958). Stat'i i materialy*. Orlov: Orlovskoe knizhnoe izdatel'stvo, 1960.

Showalter, Elaine. *The Female Malady: Women, Madness, and English Culture 1830–1980*. New York: Pantheon, 1985.

Shteinberg, A. "D. M. Leonova." *Sovetskaia muzyka* 2–3 (1946).

Shteinpress, B. S. ed. *Iz muzykal'nogo proshlogo*. Vol. 1. Moscow: Gosudarstvennoe muzykal'noe izdatel'stvo, 1960.

Shubert, A. *Moia zhizn'*. Moscow: Academia, 1929.

Siegel, George. "The Fallen Woman in Nineteenth-Century Russian Literature." *Harvard Slavic Studies* 5 (1970).

Silbajoris, Rimvydas. *War and Peace: Tolstoy's Mirror of the World.* New York: Twayne, 1995.

Silverman, Kaja. *The Acoustic Mirror: The Female Voice in Psychoanalysis and Cinema.* Bloomington: Indiana University Press, 1988.

Sipovskii, V. V. "Ital'ianskii teatr v S.-Peterburge pri Anne Ioannovne (1733–1735 gg.)" *Russkaia starina.* T. 102, no. 6 (1900).

Skal'kovskii, K. A. "Biograficheskii ocherk Odesskogo teatra." *Odesskii vestnik* (30 January 1858), no. 12.

———. *V teatral'nom mire: Nabliudeniia vospominaniia i rassuzhdeniia.* St. Petersburg: Tip. A. S. Suvorina, 1899.

———. *Vospominaniia molodosti (Po moriiu zhiteiskomu) 1843–1869.* St. Petersburg: Tip. A. S. Suvorina, 1906.

Skonechnaia, A. D. *Torzhestvo muz.* Moscow: Sovetskaia Rossiia, 1989.

Smirnov, V. I. *Arkhitektura krupneishikh teatrov Rossii vtoroi poloviny XVIII do nachala XIX vekov.* Moscow, 1950.

Smith, Patrick J. *The Tenth Muse: A Historical Study of the Opera Libretto.* New York: Alfred A. Knopf, 1970.

Smith-Rosenberg, Carroll. "The Hysterical Woman: Sex Roles and Role Conflict in Nineteenth-Century America." *Disorderly Conduct: Visions of Gender in Victorian America.* New York: Alfred A. Knopf, 1985.

Smolina, A. A. "Vospominaniia." In *Russkii provintsial'nyi teatr. Vospominaniia.* Leningrad-Moscow: Vserossiiskoe teatral'noe izdatel'stvo, 1937.

Soboleva, G. *Russkii romans.* Moscow: Znanie, 1980.

Sokolovskii. "Teatral'naia arkhitektura." *Zhurnal glavnogo upravleniia putei soobshcheniia i publichnykh zdanii* 9, kn. 1 and 3 (1849).

Solie, Ruth A. "Fictions of the Opera Box." In Richard Dellamora and Daniel Fischlin, eds., *The Work of Opera: Genre, Nationhood, and Sexual Difference.* New York: Columbia University Press, 1997.

Sollogub, V. A. "Bol'shoi svet" (High society). *Povesti. Vospominaniia.* Leningrad: Khudozhestvennaia literatura, 1988. Originally published in 1841.

———. "Bukety, ili Peterburgskoe tsvetobesie" (Bouquets, or Petersburg flower frenzy). St. Petersburg, 1845.

Stakhovich, A. A. *Klochki vospominanii.* Moscow, 1904.

Stąrk, E. (Zigfrid). *Peterburgskaia opera i ee mastera (1890–1910)*. Leningrad: Iskusstvo, 1940.

Stasov, V. V. *Izbrannye stat'i o M. I. Glinke*. Moscow: Gosudarstvennoe myzykal'noe izdatel 'stvo, 1955.

———. *Pis'ma k deiateliam russkoi kul'tury*. 2 vols. Izdatel'stvo Akademii Nauk SSSR, Moscow, 1962–67.

———. *Selected Essays on Music*. Trans. Florence Jonas. New York: Da Capo, 1980.

———. *Sobranie sochinenii* (1847–1886). T. 3. St. Petersburg: Tip. M. M. Stasiulevicha, 1894.

———. "Tormozy novogo russkogo iskusstva." *Stat'i o muzyke*. Vyp. 3 (1880–86). Moscow: Muzyka, 1977.

Stavrou, Theofanis G., ed., *Art and Culture in Nineteenth-Century Russia*. Bloomington: Indiana University Press, 1983.

Stendhal (Henri Beyle). *Life of Rossini*. Trans. Richard N. Coe. New York: Criterion Books, 1957.

Stites, Richard. "The Domestic Muse: Music at Home in the Twilight of Serfdom." In Andrew Baruch Wachtel, ed., *Intersections and Transpositions: Russian Music, Literature, and Society*. Evanston, Ill.: Northwestern University Press, 1998.

———. *The Women's Liberation Movement in Russia: Feminism, Nihilism, and Bolshevism, 1860–1930*. Princeton, N.J.: Princeton University Press, 1978.

Stokes, John. "Rachel's 'Terrible Beauty': An Actress Among the Novelists." *ELH* 51, no. 4 (winter 1984).

Stolpianskii, P. *Muzyka i muzytsirovanie v starom Peterburge*. Leningrad: Muzyka, 1989.

———. *Peterburg piat'desiat let tomu nazad (Istoricheskaia spravka)*. St. Petersburg, 1909.

Strakhov, N. N. *Biografiia, pis'ma, i zametki iz zapisnoi knizhki F. M. Dostoevskogo*. St. Petersburg, 1883.

Strepetova, P. A. "Minuvshie dni." *Vospominaniia i pis'ma 1850–1903*. Moscow: Academia, 1934.

Suleiman, Susan Rubin, ed. *The Female Body in Western Culture: Contemporary Perspectives*. Cambridge: Harvard University Press, 1985.

Suvorin, A. S. "Tatiana Repina." St. Petersburg, 1899. Originally published in 1886.

Svin'in, P. *Dostopamiatnosti Sanktpeterburga i ego okrestnostei*. St. Petersburg, 1816.

Sviridenko, S. "Russkaia opera v Mariinskom teatre za 25 let." *Russkaia muzykal'naia gazeta* 1–2, 4–5 (1912).

Tambling, Jeremy. *Opera, Ideology and Film*. New York: St. Martin's Press, 1987.

Taneev, S. V. "Iz proshlogo imperatorskikh teatrov (1825–56)." *Russkii vestnik*. T. 184, no. 8 (August 1886).

———. "Maskarady v stolitsakh." *Russkii arkhiv*, kn. 3 (1885).

Tanner, Tony. *Adultery in the Novel: Contract and Transgression*. Baltimore, Md.: Johns Hopkins University Press, 1979.

Taranovskaia, M. Z. *Arkhitektura teatrov Leningrada (istoriko-arkhitekturnyi ocherk)*. Leningrad: Stroiizdat, 1988.

Tartakovskii, A. G. *Russkaia memuaristika XVIII—pervoi poloviny XIX v*. Moscow: Nauka, 1991.

Taruskin, Richard. *Defining Russia Musically: Historical and Hermeneutical Essays*. Princeton, N.J.: Princeton University Press, 1997.

———. *Musorgsky: Eight Essays and an Epilogue*. Princeton, N.J.: Princeton University Press, 1993.

———. *Opera and Drama in Russia as Preached and Practiced in the 1860s*. Ann Arbor, Mich.: UMI Research Press, 1981.

Tchaikovskii, M. I. *Zhizn' P. I. Tchaikovskogo*, Vol. 2. Moscow: P. Iurgenson, 1901.

Tchaikovskii, P. I. *Dnevniki 1873–1891*. Moscow: Gosudarstvennoe izdatel'stvo, muzykal'nyi sektor, 1923.

———. *Muzykal'no-kriticheskie stat'i*. Moscow: Gosudarstvennoe myzykal'noe izdatel'stvo, 1953.

———. *Muzykal'nye fel'etony i zametki 1868–76*. Moscow: Iakovlev, 1898.

———. *P. I. Tchaikovskii ob opere i balete: izbrannye otryvki iz pisem i statei*. Moscow: Gosudarstvennoe muzykal'noe izdatel'stvo, 1952.

Thomas, Gail, ed. *The Muses*. Dallas, Tex.: The Dallas Institute Publications, 1994.

Tikhvinskaia, L. *Kabare i teatry miniatiur v Rossii. 1908–1917*. Moscow: RIK "Kul'tura," 1995.

Timokhin, V. V. *Vydaiushchiesia ital'ianskie pevtsy. Ocherki*. Moscow, 1962.

Tiumeneva, G. A. *Gogol' i muzyka*. Moscow, 1966.

Todd, William Mills III. *Fiction and Society in the Age of Pushkin: Ideology,*

Institutions, and Narrative. Cambridge: Harvard University Press, 1986.

———. " 'The Russian Terpsichore's Soul-Filled Flight': Dance Themes in *Eugene Onegin*." In David M. Bethea, ed., *Pushkin Today*. Bloomington: Indiana University Press, 1993.

Tolstoi, L. N. *War and Peace*. Ed. George Gibian. Trans. W. W. Norton & Company. 2nd ed. New York, 1996. Originally published in 1861–69.

———. *Anna Karenina*. Ed. George Gibian. Trans. W. W. Norton & Company. New York, 1970. Originally published in 1873–77.

———. *Voskresenie* (Resurrection). In vol. 32 of *Polnoe sobranie sochinenii*. Moscow, Leningrad: Khudozhestvennaia literatura, 1933. Originally published in 1899.

Tolstoi, L. N., and V. V. Stasov. *Perepiska (1878–1906)*. Priboi: Izdatel'stvo Akademii Nauk SSSR., 1929.

Tomashevskii, B. "Pushkin i ital'ianskaia opera." In *Pushkin i ego sovremenniki*. Vols. 31–32. Leningrad: Izdatel'stvo Akademii Nauk SSSR, 1927.

Traub, Valerie, Lindsay M. Kaplan, and Dympna Callaghan, eds. *Feminist Readings of Early Modern Culture: Emerging Subjects*. Cambridge: Cambridge University Press, 1996.

Traubner, Richard. *Operetta: A Theatrical History*. Garden City, N.J.: Doubleday, 1983.

Tsivian, Yuri. *Early Cinema in Russia and Its Cultural Reception*. Trans. Alan Bodger. New York: Routledge, 1994.

———, ed. *Silent Witnesses: Russian Films, 1908–1919*. Edizioni Biblioteca dell-immagine. British Film Institute, 1989.

Turgenev, I. S. "Klara Milich, or Posle smerti" (After death). In vol. 10 of *Polnoe sobranie sochinenii i pisem*. Moscow: Nauka, 1982. Originally published in 1882.

———. *Nakanune* (On the eve). In vol. 6 of *Polnoe sobranie sochinenii i pisem*. Moscow: Nauka, 1981. Originally published in 1860.

———. "Stoi!" (Be still!). In vol. 13 of *Polnoe sobranie sochinenii i pisem*. Moscow: Nauka, 1967. Originally published in 1879.

Turner, Victor. *Dramas, Fields, and Metaphors*. Ithaca, N.Y.: Cornell University Press, 1974.

Tynianov, Iu. N. "O kompozitsii 'Evgeniia Onegina.'" *Poetika, istoriia literatury, kino*. Moscow: Nauka, 1977.

Umanov-Kaplunovskii, V. "Iz vospominanii o E.P. Kadminoi." *Istoricheskii vestnik* (1905), no. 12.

Vakano. *Roman Adelina Patti*. St. Petersburg, 1875.

Varneke, B. "Sud'by russkoi aktrisy." *Vremennik russkogo teatral'nogo obshchestva*. Moscow, 1924.

Vasem, E. O. *Zapiski baleriny Sankt-Peterburgskogo Bol'shogo teatra 1867–1884*. Moscow-Leningrad: Iskusstvo, 1937.

Velizarii, M. I. *Put' provintsial'noi aktrisy*. Leningrad: Iskusstvo, 1938.

Vera Kholodnaia: K 100-letiiu so dnia rozhdeniia. Moscow: Iskusstvo, 1995.

Verbitskaia, A. A. *Pokinutyi* (The abandoned man). Riga, 1925/26.

Vigel', F. F. *Zapiski*. 2 vols. Moscow: Krug, 1928.

Vinitsky, Ilya. "Signora Melas, or An Italian Soprano in Russia." In Andrew Baruch Wachtel, ed., *Intersections and Transpositions: Russian Music, Literature, and Society*. Evanston, Ill.: Northwestern University Press, 1998.

Vol'f, A. I. *Khronika peterburgskikh teatrov (1826–84)*. St. Petersburg: Tip. R. Golike, 1877, 1884.

von Geldern, James, and Louise McReynolds, eds. *Entertaining Tsarist Russia: Tales, Songs, Plays, Movies, Jokes, Ads, and Images From Russian Urban Life, 1779–1917*. Bloomington: Indiana University Press, 1998.

Vsevolodskii-Gerngross, V. N. "Teatral'nye zdaniia v Sankt-Peterburge v XVIII stoletii." *Starye gody* (February and March 1910).

Wasiolek, Edward. *Tolstoy's Major Fiction*. Chicago: University of Chicago Press, 1978.

Weaver, William. *The Golden Century of Italian Opera: From Rossini to Puccini*. New York: Thames and Hudson, 1980.

Weber, William. *Music and the Middle Class: The Social Structure of Concert Life in London, Paris and Vienna*. New York: Holmes & Meier, 1975.

Weinstock, Herbert. *Vincenzo Bellini: His Life and His Operas*. New York: Alfred A. Knopf, 1971.

Weisstein, Ulrich. *The Essence of Opera*. The Free Press of Glencoe, 1964.

Wellbery, David. "E. T. A. Hoffman and Romantic Hermeneutics: An Interpretation of Hoffman's 'Don Juan.'" *Studies in Romanticism* 19 (1980).

Winternitz, Emanuel. *Musical Instruments and Their Symbolism in Western Art: Studies in Musical Iconology*. New Haven, Conn.: Yale University Press, 1979.

Wortman, Richard S. *Scenarios of Power: Myth and Ceremony in Russian Monarchy*. Vol. 1. Princeton, N.J.: Princeton University Press, 1995.

Young, Percy M. *The Concert Tradition: From the Middle Ages to the Twentieth Century*. London: Routledge and Kegan Paul, 1965.

Zhekulin, Nicholas G. "*Evgenii Onegin*: The Art of Adaptation, Novel to Opera." *Canadian Slavonic Papers* (June–September 1987).

Zolotnitskaia, L. M. *Ital'ianskii opernyi teatr v Rossii v XVIII–XX vekakh. (Lektsiia)*. Leningrad: LOLGK, 1988.

Zotov, R. *Teatral'nye vospominaniia. Avtobiograficheskie zapiski*. St. Petersburg, 1860.

Index